CHICKEN SOUP
FOR THE INDIAN SPIRITUAL SOUL

CHICKEN SOUP FOR THE INDIAN SPIRITUAL SOUL

101 Inspirational Stories to Offer Hope and Deepen Faith

Jack Canfield
Mark Victor Hansen
Veena Seshadri

westland

We would like to acknowledge the following publishers and individuals for permission to reprint the following material. (Note: the stories that were penned anonymously, that are public domain or were written by Veena Seshadri are not included in this listing.)

From Despair to Hope: The Tihar Story. Reprinted by permission of Kiran Bedi. © 2009 Kiran Bedi.

Helena's Journey. Reprinted by permission of Indu Balachandran. © 2009 Indu Balachandran.

(*continued on page 386*)

westland ltd.
Venkat Towers, 165, P. H. Road, Opp. Maduravoyal Municipal Office, Chennai 600 095
No.38/10 (New No.5), Raghava Nagar, New Timber Yard Layout, Bangalore 560 026
Survey No. A - 9, II Floor, Moula Ali Industrial Area, Moula Ali, Hyderabad 500 040
Plot No 102, Marol Coop Ind Estate, Marol, Andheri East, Mumbai 400 059
47, Brij Mohan Road, Daryaganj, New Delhi 110 002

Copyright © Chicken Soup for the Soul Publishing, LLC 2009

10 9 8 7 6 5 4 3 2 1

ISBN: 978-93-80283-27-2

This edition is for sale in India, Pakistan, Sri Lanka, Nepal and Bangladesh only

Cover Design: design on u

Typeset in Palatino Linotype by Mindways Design Pvt. Ltd.

Printed at : Anubha Printers, Noida

Contents

Contents

Introduction

The spiritual does not come scattering a bunch of visiting cards and, sometimes, we may not even be aware of its presence. But there it always is, like an undertow, deep down at the bottom of practically every aspect of our life, at least here in India. I was well aware, when I began compiling *Chicken Soup for the Indian Spiritual Soul*, that the spiritual elements in some of the stories were so inextricably meshed with the mundane, that they might prove elusive ... the secret is to relax and read with an open mind, and they will surely reveal themselves!

But first, what is spirituality? I believe that spirituality is about connecting with something that inspires us to become better, happier human beings. It creates in us the awareness that we should lead balanced lives, respecting everyone and everything, because we are all an equally special part of the whole. Jewels in the Net of Indra, as the Buddhists say, so closely linked with all the other jewels in the universe that any change in one jewel leads to a change in every other jewel.

Spirituality also encompasses ways of finding meaning and inner peace in our lives. And it is such a vast reservoir, that there is something there for anyone who wants guidance or comfort.

◆

When the stories began flowing in for the book, I was amazed at the number of people who, no matter what ordeals they had been through, believed that their lives were suffused with spiritual grace. And they were equally certain that it had given them the courage to accept and cope with whatever had happened — paraplegia, cancer, AIDS, an acid attack, a bomb blast, a hijacking, the realisation that a parent was a much-dreaded bandit....

I read the stories of a visionary police officer who changed the culture of one of the most brutal prisons in Asia by prevailing upon hardened criminals to connect with the spiritual; of a nun who gave up everything to serve the poorest of the poor in a distant land because she heard His call; of a spiritual leader who speaks of love, compassion and happiness in spite of being exiled from his beloved homeland; of a young girl from a tradition-bound village who, in spite of a series of obstacles, went on to climb mountains — literally and figuratively! I read moving accounts of love and faith in the writings of a former president of the country and that of an internationally-respected spiritual leader; of the grit and determination of a famous dancer left with a broken back after an accident, who rewrote medical history when she not only walked but danced again; of the environmental activist who was 'given' the courage to take on the might of giant multinational corporations in her fight to protect the small farmer.... And they all speak from the heart of the various hues of a rainbow spirituality conjured up from a vast palette — of love, forgiveness, faith, courage, passion, altruism and yes, humour too!

It has been said that you cannot be a truly spiritual person unless you have a positive outlook. (How could you possibly reach the heights if you are wallowing in the Slough of Despond?) So it is no wonder that the oft-repeated message in these stories — and it is relevant whether you are beset with problems, or are in seventh heaven — is this: be positive, and go find that silver lining!

Decades ago, when we were still in school, someone we knew showed us the truth of this in the way she lived, but we giggled and smirked and thought she was batty. She was an aunt of mine, a freedom fighter, who went to prison several times for her role in the Civil Disobedience Movement. She never spoke of her experiences there, but once, when we pressed her for the gory details she shrugged and said, 'Oh, the jailors were like us ... just doing their duty.'

'But prison must have been dreadful!'

As usual, there was no mention of whatever real hardships she had endured. 'Well, there were many of us women staying together, and I once found my hair crawling with lice.' We could hardly believe this! She was so finicky about her personal hygiene, and we'd always seen her in whiter than white saris. 'But one of the jailors let me go home for a day, and I got them all combed out by my mother. I also had an oil bath after a long, long time. So, in the end, it turned out to be a good thing, after all,' she concluded, a big smile lighting up her face ... and now, for the first time, I paused to think about the secret of her happiness. No doubt, you too will find that these stories rekindle many memories, and prompt you to view people and relationships from a different perspective ... hopefully, they'll help you make amends. I would love to hear how the book touched you, so do write in and tell me about it at veena.seshadri@gmail.com.

Someone once said that we are like lamps floating down a river. Sometimes, we bump into one another and journey together for a while, lighting the way. As you travel along with us, sharing the lives and insights of those whose stories you read in the book, we hope this little 'lamp' illumines your way, helps you figure out answers to your own questions and brings you hope, warmth and smiles.

Veena Seshadri

1
ON FAITH

I tell you the truth, if you have faith as small as a mustard seed, you can say to this mountain, 'Move from here to there,' and it will move. Nothing will be impossible for you.

The Holy Bible, Matthew 17:20

From Despair to Hope: The Tihar Story

Just as a mother would protect with her life her own
son, her only son, so one should cultivate an unbounded
mind towards all beings, and loving-kindness towards
all the world.
One should cultivate an unbounded mind, above and
below and across, without obstruction, without enmity,
without rivalry.

—Sutta Nipata

Tihar Central Jail is the largest prison complex in Asia. Earlier, it was considered one of the most notorious as well. It was meant to house 2,500 inmates, but around 9,000 prisoners were incarcerated there — and that included women and young children, some of whom had been born in prison and had never seen the outside world. As for healthcare and education ... well, they were non-existent. One often heard monstrous tales of corruption and extortion both by guards and criminals inside the prison. Besides, Tihar was filthy. It was lawless, and violence was a way of life there — the gang wars, the drugs, and the inhumane living conditions made Tihar a hell on earth. A place where all hope was lost.

On 1 May 1993, when I was appointed Inspector General of Prisons and assumed charge of Tihar, I was well aware that it was a 'punishment posting'. That morning, I stepped out of the staff car and walked towards my new office at Tihar, with the strange feeling that I was walking on quicksand with a mountain on my back. I was in charge of the place, but had no idea what lay in wait for me within those high walls topped by barbed wire.

My office was claustrophobic, and the rats there apparently had the right of way. And when I called my first staff meeting, I sensed that the staff were neither enthusiastic nor motivated — merely curious to find out what my agenda was. And whenever I asked a question they looked at one another through the corners of their eyes, and gave me guarded, noncommittal answers. One did not have to be psychic to realise that the task ahead would be an uphill one.

My mother would always say, 'Do everything with passion and purpose, and help others. That's the only way to live.' It had become a way of life with me — my mission, in fact — and I was determined to do just that. Ever since my early days as a police officer, I had believed that the purpose of prison should not be to punish offenders but to rehabilitate and reform them. I believe everyone (if given a chance), will try to change, and I wanted to give them that chance. Now, it had become possible for me to translate that desire into action. I was confident that we — the prison staff, the prisoners and I — would, in due course, find ways of working together as a team, for collective growth and reform. The prison would somehow be transformed into a humane place where the convicts could pick up the skills to live productive lives and stay away from crime, ever after.

I had joined the police force because of the power it gave me to change 'the system', and nudge things in the right direction. But how did one do that in a place such as Tihar? I was all too aware that I was venturing into the unknown ... walking the razor's edge, as it were ... and no, it would not be easy. My spiritual beliefs, however, have always been an enormous source of strength and comfort to me. So I decided to follow the call of my inner voice. I wanted to do more. I wanted to share more. I wanted to create more. I wanted to give more. And transform Tihar — which was now a training ground for more criminals — into an ashram.

The first time I set out on my rounds of the prison wards, I saw faces, and more faces with all sorts of expressions — angry, anxious, bewildered, despairing, blank ... They were in dire need of help, but first, I had to find a way to reach out to them and earn their trust. The question was: how?

I paused, and suddenly, I felt I had the answer, 'Do you pray?' I asked. Prayer is something that remains internally with me. If things have been good for me, I thank the Almighty and my circumstances. If I face a challenge and don't have the answer, I pray. When I asked the prisoners whether they pray, I was basically asking them whether they were seeking help.

No one answered. The prisoners looked confused and turned to the warders who looked even more confused. I repeated the question, and this time there were a few hesitant nods. I knew instinctively that prayer would prove to be the big breakthrough, but it would take a little time. And I needed something right then that would help me connect.

Did they know the popular song, *Heh malik tere bande hum*? Yes, of course, they did! I asked them to sing it with me, and at the end of the song, I felt as if they had begun to respond to me. It was a small beginning, but an encouraging one.

Quickly, I chalked out a simple routine — every day, I went around the prison, chatted with the prisoners, listened to their problems, got their feedback, sang, joked and laughed with them. And made sure that they got wholesome food as well, not the usual burnt chapatis and watery dal. For me, spirituality is clean thought, clean mind, clean action, and clean human being. So, one step at a time, we climbed the mountain — from the problem of drug addiction to healthcare to vocational education and sanitation, we tackled them all. Nothing is impossible, no target unachievable; we just have to try harder and harder ... focus on the present and do our best.

You can't steal or kill someone without generating an incredible amount of anger and hatred. So for any positive transformation a person must cultivate a moral mind first. It was evident that the prisoners needed more holistic solutions. The change had to come from within them, and touch them on a spiritual level as well. I found the answer in vipassana meditation. Why vipassana? Well, like the Tihar jail, my temple has all religions in it. It is the power of spirituality that I worship, not the form. And vipassana is not a religion, or a mantra. It helps us understand the true nature of reality and ourselves, by exploring the deepest levels of the mind. And, most importantly, in a place like prison where there are people of all faiths who hold rigidly to their views, vipassana works well because we can enter the realm of the spiritual without praying to a specific deity.

Tihar harboured hardcore criminals and was rife with feelings of revenge, anger and hatred. Yet, when vipassana meditation was first introduced, it proved to be a success and there was a distinct transformation in the men who attended the course.

In April 1994, a more ambitious vipassana meditation programme was held in Tihar, this time for over 1000 prisoners (charged with crimes from drug dealing to robbery to murder and terrorism) and staff from various religious backgrounds. With the productive and cooperative spirit now prevailing in the prison, the inmates dug drainage ditches, laid pipes, weeded and levelled a large area and helped erect a huge shamiana. To put over one thousand prisoners together in a tent such as this was a high security risk. Yet, as always, I felt that there was an invisible hand protecting me and I was grateful. At times, when I could have been killed, or hurt, something has always protected and stayed with me. To me, it is a special spiritual grace.

In the early hours of the day during one of the vipassana courses, a sudden storm struck, and the shamiana collapsed in the rain and wind. Everything was soaked and the place was wrecked.

After breakfast, the weather began to clear, and a large team of prisoners pitched in to put things in order. They dried the cushions and carpets outside, redid the wiring and baled out the water. It was a massive cooperative effort, and the tent was ready for the first discourse, on time!

During the course, the men battled their personal demons. On the closing day, many prisoners expressed their joy at their 'self-liberation'. Also, the prisoners and the jail staff began to interact much more harmoniously.

The meditation had such an effect on the prisoners that, later, one convict actually went on the stand and confessed to his crime! Another accused of murder begged forgiveness from a victim's family. And that year, two girls from the victim's family tied rakhis on his wrist. 'Today, I look after them as if they are my own family,' he says. There were more tales of remorse and gratitude … and redemption. I couldn't think of a better way to return human beings to humanity!

And my own journey…? Vipassana helped me look at my work from a clearer perspective; taught me to police myself before policing others; seek forgiveness and forgive, thus making me more effective … and leaving me with a lighter heart!

Kiran Bedi

Kareem's Dream

Abdul Kareem worked as a travel agent. First, in bustling Mumbai, and later, following in the footsteps of scores of other Keralites, in the UAE. By the accepted standards of his community, Kareem should have been a happy man. But underneath it all, a palpable discontent lurked. He found himself increasingly disillusioned with the long hours spent on demanding customers, and sensed a nagging dissatisfaction with the work he was doing. And so, in 1977, taking a long break from work, young Kareem returned to Puliyamkulam, in the coastal district of Kasargod. This isolated, sleepy village, which he called home, was far removed from the lush, idyllic picture-postcard villages of Kerala. It was rather a desolate wasteland, but incredibly, it was central to the dream Kareem had been weaving: a verdant, sun-dappled forest in the place of this forbidding stretch of land! He imagined living in a lush woodland surrounded by nature, birds and butterflies, and his pet animals.

Born to illiterate parents in a remote village in northern Kerala, Kareem completed his schooling, then did two years of junior college before ending up as a dock labourer in Mumbai. But after the riots that shook the metropolis in 1969 as a result of growing parochialism, he found himself back in his village. Before long, sensing an opportunity in the Persian Gulf boom of the early Seventies, he set up a travel and placement service for the thousands of Keralites eager to rush to the Gulf. Destiny, however, had other plans for Kareem, though nothing till then had given any indication of the man he was to become ... or of his spiritual destiny.

His work took him to the UAE frequently and soon he shifted base to this El Dorado of the time. Oddly enough, he wasn't enamoured of the glitz and glitter of his new surroundings. Instead, he found himself drawn towards the stupendous efforts being made for greening the desert country. Before long, however, he found the bustle of the big city increasingly tiresome as, deep inside, he longed for peace and quiet amidst verdant surroundings.

From the time he could remember, Kareem had always felt drawn towards nature. Shortly after his return from the UAE, as he surveyed the forbidding wasteland on the outskirts of his village, the call of nature grew more compelling. And, in a defining moment, Kareem listened to his heart, and took a decision: he would acquire part of that land. Without much ado, he invested a major portion of his savings into five acres of barren wasteland, sixteen kilometres from the coastal town of Nileswaram. The rock-strewn ground was so desolate that poor tribals were its only inhabitants. Kareem instantly became the laughing stock of the village.

Unaffected by their gibes, Kareem got to work, planting saplings in the unyielding laterite, fetching water from outlying wells.... But the seedlings were no match for the hostile environment, and promptly withered. Undeterred, Kareem planted even more of them. To the consternation of his already baffled family, he invested in another twenty-seven acres of this parched earth. Getting to work in right

earnest, he dug deep, looking for water — but came up
with rocks and rubble. Resolutely, he clawed into the sun-
scorched laterite like a man possessed, and planted more
saplings, nurturing them with unflagging passion and the
water he brought from afar. Working doggedly, as if driven
by a primordial instinct, he covered painstakingly tilled
patches with hardy saplings — and waited, and waited. In
due course, nature began to relent. A few saplings showed
signs of life!

Kareem, for the first time since he began toiling on the
land, allowed himself the luxury of a wan smile. A year went
by while he plodded on, willing the stubborn earth to yield,
even as he almost gave up on the laboriously dug wells, in
frustration, as they had remained dry. Then, one day, he was
greeted by an amazing sight: water began seeping into a few
abandoned wells. Buoyed up with hope, he planted more
saplings. Elated by the turn of events, he searched far and
wide, fetching exotic varieties of plants and rare botanical
specimens. He watched fascinated as nature, finally, began
lending him a hand and his plants gained height. Kareem was
now consumed by his mission. Infused with a new energy,
he sensed a connection to something higher than himself — a
power that was watching over him.

Soon birds and bees came calling as if following the dictates
of this mysterious power, to marvel at the result of his
doggedness. Then followed local tribals, who came looking
for work in his 'forest'. He recruited them and got to work
managing his most precious commodity: water. But Kareem
had his heart in the right place; so first, he built shelters for
them and assured them of fair wages — a first for most of
his recruits who barely eked out a living on the fringes of
society. He built low walls on slopes to hold rainwater that
had previously swept downhill carrying top soil. He dug
more pits, which obligingly filled with water. Before long,

the laterite began disintegrating, and bit by bit, over time, turned into soil.

Today, thirty years on, sunlight barely reaches the floor of Kareem's forest! The green canopy is so thick that lichens and moss grow on the forest floor amid sturdy vines entwining the leafy limbs of trees; foliage is so lush that the ambient temperature there is nearly ten degrees lower than in the surrounding areas; the once scorched land is so verdant that wells in the surrounding villages have year-long water. As word spread, environmentalists and researchers working on wasteland management converged on his land to study the 'Kareem Model'. Awards and accolades followed. Corporates and NGOs conferred honours and citations on him. The Indian Oil Corporation picked him as their mascot for their 'India Inspired' advertisements. Environmentalists named him the 'forest maker'. Trinity College, Connecticut, USA, selected his forest for research on the relationship between plants and religion. Before long, his story found its way into school textbooks.

Today, Kareem lives with his family in a modest house that he has built in a large clearing in the forest. Peacocks, deer and other animals that he introduced thrive on his thirty-two-acre woodland. It is home to diverse species of trees, medicinal plants, birds, insects, nocturnal animals and countless soil-enriching micro-organisms. Before long, Kareem had to build cottages to accommodate the increasing number of visitors. Everyone from environmentalists, scientists, university students and Ayurveda practitioners to eco-club members from schools and colleges visit his park for field experiments. And the most important thing they learn there is that, given man's ingenuity, even stubborn earth, baked by the sun and blasted by the wind, can revert to nature.

Abdul Kareem dared to dream and had the grit and conviction to make it come true. While his life teaches that even nature bows to tenacity and fortitude, his words point to the spiritual core of the man. He says, 'Much of the impatience, discontent and violence around us is due to a lack of opportunity to reconnect with where we come from. For sanity and generosity of spirit we should be able to witness nature at its unceasing, rejuvenating work.'

Profound words indeed, and they seem to sink in deeper when you are inside Kareem's park, for it seems to proclaim a truth of its own, resonating as it does with a kind of natural energy, as in a primeval forest. When you spend leisurely moments in the park, when you take in the sounds and smells of the place, the vibrations of the earth, and create an inner rapport with the surroundings, you sense that this park is indeed the result of one man's spiritual journey, no less. And as you continue to commune with nature, observing the trees, rooted in the earth yet reaching out to the skies, sheltering and feeding birds and animals and living in harmony with the rest of creation, you positively connect with the living energy of the place. John Muir had once said, 'The clearest way into the universe is through a forest wilderness.' Kareem has indeed found his way there.

Akber Ayub

Footprints

One night a man had a dream. He dreamed he was walking along the beach with God. Across the sky flashed scenes from his life. For each scene, he noticed two sets of footprints in the sand; one belonging to him, and the other to God.

When the last scene of his life flashed before him he looked back at the footprints in the sand. He noticed that many times along the path of his life there was only one set of footprints. He also noticed that it happened at the very lowest and saddest times in his life.

This really bothered him and he questioned God about it. 'Lord, you said that once I decided to follow you, you'd walk with me all the way. But I have noticed that during the most troublesome times in my life, there is only one set of footprints. I don't understand why when I needed you most you would leave me.'

God replied, 'Child, I did not ever leave you. Look carefully. During your times of trial and suffering, when you see only one set of footprints, they are mine. It was then that I carried you.'

Author Unknown

The Call of the Mountains

I was born in the small but beautiful mountain village of Nakuri near Uttarkashi in Garhwal, with the gurgling, playful Bhagirathi river flowing nearby. My parents were a hard-working and extremely self-contained couple. Even though our family was poor, my father taught us how to live with dignity and self-respect. My parents also believed that kindness is the essence of all religion.

I was the third child in the family and quite a rebel. I developed a tendency to ask questions and not be satisfied with the customary treatment meted out to girls. Even as a child, I wanted to do something wonderful with my life. For that, I knew I had to educate myself. It was no small ambition, as it was the firm belief of the people in the community that women ought only to be able to read or write a letter.

So there were breaks in my academic career, although I was good both at studies and in sports. After the eighth standard, by which time I could read and write 'sufficiently', my parents asked me to drop out of school and help around the house. But nothing is impossible if we are determined to achieve it. During the one year I spent at home, I worked hard to complete household chores during the day, and then studied on my own at night. I borrowed books from neighbours and read them. I sought help from a cousin who had studied up to her intermediate.

Seeing my determination, my elder brother persuaded my parents to let me complete my schooling. I cleared my tenth-standard examination with excellent marks … and went on to get my Bachelor's and Master's degrees, as well as a teaching degree. My family was facing financial troubles and I wanted a job desperately, but found no suitable openings.

I had always loved wandering in the Garhwal Himalayas, and had first tasted the excitement of the high altitudes when my classmates and I — we were twelve years old at the time — climbed to 4,000 metres during a picnic in the mountains. We found we could not come down by nightfall, and spent the night there without food or shelter. I was not afraid but felt a strong connection — the mountains have always had the power to lift me beyond the ordinary concerns of everyday life.

So, when I found my elder brother, Bachan, encouraging my youngest brother, Raju, to take up mountaineering, I thought to myself, 'Why not me?' My brothers were always given preferential treatment, and this made me even more determined not only to do what the boys did, but do it better

When I first expressed my desire to become a professional mountaineer, the objection that my family, relatives, and the people around me raised was that mountaineering was not something women should even think of. According to them, the only profession women should take up — if at all they insisted on working — was teaching. Naturally, my family was devastated when I chose to climb mountains instead.

The opportunity came, perhaps, due to some divine blessing, and I took up the mountaineering courses in

Uttarkashi. There was no looking back for me after that. It was a period of self-discovery, and I realised that mountaineering was not just about going into the mountains. Climbing a mountain is also a journey into yourself. Mountains make one realise where one stands in the larger scheme of things. The mountains are a power and you are like a tiny ant up there. Before I begin a trek, irrespective of the height of the mountain, I always bow my head to it in deference and humility.

The Indian Everest Expedition, in 1984, was the first mixed expedition. After I was selected, I continued with my preparation of keeping 'expedition fit' by devising my own novel methods.

We were required to bring home grass or firewood from the higher reaches. I would carry loads of stone up the mountains from my house. I would choose steeper and more difficult trails and deliberately go over boulders or climb steep rock faces to acquire better balance and get over the fear of heights. I would dump the stones up there and bring back firewood or grass. That way, I combined household work with my fitness regimen, which proved to be a boon for me later on.

When you climb a mountain, you confront all sorts of challenges. A sudden snowfall that wipes out a trekking route, or a ladder hanging loose as the crevasse it bridges becomes wider.... But such unexpected crises have helped me find out about myself — what scares me, and how I can muster confidence and determination in spite of that. I consider nature not only as a great teacher, but also as a great purifier ... it simplifies the problems, and purifies our path. It teaches us that if one way is blocked, there are many others you can take, that any problem has more than one solution. For instance, when a stream has to be crossed and there is no bridge, you can form a human chain across it.

◆

We were flown to Kathmandu, in March 1984. From there, the team moved onwards, and I had my first glimpse of Mount Everest. We, the hill people, have always worshipped the mountains and, the overpowering emotion I felt at that awe-inspiring spectacle was, therefore, devotional.

We began the ascent, and on the Buddha Purnima of 15-16 May 1984, I was at Camp III, in a colourful nylon tent perched on the ice-crusted, steep slope of Lhotse. There were ten others in the camp. Lopsang Tshering shared my tent. I was sleeping soundly, when around 12.30 a.m. I was shaken awake by a hard object hitting me on the back of my head and, simultaneously, by a loud explosion. Then I felt something cold and heavy creeping over my body and crushing me. I could hardly breathe.

A tall serac (ice tower) on the Lhotse glacier directly above our camp had cracked, crashed down and developed into a massive avalanche. This enormous mass of ice blocks, crushed ice and frozen snow thundering down the near vertical slope at the speed of an express train, devastated our camp, which was directly in its path. Practically everyone was hurt. It was a miracle no one was killed.

Lopsang was able to tear his way out of our tent, and began frantically to try and rescue me. Delay would have meant sure death. Heaving and pushing away the large ice slabs, he dug out the hardened snow and I was able to crawl to safety.

No tent had been left standing except the kitchen shelter. Groans of pain and cries for help were audible from all sides. But the expedition still had a lot of fight in it. Well before dawn, we began to dig out our equipment. I was terribly worried about the image of Goddess Durga which I had in my rucksack. Every morning and evening, I took it out and drew inspiration and strength from it. So my first act on finding my rucksack was to thrust my hand into the side pocket. To my relief, my fingers encountered the ice cold metal Durga.

I held the holy image tightly and felt that I had everything I wanted. I had Shakti in my arms. The Shakti, which had saved my life a few hours earlier and the Shakti, which, I was now sure, would lead me onwards and upwards. The experience of the night had drained all fear out of me.

The bump at the back of my head had now begun to throb. The men who had decided to return to Base Camp either due to injury or shock were getting ready to leave. When the leader asked me (I was the only woman in that summit team), whether I would like to give the summit another try, I said, 'Yes Sir, I will.'

And that decision was the turning point in my success story. I thought to myself, 'The biggest risk in life is not to take risks. God has saved my life and, perhaps, the message for me is that my destiny lies in keeping my tryst with Everest.' I felt strangely recharged, as if new strength had welled up within me.

The next morning, I got up at 4 a.m. After putting on my climbing gear, I came out of my tent at 5.30 a.m., and found Ang Dorjee, the Sherpa Sirdar, standing outside. No one else was about. I was ready physically, mentally, emotionally and spiritually too. I was carrying with me a small icon of Durga to place on the summit ... in such places one does tend to look to the divine.

The steep, frozen slopes were as hard and brittle as sheets of glass. We had to use the ice-axe and I had to kick really hard to get the front teeth of the crampon to bite into the frozen surface. I took every step very deliberately on the dangerous stretches. The rarefied air made mind and body coordination very difficult. It was now a question of surviving — the height, the cold (which, in those regions, sometimes goes down to minus 40 degrees Celsius), walking with our load on steep ice walls....

Strong winds eddied and whipped up the powdery snow, reducing visibility to nil. It was terrifying to stand erect on a knife-edge ridge, with a sheer drop on either side. There was some tricky climbing between the South Summit and what is popularly known as Hillary's Step.

The gradient started easing off noticeably. My heart stood still. It dawned on me that success was within reach. And at 1.07 p.m. on 23 May 1984, I stood on top of Everest, the first Indian woman to have done so.

Thousands of metres of near vertical drop on all sides made safety our foremost consideration and we first anchored ourselves securely by digging our ice-axes into the snow. That done, I sank on my knees, and putting my forehead to the snow, kissed Sagarmatha's crown. Taking out the image of Durga Ma and my Hanuman Chalisa from my rucksack, I placed them in the snow, after a short prayer. At that moment of joy, my thoughts went to my father and mother who had taught us the value of effort. As I rose, I bowed in respect to Ang Dorjee, my rope-leader, who had encouraged and led me to my goal.

On returning triumphant from Everest, I was caught up in a whirlwind of activities — attending receptions and dinners and meeting dignitaries. Among others, I met the President of India, Mr J.R.D. Tata, Mr Rajiv Gandhi and Mrs Indira Gandhi, and was overwhelmed when she said, 'We want hundreds of Bachendris in this country'.

I look upon my journey to the top of Everest as an opening ... a path-breaking event for other women. My parents, my family, the mountain people suddenly realised the significance of mountaineering as a sport and as a career. Thanks to the opportunities provided by Tata Steel, I am continuing my efforts to build personality and character, especially among the young.

I suppose, much of my motivation goes back to the time when I was a child, growing up in our village. The family could barely make ends meet, yet my father would invite travellers home and offer them tea. This trait of sharing what we have became so ingrained in me that I have always felt the need to reach out to others and make a difference in their lives — for there is nothing as fulfilling as that. Spirituality is using the power you have to give unselfishly. It means *doing* ... doing what is good for others. My house has always been full of people and, today, I have the pleasure of taking care of five children who came home to me in somewhat unusual circumstances.

The happiness that I derive from my work, I am able to share with other people in a way that is useful, meaningful and caring. If, as they say, 'a true measure of your worth includes all the benefits others have gained from your success', at a personal level, I feel I have been very successful as a human being.

Bachendri Pal

Once Upon a Prayer

As a child, my name was a matter of great distress to me. It was unlike the names of my classmates. To add to the confusion, I was told our family had an Indian surname — Dandekar. It had been given to us in memory of Danda, our ancestral village, where we had first landed after a shipwreck two thousand years back, while fleeing from persecutors who had taken over the Promised Land. Israel.

But, my family had discarded this surname like an old garment, folded it and put it away like a family heirloom. Sometimes brought out to be aired and remembered. Some Bene Israel families used their Indian surnames, others didn't, some still do.

For years, I did not know the meaning of my name, anyway, it became the reason for the search of the Jewish ethos, hidden somewhere within me and waiting to be discovered. And this search drove me to write.

We were not practising Jews, although some rituals existed in our daily life — they were more of the nature of reflex actions.

Slowly, however, my long-forgotten Jewishness started seeping into me at different points of life. It all started with a painful divorce. The family was in a state of shock and unable to comfort me. Perhaps this was the first divorce in the family. I wrote about this feeling in *By the Sabarmati*:

> She looked like an old book whose pages were stuck together by damp. Had I tried to pry open the pages, I was afraid she would fall apart. Between the leaves, I saw shadows of a past which was best kept hidden in the book. To me, her sorrow was almost holy, like an old Hebrew scroll at the synagogue, kept behind a curtain in a vault that faced Jerusalem and the Wailing Wall.

I felt alienated from family, society, community. That is when I met Diana. She had come from Mumbai and was employed as a nurse for the ailing head of a well-known mill-owner's family of Ahmedabad. Mother invited her often to our house and on one such visit she gave me a book of psalms.

Every night, I read fairy tales for the children and made it a habit to also read a psalm before they fell asleep. Those were difficult days, as there was not much money, no comfort, no affection, no understanding. But, the psalms comforted me, as I tried to understand: 'Thou art my shepherd, I shall not want ...'

A few years later, I met a Jewish family from America, living in Ahmedabad. They were on a fellowship to study the urban problems of the city. I was often invited to their home to celebrate Jewish festivals. As the children played, we cooked together, laughed and joked as they taught us Hebrew songs.

That was the beginning.

And, everything changed, when I met Abraham. Abraham changed my life. I wrote about him in the *Book of Esther*.

Like most Jewish tourists, he had come to Ahmedabad
to meet my father and see his zoo. As usual, my father
invited him for dinner. That evening, when I returned from
college, I saw him walking in the garden. It was winter and
he was wearing a black sweater over jeans. He looked like a
bald-headed crow as he greeted me with a warm 'shalom'.
Abraham must have been past eighty. He was thin, sprightly
and had long knotty fingers. We shook hands and I entered
the house, planning the evening meal.

I saw my father standing on the veranda and asking
Abraham if he would like some whiskey. Suddenly, Abraham
stopped walking and answered rather brusquely, 'No, I
cannot accept this.' His eyes were watery when he turned to
me and asked in a strong Israeli accent, 'Do you know today
is the Sabbath?'

'Yes, today is Friday,' I said, a little unsure of what he was
getting at.

'Then, where is the kiddush.'

'Kiddush?' I repeated, confused, looking at father for an
answer.

'Kiddush is the prayer said over a glass of wine to thank
God for his mercies, especially during the Sabbath or the
festivals. I am sorry, but I can neither eat nor drink without
doing the Sabbath prayers.'

My father tried to say, 'I am sorry, but we don't ... and you
cannot leave without eating.'

'Then, dear friend, do you mind if I do the prayers, here
in your house?'

'Yes, you can,' my father was relieved. In fact, he seemed
to like the idea.

'Thank you. Can I please ask your daughter to set the
Sabbath table?' I was embarrassed as I had never prepared
a Sabbath table. I remembered my grandmother arranging
the Sabbath table when I had been a child. It was a distant
memory.

Abraham asked me for a clean white tablecloth and spread it on the dining table. He then asked for a Sabbath candle-stand, but as we did not have one, I gave him a decorative brass plate and a candle. Abraham stood there smiling, asking me to light the candles. I protested, as I did not know how to say the prayers, but felt reassured when Abraham wrote down the Hebrew sounds in English, and asked me to light the candle while reciting them.

I covered my head with a dupatta, because grandmother used to cover her head with her sari while performing rituals. I remembered her face as I read out what he had written, and looked up in surprise as I heard my father say the prayers. He smiled awkwardly. Later, he told me, the words had suddenly come back to him. By then, Abraham had taken a clean wine glass from the kitchen cabinet, poured a glass of Port wine from father's collection of bottles. He gave the kiddush cup to my father, who held the glass in his hand, and together they recited the sonorous words.

With the men, my son was repeating the words and my daughter was also whispering them, looking pleased that she was saying the prayers in Hebrew! Abraham was saying, 'I am not religious and I have not taught you anything. Look, your father knows everything. One never forgets what one learns as a child. Let your children learn from their grandfather. I like the Sabbath and when I travel, I often find a Jewish home, like yours. If not, I just light a candle in my hotel room. I feel good. Don't you ...?'

I nodded my head happily. The house seemed to have a certain aura. Since that evening, I've started the custom of preparing the Sabbath table, saying the prayers and cooking an elaborate dinner, whenever we are all together under one roof.

A month after the dinner, I received a package from Israel. Abraham had sent us two Bibles. One for my father, the other

for me. Both were inscribed in Hebrew: 'I feel, it is my duty
as a Jew to send the Torah to you, as I did not see it in your
house.' I was deeply touched by this gesture.

While growing up, I always felt I was deaf to the sound of
the music in Hebrew prayers. Truthfully, I was often bored.
But, years later, some of these very same sounds had a great
influence on me. Like, when the Shofar or Ram's horn was
blown at the synagogue or I heard the klezmer by Giora
Friedman, a music CD my son brought from Israel, or when I
saw the musical *Golem* by Moni Ovadia. It was the same when
I saw a performance by the Israeli Baat Dor dance company
in France. The chants were in Hebrew and I was in tears, as
the sound was similar to the Hebrew prayers I had heard as
a child, while sitting in the softness of my grandmother's sari
at the synagogue in Ahmedabad.

These abstract Jewish sounds affected me deeply and
my confusion seemed to dissolve within me. I felt I had
always known the sound. The music was emotive. It stirred
something ancient within me. And, I understood the meaning
of the psalm: 'Thou maketh me lie down in green pastures;
thou leadeth me besides still waters ... thou restoreth my
soul ... thou hast anointed my head with oil; my cup runneth
over ...'

I now know that 'Esther' means 'the evening star'. I also
know, for the Jews, God is neither male nor female, but a
book. Yet, God is always referred to by male scribes as male
— He.

Jews are also taught never to pronounce God's name. The
consonants are written and the vowels are not mentioned.
It has to be G-D or YHWH. And, by the way, this God does
not have an image like Michelangelo's painting of God in
the Sistine Chapel!

Esther David

Does God Really Talk to Us?

I was on a train from Delhi to Ernakulam, Kerala. It was May 1981; I had just completed my Master's in operations research from the prestigious St. Stephen's College in Delhi, and was returning home. The journey was symbolic, in the sense that it marked the end of a rather enjoyable and exciting time in my life — my student days were over.

As I settled in my berth, my thoughts drifted towards the future. Yes, I was at the threshold of my professional career. Some of my friends already had job offers, and a few of them had even begun to work. I had decided to take a couple of months off to relax at home before embarking on my search for a job. My mother had died of cancer barely six months earlier, and I felt it was important for me to spend some time with my father.

Having studied in one of India's top colleges, I was confident of making a mark in life, and believed that finding a job would be a simple matter. As I hopped off the train at Ernakulam, I was as delighted to see my father at the station, as he was to have me back home, with a postgraduate degree to boot.

After a month or so, with my CV fine-tuned, I began my
job hunt in right earnest. I made it a point to mention that
I was visually impaired, since I was clear that my potential
employers needed to know about my disability before they
hired me.

Every morning the newspaper was scanned, jobs were
identified and applications sent. Surprise! Surprise! Contrary
to my expectations, the response was far from overwhelming.
In fact, there were just the three or four polite regret letters
that said: 'Your CV is indeed impressive; however, we do
not have a suitable opening for you at the moment. We'll get
in touch with you as soon as something comes up.' A little
disappointing, but still I pressed on.

My father sent my CV to some of his friends who had
volunteered help. An uncle of mine, who had retired from
one of India's top industrial groups, wrote to some of his
contacts. Nothing seemed to work out. I guess, people did
not want to take chances because of my disability.

My confidence, which had been sky-high scarcely a few
months before, started dwindling. I felt I was running out
of options. For the first time in life, my disability seemed to
pose a genuine challenge. I began withdrawing into a shell.
Social gatherings and family get-togethers lost their charm
for me.

To make matters worse, I could sense a change of attitude
among relatives and family friends, and I overheard some
of them share their concern with my father. They appeared
sorry for me! I heard them ask questions like, 'What about
his future? Do you have any plans? It must be really tough
on you.'

All of a sudden, I felt terribly alone. I began to miss my
mother. She had been a source of solid support and strength
during my growing years. She had been the one person I
could confide in. Frustration and self-pity started creeping

in, and I could see myself slipping to a new low with every passing day. Something had to be done. Nearly nine months had gone by and no progress had been made. Most of my friends from college had managed to get themselves jobs and were well on their way towards their goal.

My mother had always told me that there was a God above, and that nothing happened without His knowledge. She would say, 'We need to have faith, and with Him nothing is impossible. He is truly the Living God and He loves you.' She had further told me, 'Son, whenever you are in trouble, turn to Him.'

Finally, as a last option, I did just that. I spent hours reading my large print Bible and praying. I prayed with feeling. My mother's reassuring words kept coming back to me: 'Nothing is impossible with God'. I was determined to get God on my case. Days went by and nothing changed, but I persisted, for I realised that I had no other option. I surrendered myself entirely, and told Him to shape and mould my life.

Early in April 1982, I was woken up at four one morning. No, it wasn't a voice that shook me from my slumber, but a 'commanding' thought that filled me with tremendous energy and totally changed my life. I had never felt like that before. I could hardly wait for my father to wake up. For the next three hours or so, I paced restlessly in my room. Millions of thoughts and ideas raced across my mind. I was literally jumping up and down.

I believed that God had spoken to me and given me definite direction: 'Son, if you want to do something in life, go out and do it yourself. Go out in faith and the world will be at your feet.' Before long, I had made up my mind to take the first available train to Delhi, since that was the city I knew best. When I shared my experience with my father, he said 'Son, go for it.'

A week later, full of positive energy, I was on a train bound for the capital. The fifty-two hours I was on it gave me the time to take stock of things, and chart a plan of action. Given my background in operations research and mathematics, I had earlier thought of becoming a systems analyst, and had also looked at openings in marketing since I enjoy meeting people, travelling, and facing up to challenges. Now, something made me choose advertising as the career for me. The depression and despair of the past nine odd months had given way to hope and anticipation. I could not wait for things to happen

Three days after I arrived in Delhi, I landed my first job with one of the country's larger advertising agencies. That was the beginning of a new journey. Yes, the job had been waiting for me. But I needed to go out in faith to get it. Nothing is impossible with God. I have learnt that if I am prepared to surrender my life to God and live in faith, He works wonders. Who says God does not talk to us. Ask me.

George Abraham

In Memory of Mother

March 1983. I was in Rome and I remember it was a holiday. Molly and Appu, our first-born, then not yet a year old, had left for India the previous day with my sister and brother-in-law who had been visiting us. I was alone in the apartment when I received a call from my brother, Mathew, who was based in Brussels. He told me in measured tones that our youngest brother, Michael, then thirty-two, was in an Intensive Care Unit in the Sree Chitra Medical Centre in Trivandrum, Kerala, fighting for his life. It took some time for the enormity of the crisis to sink in, as Mathew told me that Michael had had two cardiac arrests in quick succession. I gained the distinct impression that the chances of his surviving were remote. The shock was far more than I could absorb. I got out of the apartment and started walking along Via Cassia and its by-lanes. Spring was round the corner, but the plants and trees lining the ancient highway, and now beginning to bloom, did not lighten the heaviness in my heart. I walked for a long time, could not get any solace, and returned to the apartment.

Something made me get into my car and drive to the
Colosseum. Nearby, the Sisters of Charity had a house, in
the stables of some ancient Roman nobleman. I knew that
Mother Teresa was in Rome visiting them, and decided to go
there. As I arrived, Mother was on the grounds of the house
talking to a few visitors. She was, I think. surprised to see
me turn up without any notice.

When I told her about Michael's condition, she immediately
excused herself to the visitors and took me inside a small room,
which the sisters used as a chapel. There she knelt with me
to pray for Michael. After a few minutes she got up to rejoin
the visitors, and asked me to continue praying. Afterwards,
when I was leaving, she gave me something for Michael. If
I remember correctly, it was a rosary, which I gave Michael
when I visited him a few weeks later.

Michael recovered against all odds and is today the vice-
chancellor of the Kannur University in Kerala. However, as
I watched Mother Teresa's beatification ceremonies on TV
two decades later in October 2003, I realised that I had not
adequately thanked Mother for her concern and prayers
for Michael. All that I could think of doing was to sit down,
despite the lateness of the hour, share this story with my
brothers and sisters over the internet and ask that they join
me in thanking Mother for kneeling with me in prayer for
our kid brother in that hour of distress, way back in '83.

Mother Teresa's primary concern was with the poor and
the hungry. She also believed that the lonely needed equal,
if not greater attention, and said, 'Being unwanted, uncared
for, forgotten by everybody, I think that is a much greater
hunger, a much greater poverty than the person who has
nothing to eat.' I did not fit into any of those categories, yet
Mother's compassion and humanity, which were the essence
of her spirituality, were boundless, all-encompassing ... and
reached out to me as we prayed together, on that terrible day

when I was alone in an alien city and needed comfort and strength. I am, forever, grateful to her.

Hormis Tharakan

Helena's Journey

Our flight was delayed by another twenty minutes. Exasperated faces looked at watches, grimaced in unison. I sent off one more message that I would arrive late at the editing studio. ...

I was on my way to Mumbai from Chennai to accomplish a very critical task (on which, apparently, our jobs — and perhaps, even our lives — depended). At least, that's what my angry client had implied. As an advertising copywriter, I had presented our thirty-second commercial for a new facial cosmetic, but our client was most annoyed with a fleeting three-second shot at the end. Apparently, our model didn't look 'radiant enough'. I was sent off to look through alternative shots at the director's studio, enhance special effects to 'salvage' the film, and return the same day.

Finally, settling in our aircraft seats, we had further cause for exasperation. The hostess mechanically announced that we'd now be making a halt en route to Mumbai, as our flight had been combined with Flight 204, which had a stopover at the temple town of Puttaparti.

What about my precious editing time! I had managed to get just two hours from my hotshot, busy film director, who might angrily leave the studio any moment ... what a crisis; hell would break loose if I didn't get the 'radiant expression' fixed by tonight.

Soon, we landed at Puttaparti. Despite my black mood, I looked curiously out of my window: this was the famed temple town, home of the revered god-man, Satya Sai Baba; a place of pilgrimage that drew thousands of devotees from all over the world.

Meanwhile, restless passengers were buzzing the call button, wondering why nothing was happening. Then we all saw why. The airline staff was struggling up the steps with a wheelchair. And on it sat a very large middle-aged lady — a foreigner — looking a bit frightened, and clutching the chair handles. The chair was finally inside the aircraft, and the lady, sweating profusely and looking apologetic, was wheeled along the aisle. The crew stopped at the two empty seats next to me, and after an enormous struggle, eased her into her aisle seat with an exhausted thump. I noticed something remarkable. The crew that had so far seemed most uncaring, was amazingly kind with this lady, who was breathlessly babbling her thanks in a strange language, punctuated by 'Sore-ee'. I instinctively reached out and pressed her plump hand. She nodded, looking grateful. A wave of curiosity and sympathy seemed to touch us all in the aircraft.

Just then a hefty European burst in through the entrance along with the rest of the passengers who were coming on board, and hurried anxiously towards the lady. Obviously the foreign lady's companion. He held her hands, and as he settled into his seat next to mine, I wondered what language they were speaking — was it Greek?

I was conscious that I shouldn't be staring at the couple next to me, yet could not help my eyes straying sideways, noting the extreme gentleness and care with which the man soothed his companion. He turned suddenly to me and said, 'Thank you help for my wife feel okay!' By now, the plane was taking off — and the man was excitedly pointing out the famous temple as it receded from our sight. Instinctively, the couple brought their palms together, shutting their eyes in a moment of faith.

I was by now totally intrigued. I simply longed to know their story. Midway through our flight, I was rewarded. Even as the lady dozed off on his wide shoulder, the man, Alkandros, turned to me in friendly conversation, mostly in broken English. He asked me how many times I had come to the beautiful city of Puttaparti. Well, I admitted, feeling inexplicably apologetic, never actually. I hurriedly asked him the same question. He gestured 'eight' with his fingers, adding with a happy smile that this was his very first visit with his wife. I exclaimed in astonishment. All the way from Greece? He told me about his unfailing annual visit to see Sai Baba. And his plan to bring his wife, somehow, to India, despite her serious disability.

The lady stirred. The wavy strands of grey hair still clung in dampness to her forehead; there was grey even on her hairy upper lip, freckles spread from her face to her ample arms. But she could have been Sleeping Beauty; that was what I saw through her companion's expression. His voice fell to a whisper as we continued our conversation: his wife was paraplegic; and this year, his dream of bringing her to see Sai Baba had come true.

My head buzzed with questions I could never ask. Had he brought her here hoping for a miracle? Did he think that Baba would make her walk again? If so, why was there such a joyful radiance on their faces, even though that wish hadn't been fulfilled?

We chatted on. This was his 'most good' visit of all, he declared. ('But your wife? She still can't walk,' said my mind.) I learnt what he did for a living: taking old discarded furniture, and renewing them with his own hands. I was delighted with his belief that all waste had a good use if you only looked for it. He asked why I was travelling to Mumbai. Oh, I'm going to correct an advertising film I said ... and then, the 'emergency' I was rushing for suddenly hit me; my life's purpose just then seemed so ridiculous.

I couldn't help noting the irony of the situation: here I was, flying across the country to 'technically correct the radiance on a model's face', when a frumpy middle-aged lady next to me — cradled in the arms of a man of deep faith, not to mention romance — had the world's most natural glow.

We landed in Mumbai. Again the big struggle to get the lady (her name was Helena) into the wheelchair. Curiously, I noticed that all the irritated, cursing passengers who'd boarded at Chennai, had turned remarkably quiet. The lady gestured to her husband to ask us all to move on — but there was a unanimous nodding of heads that said — no, please help her out first. We can wait.

Even though my questions about the real purpose of their trip to India went unasked, I got my answers in some way. Perhaps what I had seen was a demonstration of true faith — something that was sending them home with their wish completely fulfilled. Maybe, their wish was simply that the disabled woman make a very long and arduous journey to see her spiritual leader in person; a wish that didn't demand miracles but the security of knowing that they were firmly in trusted hands. A faith so genuine that it had permeated everything to touch so many of us who'd witnessed it.

Plump hands squeezed mine again in farewell. I fought back sudden tears that sprang to my eyes. We all watched in a hush as the gallant Alkandros took leave of us all with a namaste. 'Efkaristo!' he said — a Greek word of thanks I'll never forget.

I thought his glance lingered a while longer on me, with a special twinkle, before he wheeled his beautiful lady away.

Indu Balachandran

If It Is God's Will

The donation of a pair of corneas to an elderly gentleman caused a flutter at the meeting. Corneas were woefully short in supply and there were so many people who could benefit from them. Members at the meeting felt that corneas should be donated to the deserving young who had a whole life ahead, and not to the old.

'Surely if a young boy had had this cornea grafting he would have benefited in many ways and for a longer period at that. Just imagine the boy with useful eyes. He could study, go to college, gain employment, and look after his parents. In short, he could become a useful member of society,' argued one member forcefully.

Another, in an excited voice, posed the question, 'What earthly use is a set of corneas to a person who already has one foot in the grave?'

The heated argument seemed to stretch on and on. At issue was the wisdom in choosing a senior person rather than a youngster to receive the grafting of an imported cornea.

The elderly gentleman in the centre of the controversy was picked by chance. It happened one afternoon when one of the members was going around on fieldwork in a remote area, outside the city limits of Bangalore. He had made the choice, and his decision had provoked the present debate that had divided the club.

Hearing all sides of the argument, the head of the committee felt a closure on the issue was required. He assured the members that, henceforth, greater care would be taken in choosing the beneficiaries. He also promised the members that he would invite all the three recent recipients of the cornea grafting to address the club.

A few weeks later, a club meeting was convened. The three beneficiaries of the cornea project came forward to say a few words. They were all drawn from the economically depressed sections. That part of the criteria for the selection had been satisfied, and there had been no need for a discussion.

The two young boys made their speeches in Kannada, interlaced with Telugu, Tamil, and scraps of English. They were profuse in their thanks, and said how their whole life had taken on a different meaning with sight. It will open up windows of opportunity, one boy gushed. A brilliant student, he had evinced interest in computers and seemed to know a lot just from having heard educational programmes on television, or from others who were well-versed in the topic.

Both the boys said, now that sight had changed their lives, they would work hard, become worthwhile citizens and, later, when able, would reciprocate in some way the club's generosity in giving them sight.

Then came the turn of the old man. He was frail and thin, and trembled in his worn-out khadi clothes.

'When sightless and young, I didn't really miss anything. I grew accustomed to darkness and loneliness,' he started hesitantly. 'But as I grew older, not necessarily wiser, I may add, and became a grandfather, I was suddenly taken over by an urge to see. I desperately wanted my sight back.

'I wanted to see my granddaughter,' he continued, 'just once.

'Each time I had the little girl in my lap and she played with me, I forgot my pain and loneliness. She delighted me with her prattle. We'd laugh as I regaled her with stories of birds and animals. Her laughter was music to my ears. It was like listening to a cherub. After she'd fall asleep or was taken away by her mother, I'd have tears in my eyes. But I had hope. I knew God would allow me to see again — all in good time.

'To gaze at her innocence and rejoice in her birth ... I prayed very hard every day for this miracle to happen. I went to every temple, mosque and church in our village. When one of our Christian neighbours asked me whether I would go along with his family to the church of Our Lady of Health in far away Vellankani in Tamil Nadu, I readily agreed.

'For months after that my heart was filled with hope. One morning I woke up and kept my eyes shut. I had dreamt that I could see again. "What if I couldn't see," I said to myself, "Will I lose faith in God?"

'That morning, I couldn't see and cried bitterly. Later I comforted myself with the thought that a loving God knows best. So what if I couldn't see, I was still enjoying the prattle, the laughter and the company of my little granddaughter.

'That same afternoon, when one of you kind gentlemen spotted me sitting outside my hut and heard my story, you didn't sound very enthusiastic, I could tell. You said the grafting was for young people and that it may not work for people of my age.

'I smiled. I said to you if it is God's will, it will happen.

'So when you came back to me one week later, I was pleasantly surprised. I had thought you had forgotten the wretched old man. And when you took me in your car for the check-up and later for the operation, my joy knew no bounds.

'Even at the hospital the doctor said not to expect too much from the operation. There were cases where this has been known to fail. That did not deter me. I was silently praying all the time.

'After the operation, and before the bandages could be removed, I requested the doctors to allow my granddaughter to be brought before me.

'After what seemed like a long wait, the bandages were gently removed. Things were hazy and blurred in the beginning, but gradually, they began to take shape. My eyes were getting used to the light. Then I saw a vague, unclear picture of my little girl. Slowly, her form became clearer. Wonder of wonders, I could see my own sweet little baby. She was far more beautiful than I had imagined her to be! She was smiling at me. Before I could control them, tears welled in my eyes.'

He paused and looked at the members, wiping his eyes with a small piece of rag. There was a pin-drop silence in the room.

Continuing, he said, 'You have made an old man extremely happy. I have no further desires left in life. But I have one request. If possible, I would like to return the corneas you gave me. Please give it to someone more deserving. A precious gift such as this one should go to someone young. Someone who could use it profitably for improving his life....'

Janardhan Roye

A Moment of Truth

It was in the early years of my newly-discovered avatar as an outdoor person. We were at an outbound programme, at a scenic wilderness site on the banks of the river Cauvery. It was the morning of the second day of the three-day leadership programme, and the time was just right for stretching the team that extra bit, for getting them to push boundaries, break barriers. The early morning air was crisp and cool as we trekked through the forest to a rocky outcrop a couple of kilometres away. Excitement ran high and the mood was one of anticipation as we prepared for the highlight of the programme: rappelling.

Rappelling has traditionally been one of the most exciting and effective 'tools' used by climbers to descend steep rock faces, and the technique is challenging, both physically and mentally. More so as it requires the climber to step off, after walking backwards to the edge of a precipice, into what seems like thin air. This requires guts, faith in the person holding the belay or safety ropes, and, most importantly, the ability to 'let go'. For many, the moment of walking off the edge proves to be life-changing.

Since many are apprehensive about the whole exercise, we usually give a pep talk and a demonstration. Our boys were busy setting up the belays, so my mountaineering instructor and ex-army-officer husband decided to do the demo rappel. Seeing a great opportunity for some dramatic photographs, I grabbed my camera, reached a vantage point just as my husband got ready to step off the edge, and clicked.

There was a dull silence from the camera. It was the good old film variety, and the reel was over. I needed to change the film. No problem, I had another roll handy. But what about the guy hanging over the edge?

'Hey, hold on a mo,' I yelled blithely, as if he were walking down the road. 'I need to change the reel.' As I shielded my camera from the sun while reloading, I noticed my husband silhouetted against the skyline at a peculiar angle. 'Must be a tad uncomfortable,' I thought, then dismissed the notion. After all, he was an experienced climber, and had probably done this any number of times. Standing on the edge must be as easy as pie for him.

'Okay, roll!' I yelled when I was ready, and he expertly jump-rappelled down the slope as I took pictures. Then it was time for the participants to test their mettle, and the programme took over all else.

In the quiet of the evening, long after the campfire revelry was over and we sat gazing into the embers, my husband turned to me with a strange expression on his face. 'Why did you make me hang up there on the edge this morning?' he asked.

'I needed to change the film ... I told you,' I replied carelessly, intent on watching the wisps of smoke, and not really paying attention. 'Why? It must have been a piece of cake for you. You were not afraid, were you? You must have done this hundreds of times.'

His answer hit me like a bolt between the eyes. 'Of course, I've done it hundreds of times. But that doesn't mean there is no fear. Every time I go over the edge, I face the fear. And overcome it. That's where my training comes in.' My jaw dropped in surprise, and in contrition. 'The fear never goes away,' he smiled gently. 'We only learn how to get ahead of it.'

I sat in front of the fire a long, long while, thinking about what he had said. And suddenly, I understood the source of his strength.

It was that deep, unshakeable faith that made up the core of his being, a spirituality that gave him a knowledge beyond words. I had seen it on several occasions when things went wrong for us: an unquestioning calm, and an abiding belief that we were being watched over by a greater power.

It was a faith that instilled courage not just in himself, but in those with whom he came into contact. Because in the light of that faith, the spectre of fear became just a threshold to cross over.

Kalyani Candade

Way to Go, Megha!

*Trust in Him at all times, O people; pour out your
hearts to Him, for God is our refuge.*

Psalm 62:8

It was just another day — 12 April 1999 — but one which
changed Megha Tamboli's life completely. She was going to
Pune from Nagpur in a luxury coach, when it collided head-
on with a petroleum tanker. Megha was badly hurt in the
accident, and rushed to a military hospital for treatment.

After spending nineteen months at the hospital, she was
told that her thoracic spinal cord injury was so serious, that
she would not be able even to sit properly. That night, Megha,
who was just twenty-five, was understandably depressed. But
when she woke up in the morning, she was suddenly filled
with hope and decided she would not be negative or sad. 'I am
God's child. He knows what he is doing. He loves me deeply,'
she told herself repeatedly, and made up her mind not to dwell
on the accident and its consequences, or blame the rash driver,
as it would not change what had happened to her.

'I decided to look at only the positive side, which was that my brain was working and I had no head injury. Moreover, after the accident, my faith in God strengthened as I looked towards him for constant support and strength. That night, as I lay in bed and was staring at the ceiling, I asked Him to make it possible for me to earn my own living. And I made a promise to myself that I would share what I earned with those less fortunate. I took this up as a challenge and, eight months later, I began to walk with my calipers and crutches,' says Megha. And although she subsequently suffered a setback that left her paralysed below the waist, Megha refused to put on hold her dream of helping others.

It was not easy as she had to struggle with simple day-to-day activities, readjust her life and deal with sympathetic looks from family and friends. Her biggest support was her mother, who herself was a strong-willed lady with immense faith in God. Megha says, 'I never saw my mother cry, not even when I had my accident. She even consoled the families of other patients when they wept, and explained to them that they should not worry and that God is good ... that He will do good things. With my mother by my side, encouraging and inspiring me, I began to feel that it was God's way of telling me that he was with me and wanted what was best for me, although in the beginning, I just couldn't see it very clearly. With each small victory at rehabilitation, I felt his blessings grow stronger. It was as if I had risen from the ashes like a phoenix, under his guiding hand.'

It was at the hospital that she found herself reading about the BPO industry. She understood that information technology (IT) and information technology-enabled services (ITES/BPO) were a sunrise industry with a phenomenal growth rate, and that the highest standards in both competence and efficiency were a must. And she decided to target this industry and transform her life.

'I always wanted to be an entrepreneur. But how could I run my own placement and training company unless I knew the workings of the BPO industry? So for the next three years I worked in various BPO firms, right from operations to human resources,' says Megha who, through grit, determination and an unshakeable faith in God, went on to become the sole proprietor of Career Call, a one-stop shop providing recruitment, selection and training services for the IT and ITES industry.

Megha has come a long way! Today her range of corporate clients includes prestigious Indian companies and clients in Malaysia. Here too she believes that it was God's guiding hand that gave her the opportunities and strength to prove herself and fulfil the promise she made while lying helplessly on her hospital bed.

Megha has helped in rehabilitating other differently-abled people by providing job placements and moral support, and also by being the medium for spreading God's love. Four years ago, the Symbiosis Institute of Business Management, Pune, felicitated her, during their festival of entrepreneurs.

She explains, 'If you accept God, He gives you the wisdom and peace to know what is right and wrong.' With a firm belief in the Almighty, Megha adds that everything in her life has been a gift from Him, and that nothing is impossible if God is with you.

Khursheed Dinshaw

Pranitha's Story

The nights are the longest for twenty-one-year-old Pranitha. That's when her acid-scarred skin itches and burns the most. She pops a pill and tosses about on the bed, waiting, almost begging for sleep to come. But it takes three hours at least before she finally slips into a disturbed slumber, and escapes the scalded reality of her life.

It was in December 2008 that Tekalapally Pranitha and her friend Swapnika were maimed in a horrific acid attack in Warangal. Swapnika died after a fortnight, but Pranitha, after six surgeries on the neck, face, hands, back and legs, and two to repair her eyelid, soldiers on. Nine months later, Pranitha, who passed her BTech with flying colours, goes about life with such vigour that your heart trembles with awe.

'I was never scared that I would die, only had this fear that I would lose my eyesight or hearing. I lost my right ear but I can hear and, luckily, only my eyelid was damaged,' she says with a disarming smile, as if she were describing a mere pimple.

In the first three months, Pranitha was not allowed to look into a mirror. That was when she was laid up on a hospital bed and her skin was being grafted constantly. Yet she prepared for her engineering exams, with her mother and a couple of friends reading out the chapters to her. Today, she has her sights set on CAT and the Civils. A job with Infosys in Mysore is also in the bag. Pranitha landed the job before the attack, but Infosys officials, who watched her battle on relentlessly, say that it's a privilege to have this brave warrior on board.

A bandage covers her head and part of her face. Pressure garments conceal the eroded skin on her upper body and legs and yet her spunky spirit shines through. 'I have started meditating of late. Doctors tell me to play hopscotch, skip or climb stairs as an exercise. But I have to take care that I don't sweat too much. My sweat pores, in places where the acid fell, were damaged. So the minute I sweat, the skin starts itching. We bought an AC recently for the same reason,' Pranitha elaborates.

Pranitha travels to Hyderabad every week for check-ups and steroid injections. In about three months, she hopes to get a silicon ear as well.

The Warangal heroine recollects that the horror of the attack first struck her when she looked at Swapnika. 'The skin on her face was hanging and I was terrified. Then I began to feel this searing pain in my own body. It was only in the hospital that I found out it was acid.'

But Pranitha has put the harsh memories behind her with steely grit. She attributes her confidence to her family's love. 'My parents, my brother and my grandfather keep my spirits up always. My philosophy is simple. Let the doctors do their job and I'll do mine. Recovery is bound to take time.'

Asked what she seeks from God when she prays, Pranitha thrusts her chin up and answers, 'I don't ask God for anything. I need not. He knows what's best for me.'

Madhavi Tata

Shalimar

When I was a young boy growing up in Kerala, I would sometimes head for the nearby forest on a hunting expedition. (Nowadays, I shoot only with my camera!) My usual companions were a couple of men who worked for my father. And although I did pick up a few of their hunting skills during each such battle of wits between hunter and hunted, it is my love of cooking that has survived as a reminder of those forays into the wild! You see, on those hunting trips, the men would clean whatever we had bagged, throw in a few magic ingredients, and conjure up the most delicious meals, by the time the pangs of hunger struck. I was utterly fascinated by all the bubbling and sizzling, and the mouth-watering aromas, the deft touches, and the artistry that made all the difference between an ordinary meal and one fit for an emperor. After watching them on a few occasions, I began to pitch in too, adding an inventive twist here, something adventurous there, and we often ended up with a delectable new version of some humdrum dish!

◆

Armed with an engineering degree from Kerala, like many other students I went to the US in the Seventies, to study further; and later, settled down there. One of the things I really missed when I set up home in Frederick, Maryland, was a restaurant that served authentic Indian food. There were places I frequented that had a few Indian dishes on their menu, but those were a far cry from their original version. Frederick was a fast-growing town with a multi-cultural society. So I began to have fleeting thoughts of setting up an Indian restaurant there ... merely as an additional venture, of course.

In 1985, Sally (my wife) and I decided to pursue this idea seriously After looking around, we bought a very old building that happened to be in a part of downtown Frederick designated a 'historical district', so it was under certain 'rules of protection'. It meant that everything — the paint, the windows and doors, in short, all the details of the façade — had to conform to the same specifications as the rest of the buildings in the neighbourhood, which dated all the way back to the 1750s!

Sally and I spent October and November redesigning the place to suit our needs. We imported fittings, fixtures, furniture and artwork from India, and also tandoori ovens (little anticipating what lay in store for us). Meanwhile, with the people we had hired, we tackled the tedious job of transforming the first floor into an Indian restaurant.

It was spread over two rooms, and you entered through an exquisite temple door. The place looked warm and elegant and inviting. Everything was meticulously planned, down to the last detail — the tablecloths, and napkins and paintings of elephants, and so on. After weeks and weeks of hectic preparations — researching, testing and tasting food, for I wanted the menu to be authentic — the restaurant was ready to open. The sign, Shalimar, Indian Restaurant, fashioned with some of the stylistic flourishes of the Devanagari script, hung outside.

We had no dearth of customers, and our friends and guests raised toasts to our success and happily tucked into the food. From the very beginning, people were gratifyingly enthusiastic about the fare we served, in spite of Indian cuisine being alien to them. We had some excellent press reviews too!

And then, eleven days after we opened our restaurant ... it burned to the ground. The fire, which started on a Sunday morning, just before Christmas, was traced to one of the tandoors. These were built on firebricks and they burned, day in and day out, even when the restaurant was closed. So the bricks got hotter and hotter. Underneath the bricks were thick layers of wood, almost 180 years old, which caught fire, and then the blaze spread to the rest of the building. It took the fire-fighters hours to bring the fire under control. There were times when the water turned to ice before it reached the flames, and we stood by helplessly and watched everything we had worked for, as well as a couple of establishments abutting ours, burn down, causing an estimated damage of one million dollars.

This was probably one of the most traumatic events in our life. Naturally, I was devastated. All our hard work and dreams had gone down the drain ... or had they? On reflection, it struck me that, perhaps, everything had happened for the best. Maybe, God was telling us that this was not what He intended for us. We could let this catastrophe destroy our hopes, or we could look at it as God's way of pointing us in a different direction. Or, maybe, God in His infinite wisdom was testing us.

Sally and I prayed together and, with renewed confidence, we decided to go on. This was, by no means, the first setback I had faced and I found no reason to be discouraged by it. I did not think that I had failed, for I firmly believe that you grow stronger by learning to overcome adversity. When you tell yourself that you are a failure, it makes you lose sight of your goals, and that makes you lose sight of your real self. I was determined never to let that happen to me.

If we are willing to make the effort to learn through adversity, experience and hard work, those lessons will stand us in good stead throughout our life. So instead of mourning our losses, we must be willing to learn from them and try and try again to achieve what we want. What I needed to do became clear to me, and I said very calmly, 'I will rebuild Shalimar.'

God allows untoward things a place in our lives for a purpose, although we cannot always understand why He does this. We can only accept His will and do the best we can. Both Sally and I have always believed that God has a much bigger plan for everything. So, with faith and a lot of hard work and the help of friends, I began rebuilding the restaurant, which had turned into a burned-out shell. Everywhere, there were ugly, jagged, gaping holes, tangles of wires, splintered beams hanging askew, and furniture strewn at crazy angles over floors littered with debris. Clinging to everything still was the acrid odour of smoke. It was mind-boggling!

I took stock of it all and wondered, 'How are we going to put this right?' But the outpouring of support and sympathy from the community gave us great confidence, and so we moved our restaurant and all the belongings that had been salvaged to another place. Phoenix-like, the Shalimar emerged again, about six blocks away.

Everybody persevered — our waiters, our cooks, our manager — and although we worked hard, there were lots of laughs too. Thankfully, no one had died in the fire, and we opened our home — we had a small three-bedroom house at the time — to all of our staff. Where else could they have gone? And so our house was overflowing with cooks and waiters and our staff, and they clustered together and slept on the floor. All this had happened during the Christmas holidays, and we were soon like one big family. Everything was everywhere!

The compassion of friends, neighbours and customers was overwhelming. Some people hugged us, others offered their condolences, and all of them volunteered help. They plied us with cartons of cereal, soap, milk, rice, clothes, fruit ... they just kept coming and delivering them. Soon we had a surfeit of everything under the sun!

Most inspiring of all were those vivid memories of teamwork, the rapport and joy we felt because we all shared the common mission of rebuilding the old Shalimar and running it again. And so, we kept at it, and kept at it, and kept at it ... and it was a long, long haul but we did it in the end!

The day we opened, we hung balloons out of all the windows. And the building looked beautiful with new carpets and fixtures. The insurance did not cover all our losses, and that cloud loomed over us for many months. Sally prayed repeatedly for one thing, 'God, please make it possible to pay our mortgage.' And we never missed paying a single instalment — I think it was some 632 dollars and 46 cents or so — on time. That was a miracle.

Then, after we had gone through all the stress and trouble of rebuilding Shalimar, we had an unexpected setback, and I found I had to sell it after all. I had planned things ... but He disposed of them. 'God, what is happening to me?' I agonised, but my faith was never shaken. I knew that He would show me the way, all in His own time. And He did! A year later I was given the opportunity to pursue my dream of starting my own company.

Initially, I had not been able to get the funds I needed. Then, I had an unexpected lead, and contacted the person I had been told about (everyone called him 'Doc'), to find out whether he would consider investing in my company. When I explained what I had in mind, he seemed interested in my project and invited me to his home. As soon as I parked the car and got out, my eyes were drawn to the name of his house. It was Shalimar! My own Shalimar had been reduced to ashes and another Shalimar had drawn me towards it! I was sure that God had brought me there for a reason. I wondered if it was some kind of a marker to point out my path. Or whether He was testing me so that I would learn to push myself to pass the test, and then keep on growing. I did not question His reasons but went ahead with what needed to be done … and in the end, it proved to be a bit of both! But that's another story.

With His hand guiding me gently through all my trials, I did achieve my dream, and started the Maryland Paper Company, which has grown into one of the biggest producers of roofing felt from recycled paper, in the US. It was, and still is, my company.

Today, I do all my Indian cooking at home!

Mathew Chakola

Hockey and the Eucharist

When I was in school, Jesus was as vivid to me as my school friends and companions. The feeling faded at around the time I entered college, though my interest in and attraction to the faith of my childhood continues. Even today, committed as I am to vedanta, however relentless and powerful its logic and philosophy, Jesus is my ishta devata. Believe in me, you will be saved. Everybody is as important as you are. Treat others as you wish to be treated. God's Kingdom is within you. The messages of Christ were so simple that even a child could understand them.

Because Hindus confidently accommodate other religions and do not have an either/or attitude to faith, I had no difficulty reading or talking about Christianity at home. I stuck a picture of Jesus in my compass box and a rosary lay by the copy of the *Ramayana* on the puja shelf.

When I was eleven years old, I was selected for the school hockey team. My games mistress, Deana Thomas, had me playing right extreme. Anyone who knows the game will know that the players who have to run the most and fastest are those positioned on the extremes of the field. As the youngest player, I was good-humouredly teased about everything. I was called the Stick Insect, I was so thin. My diet, particularly, was the object of much laughter because all the others were non-vegetarians, much better built than I was, and much stronger, though not necessarily for that reason. 'You better eat some meat if you want to build your stamina,' was something I was told every day. It was true that I tired faster than the others, and I was sure it was because of my *erasheri* and all those useless vegetable thorans and upperis.

I thought about it. Beef and other sorts of meat? No. It had to be something else. What was the last meal Jesus had had with his disciples? Bread and wine. Yes. That was it. He had also told them to remember Him. My body and my blood. What could be better? I asked about the bread and wine my friends received in church. Alas, it wasn't for sale.

Why was his body and blood available only in church?

That evening, after everybody had bathed and the lamps were lit, I took careful aim and announced, 'From now onwards, may I have some bread and wine at this time? I have to build my stamina.' There was the kind of silence that made me regret my words as soon as they were out, but it was too late.

Breaking the silence, my aunt, Echu Edathi, said smoothly, 'Yes of course. You can have Indian wine.'

'Will it be from crushed grapes? It has to be crushed grapes.'

'Why? Dasamoolarishtam is just as good. I will give you that. And bread ... like, er ... like they distribute in church.' My aunt understood what I wanted. 'It will make you strong,' she said persuasively.

I brightened up immediately. Whatever bread I ate, I believed He would be in it. And since my life was about to change, I compromised on the brand of wine.

And so it happened. Echu Edathi used to freeze the bread, slice it fine, trim the crust and give me a slice along with an ounce-glass full of dasamoolarishtam. My mother's face was expressionless as she brought this strange snack from the puja room, where I felt it had to be placed before I ate it in the evening. The point is, every time I thought of it, I felt strong. My game improved, I didn't feel tired, and my team mates congratulated me on what they thought was my new diet.

Only my understanding family knew what my faith-food was. Years later, I read about auto-suggestion and the power of faith. Jesus too had said that if you had enough faith you could move mountains and uproot a tree and plant it in the sea.

I certainly moved the hockey field on the faith that I was eating what the disciples had eaten.

Mini Krishnan

Fate or Faith?

During the last Diwali holidays, my husband and I, along with our seven-and-a-half-year-old son, Sarthak, his cousin, and another couple went on a picnic to Murud Janjhira in Alibaug, located on the coastal belt of Maharashtra. It is a quiet seaside resort on the outskirts of Mumbai. Our journey in our Toyota-Qualis was quite comfortable but uneventful. So, the next day, on our way to the beach, we decided to kill the monotony and got a bit adventurous. Instead of parking our vehicle in the parking area, we drove down towards the shoreline. I curled up my nose at the sight of a few people, here and there. But for them, it could have been my own private beach, I thought!

We got a bit carried away and did something crazy. We made the children sit on the carrier, on top of the Qualis. We ladies sat on the bonnet, the men piled in and the one behind the steering wheel set the Qualis flying along the shoreline, parallel to the sea. Suddenly, my imagination soared. Though I have neither the face nor the figure of a Miss Universe, I imagined myself shooting for some international advertisement campaign! The guys looked like daredevils right out of a James Bond thriller, and the children had all the powers of their favourite hero, Superman.

After this crazy drive, we parked our vehicle a little away from the shoreline and jumped into the sea. Ten minutes later we had the shock of our lives. The seawater had reached our parked vehicle, and it had started subsiding into the wet sand. By the time we reached it, its rear wheels had gone deep down. As my husband started the car, pressed the accelerator and revved the engine, the wheels rotated in the same place and sank down by half a foot. I felt ashamed of myself when the same people whom I had looked upon as intruders in 'my' space, came running to help us. Thank God, it was not a private beach and we had people around, I thought.

Though there were about thirty of us, the Qualis would not budge. It was like pushing against a wall. There was a huge commotion and instant panic. One of the locals said that he could arrange for a crane to pull out the Qualis, but that it would cost Rs 2,000. Another gentleman suggested that we put rocks underneath after lifting the rear wheels so that the wheels would be on firmer ground. No sooner had he uttered those words than all of us started passing the rocks we could find around us, towards the Qualis.

My son Sarthak puffed up his cheeks like a monkey, and remarked, 'Mama, we are just like the vanar sena, trying to build the bridge to Lanka, across the sea, so that Sri Rama could cross over!' Under normal conditions, I would have complimented him proudly on this excellent mythological analogy, but anxiety had dimmed my sense of humour. Instead, I screamed at him to stop being 'smart', and to keep his comments to himself.

We lifted up the rear wheel and put small rocks into the pit. To our delight, this time the Qualis moved forward suddenly and, for a second, we thought it would come out. But our hopes were short-lived. The vehicle kept moving back and forth, but refused to come out of the pit that had formed below the wheels. As we were thinking of requisitioning a crane to lift out the Qualis, Sarthak came to me and remarked, 'Mama, how is it going to work? You forgot to write "Jai Sri Ram" on the rocks!'

He sounded desperate. I remembered how I had screamed at him for no fault of his, and it pricked my conscience. Before I realised what I was doing, I rushed to the first rock in sight and made my son write 'Jai Sri Ram' on it with a brick. The onlookers stared at me as if they were watching a mad woman, and I found myself saying, 'Please let us try it once again, for the last time.'

This time, as the crowd lifted up the rear wheels, the atmosphere echoed with a spontaneous chorus of 'Jai Sri Ram!' from everybody. As my husband floored the accelerator, with a sudden jerk the Qualis lurched forward and inched its way out of the pit! There was an instant cry of relief from everyone. As we thanked the crowd profusely, they all remarked on what seemed like a miracle: what many rocks had failed to do, one rock with God's name on it had accomplished!

'See? I told you it doesn't happen only in *Ramayana*,' I heard my son telling his cousin. 'My mother is a teacher and she knows everything,' he beamed!

I ran to my little angel and held him close as tears rolled down my cheeks. He seemed unaware that he had taught his mother the greatest lesson of her life, something that she had been preaching but not practising herself:

If you don't lose your faith

You can indeed change your fate!

Preeti A. Bhatt

The Weekend Surprise

On a visit to London in 1986, my husband and I found that we had a weekend free, and decided to visit the famous shrine at Lourdes, in the south of France. We were lucky to get train tickets at short notice — and only later was I able to see that it was all part of a magnificent miracle, at least for me.

After a comfortable journey, we reached Lourdes; from the station, we took a shuttle bus to the shrine and there we were told to go for the baths. Separate sunken baths have been made for men and women where one can have a dip in the holy waters of the spring, which is visible under a glass sheet. On that day, it was very crowded because all the military cadets of Europe were there for a special blessing from the archbishop, who was coming from Rome for the occasion.

I was sitting on the pews on one side where all the women were seated. On a small podium, mass was being read in various languages — Russian, Polish, German, and French. Suddenly, a woman came on stage and spoke in French, asking if there was any English-speaking person in the crowd. Since I had learnt French in school, I understood what she was saying, and I raised my hand, expecting that she wanted some instructions to be conveyed in English for the sake of those who understood only English. On seeing me, the woman said, 'Come here, come up quickly,' and when I ran up to her, she thrust a huge book — the Bible — in my hand, told me that I must read from it, and disappeared.

Fortunately, I was somewhat familiar with the Bible, as I had studied in Christian schools and colleges. I sat on stage, listening to a man reciting something in a language that I did not recognise. As soon as he finished, I was asked to read, and did so next. Surprisingly, I remembered even the hymns that were sung, as I had learnt them back in my schooldays!

Later, after a dip in the baths, my husband and I sat on the lawns to eat lunch — chapati and alu curry which I had cooked and brought from London. My husband said that on hearing my voice over the mike he had got the shock of his life; and had had to crane his neck to see if it was really me on the stage. He laughed and said that a typical Tam-Bram mami, in silks and diamonds, reading out the mass in Lourdes was a unique sight indeed.

After that beautiful experience, I wanted to share my joy with one and all, and started looking around to see if I could find someone who would share my food with me. My husband tried to dissuade me saying that, in France, one cannot find beggars, and that I should go ahead and eat my food quickly. Just as I was reluctantly tearing a piece of chapati, an old man suddenly came up and asked if I could give him some food! I was overwhelmed and, feeling utterly blessed, gladly gave him what I had.

That night, on the train back to England, as we sat eating bread and jam, my husband was telling me in Tamil that he was sick and tired of eating bread all the time, and that he was waiting to get back to India just to eat proper food — by which he meant sambar, rasam, appalam … the lot. Suddenly, we were startled out of our skins when, seemingly out of the dark, someone spoke to us in Tamil, and invited us to dinner at his home in London the following evening! Recovering from our surprise, we noticed that the person who was stretched out in the seat across the aisle was an Indian, a military attaché, posted in London. We quickly struck up a conversation and said that we could not impose on him, but he would have none of that. The next evening found us — a little apprehensive and embarrassed — ringing his doorbell. But all our misgivings vanished when our new friend opened the door smilingly, and out wafted the delicious aroma of a south Indian meal. The table was laden with a veritable feast — sambar, puliogere, payasam — the works.

Even now, when I look back on that 'miraculous' weekend, I am struck with wonder at His mysterious ways ... at how He understands and fulfils our smallest wishes, at the right time.

Raji Ratan
(As told to Karuna Sivasailam)

Full Circle

When a child is delivered to your doorstep, you have no choice but to put your faith in the unknowable. That's how my friend, Jyoti, felt when she discovered a tiny, dark boy, about eight months old, early one morning as she arrived at her orphanage in Bangalore.

In over a decade of regularly visiting Jyoti's orphanage, I had seen and heard the stories of countless children, willed into this world by accident, left to find life in the care of fate. And Jyoti.

Jyoti looked at this child in wonder, like she had so many times before. Every child has a certain 'something', she's often told me. This one had deep, luminous eyes! They shone through the dirty rags that covered his body. Fierce, black, gleaming eyes.

The little boy was soon introduced to five other little children at the orphanage, who were between a few months and five years of age. The naming ritual went into action. The maid proclaimed that the baby looked like a jewel in the dust, so they called him Ratan.

In a few months, the doctor diagnosed that little Ratan was spastic and had polio. The maids despaired ... he would never be adopted. Ratan was, like all kids, oblivious to the future. He flashed his dazzling smile, and his shiny eyes sparkled. He won over hearts with his special laughter — a full-throated triumphant gurgle that set off a chorus of giggles from the other children.

Over the years, the oldest girl there, called Kaveri, instinctively played a protective role, admonishing Ratan for not eating, complaining to the maids, and fighting off other kids for him.

But for eight long years, Ratan and Kaveri saw their brothers and sisters leave them for new homes. Our hearts would break to see them cling desperately to the legs of every person who came visiting the orphanage, in the earnest hope that they would be picked. But ready-made parents never came for them. 'It's their fate,' moaned the maids. 'Jyoti-ma will have to keep them forever.'

But then, one day, a young lady from America came calling.

Jane, a long-time colleague of Jyoti's, a single mother working in the US, was looking for a companion for her daughter. She picked out Kaveri as a perfect sister. At long last, Kaveri's hope of adoption had come true!

On Kaveri's last day at the orphanage, I was invited to a party. Ratan laughed and yelled with joy as if unaware that Kaveri was leaving him. 'Perhaps he's being spared the awful wrench of knowing what separation is,' I thought anxiously. At such times, was it a blessing to be spastic, I wondered.

Then in a few months, Richard, a widowed father, came visiting from America. He was captivated by Ratan's boisterous spirit and sparkling eyes. We cheered as Ratan was picked for adoption.

This could have been the happy ending, but for an astonishing quirk of fate.

A few years later, the adoptive American parents of the orphanage children all came together one day, at a networking party arranged by Jyoti in New Jersey. They arrived from everywhere — to meet and to share stories and marvel at the karmic bond that linked them all.

And that's where Richard met Jane for the first time. The friendship grew into love. And in a few months, they were married.

Incredibly, Ratan and Kaveri were back, full circle, as brother and sister under the same roof!

'How amazing,' I said to Jyoti. 'You made that happen, you know. If it wasn't for that party you organised ...'

'Don't know about that,' Jyoti said with a twinkle in her eyes. 'Ratan's exultant laughter on the day Kaveri left the orphanage meant he knew something we could never have guessed.' I thought this was a most charming interpretation of the term 'leap of faith'!

Over the years, Jyoti has placed over two hundred abandoned children in homes around the world. She calls it her karmic due, and is guided by sheer optimism, for she believes that faith can make things happen.

Shubha Priya

When He Calls

At the end of the nineteenth century, my great grandfather ran away from home, leaving his village forever, and landed in Bangalore. His forefathers had been Vedic scholars, but my great grandfather had set his heart on a 'Western' education. According to family lore, he found distant relatives in the city, who allowed him to stay with them and, in exchange, he taught the children in the family something he was good at — maths. Later, with a scholarship to back him up, he went to college and emerged an engineer.

Bangalore, then, was a vast palette of many greens, spiked with fiery gul mohars and purple jacaranda, and people had begun to build and live in bungalows surrounded by huge gardens. My great grandfather soon got into the act and he too began building the colossal stone buildings that Bangalore was once famous for. In course of time, when the Sringeri Shankara Mutt decided to construct their buildings in Bangalore, the project was entrusted to him. When the project was completed, His Holiness was so pleased with the results, that he called my great grandfather and presented him with a murti of Ganapathy, made of metal.

My great grandfather was in a bind. In those days, a murti (especially one presented by someone as revered as His Holiness) could not be deposited in the living room as an object d'art. Once you had such a murti in the house, it *had* to be installed in the puja room and properly prayed to in accordance with certain rules of worship. Now, a brief namaskar after his bath was about the extent of my great grandfather's spiritual dealings, and he had no intention of mending his ways.

My great grandmother could, of course, have acted as his proxy in the puja room, but she thought there would be plenty of time to worry about the afterlife after she got there. Meanwhile, there were more pressing concerns here and now — daughters-in-law to be chivvied, servants to be chastised, marauding monkeys to be outwitted, and so on....

So how could he decline the icon without offending His Holiness, wondered my great grandfather. He could think of no plausible reason, so he decided to come clean and confessed that he, his wife and his sons were all — sad to say — spiritually challenged. So could His Holiness please take back the icon?

His Holiness smiled gently, looked at him with luminous eyes, and said, 'When the time is right, it will happen. Whomsoever He calls will go to Him. In the meantime, keep the murti in your puja room.'

For years, the Shankara Ganapathy gleamed benignly in the light of the oil lamps that were lit in the puja room, every day. As usual, my great grandfather and his three sons bobbed in for a brief namaskar in the morning. A little later, a priest came in to do the puja, and steaming hot offerings were dispatched to the puja room on time, so Ganapathy had no cause for complaint, if He was prepared to overlook the fact that the family was not spending quality time with Him.

Then, all of a sudden, for whatever mysterious reason, my great grandfather's second son — my grandfather — found himself drawn to the puja room, and began to spend more and more time there. He brushed up his Sanskrit with some help from the priest and began to participate in the pujas. And after my great grandfather died, the Shankara Ganapathy migrated with my grandfather to the house that he built, and occupied pride of place in the puja room.

My father chose to have nothing more than a nodding acquaintance with all things spiritual, and my only brother, not even that, thank you very much. He did not trust anything unless it had been proved conclusively and scientifically, and had a Q.E.D. slapped on its tail. So, after my grandfather died, my mother worried about what would happen to the Shankara Ganapathy in the years to come. Who would continue the puja? Alas, she found no answer. My mother eventually did the smart thing — she focused on managing her arthritis and stopped worrying about His future.

Like all NRIs living in the US, my brother and his family have been coming to India during the children's summer holidays, to visit family and friends, eat street food, and watch the latest Hindi movies. It was all a set routine. Then, when the kids were teenagers, something strange happened. During one of the visits, my nephew, Hari, began to disappear every morning after his bath. Was he meeting a girlfriend — he was only thirteen, for goodness sake! It was his mother who finally butted in and asked, 'Hari, where do you go every morning?'

'To the Ganapathy temple on the next street.'

My brother was bewildered. 'Did your grandmother ask you to go?'

'Of course not! I go because I want to.' My brother should have seen it coming when Hari began to show a heightened interest in the puja room and its contents — particularly the Shankara Ganapathy — that visit.

Nevertheless, such behaviour was quite unexpected. The children had all been brought up in nice, rational, secular surroundings, and here was this boy haring off to the temple without so much as a by-your-leave. Sheesh! Teenagers! Anyway, there was still hope. Back in the US, it was all bound to wear off — peer pressure would take care of that.

But it didn't. My brother's house is near the famous Pittsburg temple, and Hari not only continued to march to the beat of a different drummer, he decided to be that drummer himself! And as he can be mighty persuasive when he puts his mind to it, soon, a whole group of kids had signed up for bhajan classes and various other weekend activities at the temple! And my brother was roped in as part of the temple-going car pool....

Hari's grades were excellent and as he did all the usual teenage stuff — painted his nails black, listened to eardrum-shattering music, left his dirty clothes strewn all over the floor, and pigged out on Mexican food — the alarm bells stopped ringing and his spiritual predilections were largely ignored.

◆

Years passed ... and, like all his friends, Hari got his driving licence one winter. Now, my brother's house is on a hill. The roads that wind around it have safety barriers only at the sharp hairpin bends. And in winter, when there's ice and snow all over the place, they can be dangerous and difficult to navigate. So when Hari insisted on driving to his best friend's birthday party hardly a week after getting his licence, everyone was concerned. But, as usual, he somehow managed to persuade his parents to let him go.

Snow had been falling for days, and as he drove down the winding road, some animal, maybe a gopher, crossed his path. He braked to avoid hitting it, and the car skidded furiously, zigzagging across the road, from side to side, alternately slamming into the side of the hill and the safety barrier, beyond which was a dizzying drop with the bottom barely visible. Eventually, the car turned turtle several times before spinning to a halt. Passers-by who saw the accident called the police. And things moved fast after that.

My brother and sister-in-law, who had been alerted, rushed to the scene of the accident to find police cars, an ambulance and paramedics swarming everywhere. Hari's car was a pulverised wreck. Mangled car parts and glass shards were strewn all over the place. And there was no sign of the boy.

'Is our son alive?' My sister-in-law says that, after looking at the crumpled remains of the car, she was prepared for the worst.

'Amma!' Just then Hari emerged from the ambulance, with nothing more than a couple of scratches. The paramedics had checked him out and found nothing damaged or broken!

'A miracle … that's what I say. Never seen anything like it before.' The policeman looked at Hari and shook his head in wonder. 'Can you believe this … hardly a scratch on the boy!'

'Hari, I think you'd better come home and rest.'

'No, Amma,' Hari said firmly.

'You still want to go for the party!'

'No …'

'A miracle, praise the Lord,' repeated the policeman, and I suppose Hari agreed with him. 'Amma, I want to spend some time at the temple,' he said. 'Can you drive me there?'

My brother, I believe, went home and got it all off his chest by writing to the car manufacturers, commending them on the design of Hari's vehicle, which he called 'a miracle of automobile engineering'!

Veena Seshadri

2

ON LOVE AND FORGIVENESS

God doesn't look at how much we do, but with how much love we do it.

Mother Teresa

Son, Mothers Only Give

God could not be everywhere, and therefore he made mothers.

—*Proverb*

This is a story about my mother who lived ninety-three years, a woman of love, a woman of kindness and above all a woman of divine nature. My mother performed namaz five times every day. During namaz, my mother always looked angelic. Every time I saw her during namaz, I was inspired and moved.

When I look back at my childhood, a beautiful kaleidoscope of good human values, simple and joyous people, sea waves, hovering seagulls, golden sand, a crowd of faithful pilgrims arriving from distant places, the Mosque Street prayers, school, petty shops, and horse carts emerge. Everything then merges into the figure of one graceful pious lady — my mother, Ashiamma.

My childhood was quite comfortable in the sense that my parents, absorbing all problems, provided us with all the basic amenities — shelter, food, clothing, education and, above all, a loving environment. During World War II, however, there was scarcity all around presenting challenges and toil. I would get up quite early in the morning and watch my parents offer their fajr (daybreak) prayer. Even before the sun arose from the blue waters of the sea, my father would go to a coconut grove he owned, about four miles from the house. I would walk many miles to the house of my saintly teacher. I would also attend an Arabic school.

After the two learning sessions, I would collect newspapers at the station and go door-to-door distributing them for my cousin, who would pay me an anna for this effort.

I would proudly take the coin to my mother and deposit it with her. I didn't ever need that money, but when I had to go to Ramanathapuram for my high school education, my mother produced all the coins, now a significant amount, she had so jealously treasured. Tears welled in my eyes. She ran her fingers through my hair and quietly said — 'Son, mothers only give.'

Dr A.P.J. Abdul Kalam

Stop!

Not by enmity is enmity ended; by friendliness enmity is ended.

—*Dhammapada*

Long ago, in ancient India, people feared going anywhere near one particular forest because a dreaded bandit was at large there. He not only robbed people, but also had a perverse pleasure in cutting off their fingers and stringing them in a fearsome necklace, which he flaunted proudly.

'Anguli-mala', the one with a necklace of fingers, invoked fear in the hearts of all the people and virtually controlled the whole forest. Once, the Buddha set off on the route frequented by Angulimala. 'Please do not take this route. Angulimala does not spare anyone,' the people begged, but the Buddha merely smiled and told them to be at ease.

As soon as the Buddha had traversed some distance, he could hear thundering footsteps. Angulimala had seen him and was trying to catch up. Buddha walked steadily while Angulimala ran desperately. Strangely, Angulimala was just not able to do catch up with the Buddha. Utterly frustrated, he cried out, 'O bhikkhu (monk), stop, stop!' He did not really expect the monk to stop, thinking there was some magical power in the monk.

Much to his surprise, the Buddha stopped, turned and replied calmly, 'I have stopped. It is you who has not stopped.' Totally bewildered, Angulimala looked on as the Buddha continued, 'I say that I have stopped because I have given up killing all beings. I have given up ill-treating all beings, and have established myself in universal love, patience, and knowledge through reflection. But you still have not given up killing or ill-treating others and you are not yet established in universal love and patience. Hence, you are the one who has not stopped. You could, however, stop any time you wish to.'

Nobody had ever spoken to Angulimala in such a calm, compassionate manner. The peace that he felt just by being in the Buddha's presence was overwhelming. With tears in his eyes, he threw away the necklace of fingers and his weapons. Choked with emotion, he pleaded with the Buddha to admit him to the order of the bhikkhus. The Buddha willingly did so.

Many in the order were aghast. Bound by Buddha's order, they did not oppose the decision but avoided interacting with Angulimala, the dreaded bandit. Observing this, the Buddha counselled Angulimala, 'Be patient. Your bad karma will cease to haunt you if you remain calm and composed.'

Angulimala understood and continued serving in the community patiently and lovingly. With time, he realised he was especially skilled in helping women in labour, as blood, pain and shrieks did not unnerve him. Gradually, his past identity dropped and he became known as the person who was very skilled in helping women deliver babies.

This tale gives me new insights every time I read it.

The statement of the Buddha, 'I have now stopped', that was crucial in effecting Angulimala's transformation, is a wonderful message of compassion and empathy, saying effectively, 'I have been there and I understand what you are going through.'

Once transformed, Angulimala still needs to struggle to be respected by the others. The Buddha counsels him to keep going, and it is by not swerving from the path that he finally gains acceptance from the community. This shows us that penitence may be tested severely but, if it is genuine, there is acceptance at the end of the struggle.

At the societal level, this tale is eternally relevant in showing us that even a hardened miscreant, be he a burglar, murderer or terrorist, can turn over a new leaf if he is approached with understanding and empathy. In fact, the skill he had acquired was now used in a positive manner.

Above all, the core message that I get from the tale is that we all go through several stages of growth in our various lifetimes, and Buddhahood can be attained by any of us, no matter where we currently stand.

Jamuna Rangachari

The Blessing

When I was a girl, my grandmother was my idol. I loved her fiercely, with the mix of awe and complete surrender that children are capable of, and a slight unease of incurring her displeasure. What I looked forward to most, throughout the year, was going home to my grandparents' for summer. As we rode from the railway station in a tonga, covering the short distance to the house, I pictured her sitting in her cane chair in the deep veranda, waiting for me, her strong-coloured silk sari ablaze against the morning sun; I felt the soft, heavy, much-washed pleats between my fingers, I inhaled the faint woody fragrance of the chest of drawers in which her saris always lay neatly folded, I felt her hands holding my face, I heard the lilt in her voice as she called my name. By the time I reached the gate, I was ready to burst; I could only run in and throw myself into her lap.

My grandfather was a lawyer of some eminence in the small town, and they lived in a grand old house that was teeming with people and pets. Running that household, I realised later, must have been like running a medieval military camp, an unwieldy establishment in a constant state of flux. My grandmother ran the household effortlessly, or so it seemed. But for the month that we were there, she was there for us, for me, to go to the shops, on picnics and walks, to the library; I remember shared afternoon naps and late night stories.

I am a lot like her, I see that now — from her love of strong colours and heavy textures, her measured way of speaking, her taste for certain flavours in food, her nice discrimination and, perhaps, even her prejudices. But what I owe most to her, is her love of reading. One of the most enduring images I carry is of her sitting in the wicker chair in the veranda, immersed in the confidences of Ladybird Johnson or even an Edgar Wallace, oblivious to the hurly-burly of the household to which she would return at the end of the afternoon, as if woken from a trance. She was my first guide to books — she would surprise me with the most unexpected parcels. At the height of my infatuation with Enid Blyton's Famous Five, I remember Monica Dickens's *Summer at World's End* arriving in the post, after which the adventures of children on their own, with their animals, meant something completely different. When I reached out for Nabokov's *Lolita* in my grandmother's library — I was in high school then — she made me put it back. Not now, she said, you can read it after you are married.

As I grew up, I had new friends, went to new places and encountered new ideas and new books. My holidays grew shorter. I also learnt to see my grandmother differently. I saw her as a mother-in-law and an employer; as a human being capable of only that much, and not as a repository of all that was good and true and exciting. When I got my first job, my 'summer holidays', as I knew them, were over. And then I got married and started a family of my own. We met more and more only on social occasions, in the crowded presence of others.

As I spread my wings, she started retracting hers. She gave up the reins of her household, and went, officially, into the care of her sons and daughters. We met less often and more briefly than before, but every time I saw her, there she was, straight, tall, proud and soft-spoken, and I felt again a clutch at my heart, the clutch of my girlhood, and I was back running up the stairs to greet her as she sat in her wicker chair in the veranda.

When she died, I could not go to see her. But that night, I remember lying awake in my bed in the small hours of the morning, thinking of her, filled with regret at not having gone to see her, at having allowed her to slip away when it was my turn to take command, wishing I could roll back twenty years and relive them ... when the strangest thing happened. I was suddenly suffused by a warm glow, a glow that spread from head to foot, a feeling of such pure happiness and peace and well-being that it could only have been a blessing of love.

I think of my grandmother often and I have often tried to re-experience that feeling, but I have never had another 'visitation'. But the memory of that night is very strong, and I recall it often. I consider myself a rational being, bound firmly to terra firma, loath to use words that dandle the extra terrestrial, but this much I have learnt — we must acknowledge and bind the love of those closest to us, while there is time. For that is what makes and sustains us.

K.R. Usha

Hug Your Enemies

Repel the evil of another with your good deeds. You will see that the one with whom you had enmity will be your close friend.

— *The Holy Qur'an 41: 34*

'I hugged him in my imagination ...' the well-pitched and well-modulated voice of KS echoed in the conference hall of Fairmont Hotel in San Francisco. When KS speaks about spirituality, he always speaks from his heart.

The session was on 'The Universe Within'. It was part of a ten-day spiritual convention on 'Creating a Sustainable Compassionate Society and Culture of Peace', where more than eighty per cent of the delegates were from the corporate world. The panel of experts that included both spiritual celebrities and renowned scientists, after sharing their thoughts, invited the participants to share some of their unique experiences on something unexplainable or unbelievable. K.S. Raju, chairman of the Nagarjuna Group, was the first to get up and share his unique experience.

When KS speaks, he seems to fall into a trance; each word that comes from him strikes directly at the heart of the listeners. There was silence.

'I am an entrepreneur and I manage a small group of enterprises called Nagarjuna, in India,' KS began. 'Due to some policy interpretation, a senior bureaucrat withheld a huge amount of money and my every argument with him went unheard. Even before hearing me out, he would look at his watch, making it evident that he was waiting for the allotted time to be over. It was quite a painful experience and I gave vent to my frustrations in private. Then something strange happened.' He paused — a long pause. Then KS turned and looked at his daughter.

'One fine morning, Laxmi, my daughter, made me realise that what I was doing was not my natural way. She explained that, maybe, the bureaucrat was carrying out his dharma, the duty allotted to him! Why should I feel bad about him if my logic didn't appeal to him? Both of us were looking at the same issue from different perspectives.' KS turned to the panel of experts and looked directly into their eyes. He was absolutely calm and the people were eager to hear more from him.

'Then a miracle happened!' KS started after a brief pause. 'The awareness created by my daughter brought me back to my senses. I started loving the bureaucrat and hugging him in my imagination. In my prayers I prayed for his well-being. I filled pure love for him in my heart. And when the time came for the next meeting after a month, I greeted him with pure warmth and, at first he looked into my eyes and made some personal inquiries that were really soothing to me. Then he patiently heard my viewpoint without looking at his watch this time. I took more time than was allotted. After hearing me fully, he said, 'Mr Raju, it makes a lot of sense to me. I will send my team to review the matter and let me then see what I can do to resolve it.' When the meeting was over, he got up and came to the door and shook my hand with unprecedented warmth. The matter was soon resolved.

'Hug the guy in your imagination if you want to create a pure relationship without any selfish motives. Generate positive vibrations to drive out negativity,' he concluded, and people began to get up spontaneously to give him a standing ovation.

Jesus Christ said: 'If someone strikes you on one cheek, turn to him the other also.' Buddha's thoughts are no different when he says, 'Negativity cannot be countered with negative thoughts.' According to Hindu philosophy, 'Good (positive) deeds produce good results and bad (negative) deeds produce bad results.' So, be positive in thoughts and actions and, for sure, the results will be positive. All scriptures say this. We read them but do not trust our own scriptures.

The power of a pure relationship is immeasurable. Just hug in your imagination and you will find the bonds of relationships getting strengthened. The only way to drive away the negative waves is by creating positive waves of thoughts. Hug even your enemy in your imagination and you will find foes turning into friends.

You cannot hug in your imagination without loving someone, without having good feelings for someone. It is such a powerful process! I have learnt the art of living and developing pure relationships — managing from within!

Relationships are nurtured by taking care of others. When you do so, you are already taken care of by the unseen. This is what Ralph Waldo Emerson meant by his famous words: 'It is one of the most beautiful compensations of life that no man can sincerely try to help another without helping himself.'

Hug your enemies in your imagination and turn them into your friends.

Moid Siddiqui

Give Till It Hurts

Lord, make me a channel of Thy peace that where there is hatred, I may bring love; that where there is wrong, I may bring the spirit of forgiveness; that where there is discord, I may bring harmony; that where there is error, I may bring truth; that where there is doubt, I may bring faith; that where there is despair, I may bring hope; that where there are shadows, I may bring light; that where there is sadness, I may bring joy.

St. Francis of Assisi

The poor can teach us so many beautiful things. The poor are very wonderful people. One evening we went out and we picked up four people from the street. And one of them was in a most terrible condition — and I told the Sisters: You take care of the other three, I (will) take of this one that (looks) worse. So I did for her all that my love could do. I put her in bed, and there was such a beautiful smile on her face. She took hold of my hand, as she said one word only: Thank you — and she died.

I could not help but examine my conscience before her, and I asked what would I say if I was in her place. And my answer was very simple. I would have tried to draw a little attention to myself, I would have said I am hungry, that I am dying, I am cold, I am in pain, or something, but she gave me much more — she gave me her grateful love. And she died with a smile on her face. As that man whom we picked up from the drain, half eaten with worms, and we brought him to the home. 'I have lived like an animal in the street, but I am going to die like an angel, loved and cared for.' And it was sc wonderful to see the greatness of that man who could speak like that, who could die like that without blaming anybody, without cursing anybody, without comparing anything. Like an angel — this is the greatness of our people.

◆

Love begins at home, and it is not how much we do, but how much love we put in the action that we do ...

Some time ago, in Calcutta, we had great difficulty in getting sugar, and I don't know how the word got around to the children, and a little boy of four years old ... went home and told his parents: I will not eat sugar for three days, I will give my sugar to Mother Teresa for her children. After three days, his father and mother brought him to our home. I had never met them before, and this little one could scarcely pronounce my name, but he knew exactly what he had come to do. He knew that he wanted to share his love.

And so here I am talking with you — I want you to find the poor here, right in your own home first. And begin love there. Be that good news to your own people. And find out about your next-door neighbour — do you know who they are? I had the most extraordinary experience with a Hindu family who had eight children. A gentleman came to our

house and said: 'Mother Teresa, there is a family with eight
children, they have not eaten for so long — do something.' So
I took some rice and I went there immediately. And I saw the
children — their eyes shining with hunger — I don't know
if you have ever seen hunger. But I have seen it very often.
And she took the rice, she divided the rice, and she went
out. When she came back I asked her — where did you go,
what did you do? And she gave me a very simple answer:
'They are hungry also.' What struck me most was that she
knew — and who are they, a Muslim family — and she knew.
I didn't bring more rice that evening because I wanted them
to enjoy the joy of sharing. But there were those children,
radiating joy, sharing the joy with their mother because she
had the love to give. And you see this is where love begins
— at home.

Because I believe that love begins at home, if we can create
a home for the poor — I think that more and more love will
spread. And we will be able, through this understanding
love, to bring peace, be the good news to the poor. The poor
in our own family first, in our country and in the world ...
let us always meet each other with a smile, for the smile is
the beginning of love, and once we begin to love each other
naturally we want to do something ... What we have done
we should not have been able to do if you did not share with
your prayers, with your gifts, this continual giving. But I don't
want you to give me from your abundance, I want that you
give me until it hurts.

The other day I received fifteen dollars from a man who has
been on his back for twenty years, and the only part that he
can move is his right hand. And the only companion that he
enjoys is smoking. And he said to me: 'I do not smoke for one
week, and I send you this money.' It must have been a terrible
sacrifice for him, but see how beautiful, how he shared, and
with that money I bought bread and I gave to those who are

hungry, with a joy on both sides; he was giving and the poor were receiving ... It is a gift of God to us to be able to share our love with others.

Mother Teresa

Not in the Words
We Speak but in Our Deeds

I knew that I was not exactly the image of the ideal daughter-in-law Amma had in mind. Her first-born son, on whom they had placed all their expectations, wanted to marry a girl he had met in Mumbai. She was from a different community, spoke a different language, and was modern and unconventional. Amma must have tried to convince him otherwise, but when he didn't give in, finally, she consented to our marriage. It was perhaps more not to displease him than anything else.

In the beginning, she would visit us in Mumbai — she lived in Bangalore — and stay for a short while. We got to know each other, and I realised how non-interfering she was. I respected her for this, and though we were clearly two very different women belonging to two diverse worlds, we learnt to value each other's space. As the years passed, we developed a kind of relationship that was mutually cordial and considerate. It slowly turned into admiration for each other, infused with affection.

I remember certain relatives visiting us when we were living in Bangalore. They were from my father-in-law's extended family, and I could sense the authority and the air of superiority they exuded during their visit. Amma was always very hospitable, warm and friendly with them. I wondered why. She would go out of her way to be generous with them. Often, they would praise her while leaving, and were clearly envious of her being surrounded by her family, especially her daughters-in-law and grandchildren who loved her. Clearly they must have lacked it all.

When my husband and I stayed abroad for a while, she spent several months with us, and it was then she would talk about her life at length to me. I could see how harsh it had been. Her childhood in a small village, just a few years' schooling, her marriage at the age of fifteen to a much older man who was a widower with a son, and her long journey to a far-off land at that age, as a new bride. She survived as a refugee during the time of the Partition, with her first-born son, not knowing if her husband would follow safely, later on. Fortunately for her, he did. Life improved once her family settled in Bangalore, with more children, stability and financial security.

The thing which struck me most was her way of telling her life stories. In spite of all the hardships she had endured in her life, her tone was never bitter. She never talked ill of anyone. I often wondered where she must have collected her wisdom.

Once she narrated what had happened at a family wedding. She was young then, with small children. Those relatives who were celebrating the wedding were rich and highly placed in society. Amma was the wife of a lower middle-class brother, a clerk of meagre means. She was supposed to be around only to shoulder the burden of the innumerable wedding chores. Then, suddenly, all hell broke loose when it was discovered that some pieces of wedding jewellery were missing. In such circumstances, as suspicion usually falls on the poor relatives, Amma was called and asked humiliating questions. She, of course, told them that she knew nothing about the theft of the jewellery, but the rich relatives didn't believe her. They asked her to prove her innocence by opening her bags in front of everyone. How crushing it must have been for Amma. It was not enough that she was innocent, but she had to prove it in the most humiliating way. She remembered, 'I opened my bags. Showed them I was not a thief. Only I know how I endured the shame.'

My heart went out to her while listening to this. But she was calm and composed. Then it occurred to me that those were the same relatives who often visited us now. Times had changed and she was living in a big house with her grown-up children and their families. Her sons and daughters-in-law respected and loved her. Yet, how hospitable she was to those same relatives who had disgraced her. How could she forgive them? How was it possible for her to forget the past humiliations so easily? Why did she not ignore them now? Or put them in their place? She could have done that so easily now. I often wondered about it. Wasn't the taste of revenge sweet?

The answer was revealed to me when she was reminiscing about her childhood, once again. She said, 'Do you know why people behave badly with us at times? Why we have to face such incidents? *So that we know how not to behave.*' I was astounded for a moment. She was ever so casual about it. It seemed so simple! A lesson learned so that it makes you a better person. You are not concerned about your own humiliations and insults. You learn from it and you shine with your own virtue. You forget the bitterness and bring peace into your heart.

Her attitude was a blend of simplicity and high thinking, and she imparted her wisdom to us without the jargon of great spiritual sermons. In her way, she was a simple, religious woman. Yet, she never questioned me when I didn't follow the rituals. Amma was a spiritual person in the real sense of the word. After all, a truly spiritual life is one of acceptance. It is a path of love and forgiveness. And the true essence of spirituality is reflected not in the words we speak, but in the deeds that make up the life we live.

Saniya

Doing the Right Thing at the Right Time

My father's mother lived with us till she died at the age of seventy-five. When a stroke left her bedridden during the last five years of her life, my mother chose to care for her.

We shared a bedroom—my grandmother and I—and since I was supposed to be a spitting image of her, she had always been partial to me. Before she fell sick and became incommunicado, we had been good friends, often talking late into the night about the politics in my school, her past and even my crushes! She came to live with us when I was eleven, the age when she herself had gotten married! From then until she died — when I was in the eleventh class — we were roommates.

Where my mother was soft-spoken and mild-mannered, my grandmother, whom we called Ammamma, was a complete firebrand, saying that aggression had to be met with aggression. In a way, Ammamma was like a child, and often grumbled to my mother when things did not go her way.

During Ammamma's sickness, when she lost her memory and I had drifted away from her emotionally, my mother took charge of her wasting body, not relegating it to a maid, nurse or dependent relative. Our room smelt of a strange mix of Dettol and pee most of the time. I often pleaded for another room, but my brother had the spare bedroom.

Since caretaking was a 24/7 job, my mother had no social life. Such hands-on hygiene was alien to me, even repulsive. Plus, the departure of memory and the onset of dementia had made Ammamma not just a stranger, but also unlovable to me. Not once did my mother ask me to share her duties, only proving by example how important the physical was in terms of spiritual growth.

Since mom had stopped going out, church too had become a casualty. Once, during a church festival, one of her friends insisted she go. But my mother was firm about not leaving Ammamma alone. What troubled me then was the joy and cheer she brought to this thankless and — as I saw it — endless job. So after the friend left, I said, 'Mommy, you could have gone. At least to the church … no one will grudge you an outing! You could have escaped all this for an hour and people would have only said what a good woman you are for praying.'

My mother said, 'Which god asks for empty worship? This is my worship — through someone I can touch. If you want to see things in terms of religion, her room is my church and her bed my altar. Of course, I can go sit for hours in the church, but that would not be practical piety but an impractical, self-pitying piety, and not facing up to my responsibilities in life.'

She thus redefined religion to me — I was fashionably atheist then (I have since turned agnostic) — that it had more to do with doing one's earthly duties and less with showy rituals. Her Holy Mass did not involve wearing her Sunday best and kneeling in pews at the right cue. There she was in her home clothes, kneeling with bedpan in hand. Feeding

Ammamma was another messy job despite the bib and tray—most of the time she petulantly spat out or shoved her plate violently away—but my mother, never losing patience, would murmur affectionately and chat on as if Ammamma was responding normally to her.

Through those years, I learnt that hygiene was best turned self-reliant; from washing your own clothes, sheets, cleaning your own toilet, washbasin, etc., you could proceed to washing others. I learnt that kindness was not a one-time outburst of birthday gifts or flowers, but an ongoing everyday business. That our personal interpretation of religion makes us the person we are — we can take the easy way out and learn all the prayers by heart, or we can one put our shoulder under the bus-tyre stuck in slush, and live in the constructive here and now. And that spirituality began and ended with the physical, that the body did not suddenly melt into air leaving a pure wick-like soul behind, but that the spirit was moulded via the actions of the body and the words in one's mouth.

Till today I have not heard my mother whine, 'I had to look after my mother-in-law'. It was just something she did between her cooking and joking, a matter of routine and self-fulfilment.

I asked her recently if she did not regret the waste of her youth in this manner and she was surprised. 'I am glad I did the right thing at the right time. It would have been hell if I'd had to look back with regret, thinking I should have done this or that, when it was too late.'

Shinie Antony

Beyond the Call of Duty

When my husband was very ill and in the ICU at the Christian Medical College and Hospital, Vellore, the doctors allowed me to sit beside him and hold his hand. The bright lights in the room glared at me. The *bleep bleep* of the many monitors and machines scared me. I noticed that the woman in the next bed was very sick. Twice during the night her heart had stopped and she was revived. I heard the nurses whisper to the trainee nurse beside her, that the woman's pulse was slowing again and that it would soon stop, and that would be the end of her life. The trainee nurse on duty kept a close watch on her. She would come and take her pulse, check the monitors and adjust her pillows quietly. After a while, I saw her bring a bowl of water and sponge the dying woman's face tenderly. Then she pulled out a comb and carefully combed her matted hair. Finally, very gently, she put some kumkum on her forehead.

I sat watching this with rapt attention. Nobody else saw what the nurse did. The woman in the bed certainly was not aware of it. In fact, a few minutes after the nurse left her side, she died. So why did the young nurse bother at all? The love, the gentleness, the tenderness, the look of compassion and concern on the nurse's face was awesome.

At that point in time, I wasn't even sure if God existed. Would a God of love send such pain and suffering to those he loved? My prayers for my husband's healing were unanswered, I was exhausted with nursing him and felt frozen and miserable all the time. God, if He did exist, was far, far away. That morning, though, I had a glimpse of God through this nurse's face and her loving actions, and my dying faith was restored.

Usha Jesudasan

3

ECLECTIC WISDOM

Stop leaving and you will arrive.
Stop searching and you will see.
Stop running away and you will be found.

Lao Tzu

Me, My Bike and the Road Ahead

The unalloyed truth ... I love to ride. The feeling of freedom is an absolute chant. Addictive ... thrilling ... a head rush, once experienced, it never leaves you. That said, I will have you know I am NOT a biker babe! I don't ride with a club; I hate grunge, dirt and grease. I don't wear leather jackets and carry knuckle guards and I even worry about how my hair looks every time I take off my helmet!

But that's small change. When it's you, your bike and the road ahead, all things cease to exist. So, when I landed up for the Himalayan Odyssey with a cameraman and a pink scarf, I wasn't expecting anything other than pure feeling.

Now, an Enfield is a bike that takes its own sweet time to 'get to know you'. You can't stake a claim, you can't wrangle over ownership. The courting is slow, even for a girl! Unfortunately, I had just half an hour to say hello to my bike, before we took off on the world's highest motorable road.

The Machismo 500 LB is not designed for a small person, and the roads at 18,000 feet are not easily navigable. The air is rarefied and freezing cold and, to top it, I had to shoot, as our journey was going to be televised. With my toes barely touching the ground, my focus was to stay astride and not ride off the cliff!

The view was breathtaking, but you didn't dare look up from the road. My camera person, Vilayat, who is not a rider, was so spooked by what we were doing, that he point-blank refused to get on a bike. He shot the entire sequence from a car, and alternately, on foot.

Of course, we weren't alone. There were fifty-five other bikes riding alongside. And when you watch someone else manoeuvre and come out alive, that's all the assurance you need to know it can be done. And, in my book, if it can be done … I can do it. But knowing yourself is not worth a paisa. In Biker Law, you have to prove your mettle on your machine before anyone knows you exist. And being from the media, with the camera pointing at my face, wasn't helping either.

The minute we got back from Khardungla, the height of my bike was reduced. A few days on, 'we' (I and my bike) became more companionable in a sea of mankind. Did I mention the riders were male, apart from me and two other women riders?

And men being men, a heavy ladle of free advice was always at hand. There were so many voices telling us how to shoot, which angle to shoot from and so forth, that I was actually shooting on the sly! One of the loudest opinions came from a guy who didn't even own a TV! The ride was turning into a sting operation.

Hordes of riders had come from across India, and each day, the distance and terrain demanded you rode at a steady pace. That meant the moment one shot of the bikes was through, we got left behind. Slowing us further was my camera person, who was travelling by car on a biker-friendly terrain.

While I sweated over the shoot, the organisers had anxious moments over completing the route safely and on time. And then, I arrived at my favourite part of the journey —

the camaraderie that sets us riders apart. This is something those on four-wheels are never visited by. Fellow riders volunteered to give us all the shots we needed. Little stops along the way … just enough for the camera car to catch up, or the tripod to be set. Lunch breaks were a little longer than before, and tea breaks got more frequent. I had been accepted in the hood.

It had been a stressful time in my life, and I discovered that pushing boundaries helped me connect with something that strengthened and reassured me.

♦

My trip to Ladakh left me with a lust for riding, and memories that made my imagination turn buses on the Delhi roads into mountains, and small potholes into raging water crossings.

I swerved and steered my imaginary bike over them, gripping the steering wheel of my car in a desperate bid to keep my balance.

I checked out random bikers on the road, looking for a hint of the riders who'd dare to brave Ladakh, in their silhouettes. I had returned from that trip gasping at my own accomplishment, thrilled about making it home in one piece, and happy to have finally crossed Ladakh off my To Do List for Riding.

It was time to move on to other things....

Then, before I knew it, there was this show I was talking about. A tougher, more challenging ride. One of the toughest routes in the world! Brainwave: let's do the Ladakh lake circuit. And it was decided. Once more I was heading back to the mountains.

It started with picking a handful of riders from across India, who shared the same obsessive headspace for riding. A task that was easier said than done. I met many a crazy bike enthusiast who pledged undying loyalty to the call of riding, but few could hold their own on the road. It was also a task to separate the reality TV-show hopefuls with stars in their eyes from the real riders, since this was one road-trip we would not be voting anyone out!

One by one, the eight other riders came on board. The first time all of us met was at Chandigarh, the day before we were due to leave ... I was more than a little apprehensive about how we would get along. This wasn't some massive event with tons of people behind the scenes. We were pretty much taking off on a road trip, except that we planned to shoot as much of it as possible.

Being on the road with someone you don't like or trust is not a happy proposition. I had picked riders with completely unique identities, and by default we were a headstrong lot. I saw plenty of raised eyebrows and puffed chests as we all sized each other up, and thankfully, nobody got killed.

It took all of one day of being on the road for the creases to smoothen themselves out. Finally I could uncross my fingers ... it looked like we would survive the road trip after all.

And that we did, and more! They say you don't take the trip, the trip takes you... not just across the world's highest mountains, icy river crossings, stretches where, perhaps, no one has ever set foot before. Most important of all, it takes you on a journey of discovery within yourself. Making you aware of what a tiny speck you are, yet helping you expand until you become a part of everything that's around you, and beyond. And you feel you've been given the courage and the fortitude to weather any adversity that comes hurtling towards you.

You ride along the shore of a prehistoric sea, many thousand feet above the plains ... and it puts your life in perspective. Being there, is a huge clean break ... it's like putting your mind through a washing machine (as imaginatively described by one of my fellow riders) you emerge cleansed, renewed, regenerated, and ready to push against all odds to do the best you can, and be the best you can be.

Ayesha Sharma

Daffodils in December

There is a quote that says, 'God gave us memory so that we can have roses in December'. I had never heard of, or seen daffodils in December, either in India or abroad. Roses, yes ... but not daffodils. On the contrary, it is common knowledge that daffodils are a spring-flower in the West. But a daffodil bloomed in my garden (I live in Ooty) last December. I like to think of it as Nithya's gift.

He came in out of the mountain mists, and I sensed his presence before I saw him. I was pottering in the garden, as I usually do, after breakfast. I bent down to sniff at a narcissus, musing that October was an unusual month for narcissi to bloom. I then turned to the pot which had held my prized daffodil bulb. I groped around for the bulb, but my fingers failed to locate it. So my mali had been right — it must have disintegrated. I was very disappointed, for daffodils are rare in India.

I straightened up, and looked around — the garden was a jungle of weeds, what with the rains, and the continued absence of my mali; labour was scarce and I wondered when and how I could get the garden cleaned. It was then that I saw, or rather, sensed his presence. He was a stranger ... there was a beatific smile on his face, and he could have been anything from fifteen to nineteen.

'Where have you come from?' I asked him in Tamil. He continued to smile. I repeated my question, but there was no answer, only a wide smile. Realising that he was differently-abled, I tried sign language, and he pointed a hand over the mountain. Communicating by sign language, I understood that he was looking for work ... and soon, he was cleaning up the garden.

At eleven o'clock, I went to call him for tea. And he came with the alacrity of a child. In fact, there was a childlike innocence about him. 'What is your name?' I asked him in sign language, and he gestured for pen and paper, which I gave him. I was more than a little surprised to see him write 'Nithyananda' in a childlike hand, in English. From then on, we started communicating by writing 'notes' to each other.

The next day, when I went to call Nithya for morning tea, I was pleasantly surprised to see that he was weeding the flower-pots, even though I had not asked him to. Drawing nearer, I saw that Nithya had cleared the weeds from the pot that had held the daffodil bulb. I bent down, and my heart surged to see a sliver of green. So the bulb had not disintegrated, as my mali would have me believe. My relief was a measure of how much it meant to me. I had nurtured it with attention, affection and even poetry, and I wondered what ESP had guided Nithya to the soul of the daffodil amid the tangle of weeds.

The following day, I needed Nithya to dig a garbage-pit, and pointing to the spot where I wanted it, I began to walk through the thick grass when Nithya held up a hand. I halted in my tracks, perplexed. Within minutes, Nithya pointed to a snake that was slithering right across the path I would have taken. How did he know it was there? Do the differently-abled have an extra-sensitivity? I was shaken as I walked back to the bungalow. Was it a poisonous snake, and had Nithya, perhaps, saved my life?

That evening, I paid Nithya, and wrote in the notepad: 'Take leave for three days as it's the puja season, and come back on Friday.' Later, I spoke to my daughter, Roshini, who lives in Italy, and discussed the celebrations I was planning for the puja. I also told her about Nithya and the daffodil bulb, about his childlike enjoyment of food, his knowledge of English and about the snake.

'What's the use of giving him only food for his stomach, Mummy? Why don't you give him some food for the soul as well? I mean, why don't you buy him some books for Saraswati puja?'

Early next morning, I woke up to the strains of the Saraswati stotram from a nearby ashram. As I came out of the puja room and got ready to go to town to attend the puja celebrations at one or two places, and to buy some books for Nithya, I sensed his presence in the garden before I saw him. Even though I had given him a few days off, Nithya had come to greet me with the traditional offerings for Saraswati puja — a coconut, fruit, betel leaves, limes, puffed rice and chrysanthemum flowers. I was deeply touched.

In town, after the puja celebrations, I went to a bookshop, and chose a copy of the *Panchatantra*, Aesop's fables, and a book of folktales for Nithya. I could not wait to see him after the puja holidays and, after work, I gave him the books. The joy on his face was indescribable, and he kept pointing to the books, and to himself, and asking me in sign language, 'For me? For me?'

After a week, Nithya stopped coming. By then the garden was spick and span. Eventually, my mali returned. Then, one crisp December morning, my daffodil bloomed. As I gazed enraptured, I thought about Nithyananda, and reflected,

'How aptly he has been named Nithyananda (eternal joy).' I thanked him silently for bringing me daffodils in December ... at a time when I really needed something to brighten my life.

From the nearby ashram came the strains of a mantra from the *Taittiriya Aranyaka*:

May the winds bring us happiness.
May the rivers carry happiness to us.
May the herbs give happiness to us.
May the heavens give us happiness.
May the trees give us happiness.
May the sun pour down happiness.

The blessings of nature were all around me, yet I needed a catalyst — a differently-abled child who slipped into my life and slipped out of it like a gentle breeze — to make me aware of all that He had showered on me. And make me reflect on the inter-connectedness of all forms of life, and the Master Hand behind it all.

Sometimes, on a misty morning, I gaze across the mountains, wishing, hoping, Nithya will come. As I walk in the garden, I reflect that he had come into my life when I needed him, and that, with his special gifts, he was probably spreading light and joy to others who were in need of it.

Indu Mallah

The Spirit of Silence

I cannot now recollect the order in which the sounds of early morning announced the arrival of a new day (when I was a young boy). Was it of sweeping and cleaning? Or the churning of yoghurt in giant clay pots, the rhythm of it almost a lullaby in that drowsy half-light of early dawn, and this had to be done in the cool of dawn or the butter would not set. The pounding of spices in a mortar, for spices had to be crushed, ground, and prepared daily. It was inconceivable to use a stale lot. Besides, each dish needed an altogether different combination of them, their prickly fragrance mingling with the incense of dawn prayers. The grinding of wheat for flour was in the afternoons, stone grinders rotated by hand producing yet again a soporific, siesta sound. The camels carrying water pakhals would arrive early, while it was still dark, and an announcement was made by the carrier from just outside the zenana deodhi gates. An untidy scrum of maids then always occurred, for missing this early morning delivery meant a wait for at least another hour, the time it took for the cameleer to go back to the sweet water well in the river-bed, fill the pakhal — capacious leather pouches slung on both sides of the camel's back and balanced, or they would tip over (a tedious job, each bucketful had to be yanked up by hand) — then take a breather, a conversational smoke perhaps, even a detour home, and return. Fresh milk from the bagur also arrived then, the herdsman carrying a large urn on his turbaned head as well as milk containers in his hands.

Dust particles danced on the slanting rays of the early morning sun as I lay in bed and gloried in the luxury of the day that stretched ahead. A whole day! What an unending infinity that is in childhood! Time had altogether a different dimension then, a measure that is its own. As life advances this 'measure' loses its generosity, shrinks in experience, passing so rapidly. Perhaps, because by then watches and clocks begin to devour time by the micro-second, and that too insatiably.

Those great, endless afternoons when heat rose from the earth in waves, when shade was scarce and, drowsily, even the great House and its ceaseless bustle paused, the maids dropped work, lay down, gossiped, yawned and napped. Mother would then sleepily admonish me to lie down, not to do this or that or those endless many things that children must not do. In the overpowering silence of those afternoons, it was only the wind that soughed through the bush and endlessly across the sand, rippling its surface in ridges and troughs. The pigeons, though, strutted and gurgled amorously in the eaves, upon roof corners, and on the ledges, the males ceaselessly trying their luck with reluctant and uncooperative females. I would sit in the balcony and watch and listen and see the shadows shift until the afternoon heat eased, the sun rode lower in the sky and the first of the traders reached: the bangle-sellers, the village goldsmith or the gandhi (perfume-seller) to tempt the women in the zenana. On one such afternoon, my ear lobes were pierced, I cannot recollect by whom. I have no recollection of any pain either, but very soon after that, like the others, I too remained adorned with tiny ear-studs.

Dusk would arrive with more milk and water deliveries, and then that hour of the lighting of evening lamps. The convenience of hurricane lanterns had arrived by then, and all were lit at one spot, for economy in fuel use, I suppose. And then, at dusk, the lantern carrier, clutching several of them in each hand, would emerge in the gathering dark and greet all for the evening, by sharing a salutation in the name of a saintly forefather of mine. Ancestors, for us, are naturally a part of our veneration and though not in the pantheon of gods, they have always been a part of our devotions. For a half hour or so after that followed a mandatory period of evening silence — maun. For us this was agony In childhood to sit silent and pray and meditate every evening, compulsorily, was a near impossible demand. And every evening at that hour, the entire House would fall reverentially silent, all inhabitants of it observing that half hour of quietude. I do not know if memory plays tricks but no sound then broke the silence, until all light faded from the sky, lanterns cast pools of dark shadows and stars dotted the heavens again. The ending of maun was announced by a handclap from someone senior, and then a loud greeting to all, again in the name of my saintly forefather.

Maun and its imposition in childhood helped me discover myself, but only in time, and with time, for an 'inner sense' gradually evolved, like water slowly rising in an open well, and I understood that maun, silence, contemplation, meditation, all are, in reality, synonyms. Besides, silence is the most evolved, intense mode of expression: it is the 'voice' of the spirit that inspires 'learning' or gyan, an inner illumination, seldom a flash, much more a slow awakening. That is what maun or silence does ... did in my case.

Jaswant Singh

The Songs of Kabir

O servant, where dost thou seek Me?

Lo! I am beside thee.

I am neither in temple nor in mosque: I am neither in Kaaba nor in Kailash:

Neither am I in rites and ceremonies, nor in yoga and renunciation.

If thou art a true seeker, thou shalt at once see Me: thou shalt meet Me in a moment of time.

Kabir says, 'O Sadhu! God is the breath of all breath.'

◆

Within this earthen vessel are bowers and groves, and within it is the Creator:

Within this vessel are the seven oceans and the unnumbered stars.

The touchstone and the jewel-appraiser are within;

And within this vessel the Eternal soundeth, and the spring wells up.

Kabir says: 'Listen to me, my Friend! My beloved Lord is within.'

◆

I have known in my body the sport of the universe: I have escaped from the error of this world.

The inward and the outward are become as one sky, the Infinite and the finite are united: I am drunken with the sight of this All!

This Light of Thine fulfils the universe: the lamp of love that burns on the salver of knowledge.

Kabir says: 'There error cannot enter, and the conflict of life and death is felt no more.'

Translated by Rabindranath Tagore

Tara

When Tara was small she was afraid of *everything*! A pair of pigeons on the window ledge scared her. Was it their beady, red-ringed-with-black, staring eyes? Mother told Tara they were soft and gentle creatures that meant her no harm. 'Look at their throats Tara,' she said. 'See that silky green, blue, purple and silver all mixed up. Have you ever seen such a beautiful colour?' But Tara continued to be afraid of them.

Mother sighed.

Tara was afraid of bees. Sometimes she had nightmares of them swarming and buzzing around her and woke up terrified. Then she would take Bluey, her beloved old teddy bear, and crawl into Mother's bed and go to sleep. Mother called Tara her 'Christmas present', because when Mother woke up in the morning she found Tara there, all wrapped up in her quilt just like a gift.

Mother said bees were quite wonderful. Without them we would not have flowers. They gave Tara honey to put on her bread. What's more, said Mother, bees were very clever, much smarter than people. When Tara grew older she tried to love bees. She succeeded for a little while, until one or two stray ones flew into the room and circled around the lamp at times, when Tara sat down to do her homework. Then, Tara would jump up and scream. Mother would hurry out of the kitchen and chase the bee out of the window with a newspaper. 'They will not sting you, Tara,' said Mother. 'They are only attracted to the light.' But Tara screamed and flapped, anyway.

Mother sighed.

Tara was most afraid of the big green municipality dump-trucks that collected the garbage. Leena, in kindergarten, had told her that if one of them even came *near* her, she would die! Mother told Tara not to be so silly! She made up a story about the man who drove the truck, his wife and his children. He was a person just like Daddy, she said. He was only doing his job. Did Daddy run his car into people and kill anyone? NO! Tara wanted to believe Mother. But she still held tight to Mother's hand whenever she saw one of the green monster trucks at the far end of the street.

Mother sighed.

When Tara was a baby she was afraid of big, tall people, especially strangers. She cried and buried her face in Mother's neck when six-foot-four-inch-tall Uncle George came to visit. Mother got Uncle George to play pat-a-cake with Tara, but Tara did not want to play.

Tara was afraid of elephants, even the gentle giant, Ram, the temple elephant. Tara watched fearfully from a safe distance as Ram 'blessed' Mother with his trunk when she gave him coconut, bananas and jaggery.

Tara was afraid of school, especially of P.T. Sir's booming voice, of Vasanti Madam's vice-like grip on her arm as she shoved the children into the auditorium. Mother watched helplessly from the school gate as Tara tried to make herself invisible by shrinking into the wall, as a herd of children thundered down the corridor.

Tara even had an imaginary place she would retreat to, called Rose Land. Its imaginary citizens, all paragons of virtue, apparently, 'spoke kindly and softly to each other'. She even led Mother to the dining room window and pointed to the distant blue hills. 'There,' she said, 'that is Rose Land over there!'

Mother wondered. Why did life so frighten the child? Why would she not allow the cool voice of logic and reason to soothe her fears? Did she have too much imagination? Those were the questions that kept Mother awake some nights.

Time passed. Now Tara is all grown up. She is afraid of nothing!

She chose to study in a college far from home, and live in a hostel full of strangers. After leaving college, she took up a job on the west coast and lived with just a shaggy, tawny dog, in a derelict guest-house on the deserted beach where her only neighbour was a poor, sad, mentally ill woman, whom she took under her wing. When Tara was asked by Mother's friend to deliver a package to old Mr Perez, whom she did not know at all, she pushed open the gate and walked straight into his large and notoriously fierce Doberman! 'The dog *likes* her,' the astonished owner reported to Mother. 'It's amazing, because Rocky does not like *anybody*!'

Tara is not afraid to trek through leech-infested jungles. Last month she helped a mahout to bathe his elephant in the river during an interactive session at the Dubare Elephant Camp. She is not afraid to live in a rough, rat-infested hut on the beach, and dive into the sea off the Andaman Islands on a snorkelling trip. Mother listens in awe when Tara describes the marvels of the silent and fascinating undersea world of exotic, multi-coloured fish and delicate coral, a world that Mother can imagine only with a lot of help from the Discovery Channel! Tara laughs when she tells Mother how rats ate her room mate's contact lens container and all their food and their soap!

Recently, Mother paled when Tara showed her a photograph taken with her new-fangled phone. It shows Tara, small and upside down against a big blue sky, dangling at the end of a rope. She had gone bungee jumping! Tara is not afraid to drive back alone at midnight after working late at the office.

And Mother? She lies awake and worries.

'Oh, my Mother is afraid of *everything*,' Tara tells a friend. Mother hides a smile.

Mother is in Tara's room watching her pack her travel bag. She has an early start tomorrow. A memory is taking shape in Mother's mind. It is of Tara, aged nine, getting off the school bus with her bag. Her favourite bedtime ritual then (and now, for all Mother knows) was to recite the shanti shloka which she had been taught at school. A simple, much-loved prayer from the Upanishad, which means: 'Lead me from Untruth into Truth, from Darkness into Light, from Death into Immortality'.

Mother is lost in thought. When did Tara emerge from that dark and fearsome cocoon she had made for herself and become the brave, rational, independent person she is today? Mother thinks the transformation must have happened when they were all busy just living their lives.

Mother goes into her own room and quietly shuts the door. She knows Tara will be all right. She is sure of it. She stands by the window and looks out into the quiet night and says softly, '*Tamasoma jyotirgamaya ...*' — lead me from Darkness into Light.

She sighs, but this time it is a sigh of heartfelt gratitude for a child's prayer that was heard.

Leela Krishnamohan

I Am a Lotus

My neighbours probably wonder what the strange chant they hear every morning coming from my bedroom window means.

For the past three months, I have been chanting regularly, either at home or in other lay Buddhists' homes, with the consequence that my mood is constantly elevated all through the day.

A friend of mine in Delhi introduced me to Nichiren Buddhism many years ago. I couldn't help but notice the transformation in him over the years that I have known him. Earlier he used to be self-absorbed and unhappy, but soon he had this glow on his face that evoked a response in me. What was the secret of his newfound happiness? He invited me home for a chanting session.

In an inner room in his flat, he had a scroll enshrined in a wooden case. On the scroll were three lines of Japanese words. The centre line, he explained, reads: Nam-Myoho-renge-kyo. These words are the essence of Nichiren Buddhism. They literally mean: 'I devote my life to the Mystic Law of cause and effect'. It is derived and translated into Japanese from the Sanskrit title of the Lotus Sutra.

Hearing the words chanted had a magical effect on me. It was almost as if a lotus inside me began to emerge from muddy waters and was ready to bloom. I wanted to know more about the practice.

Over two thousand years ago, Gautama Buddha taught that all human beings are already blessed with enlightenment or Buddhahood. Life's journey is to understand what we already possess. Buddhism survived in other regions of Asia, in various forms through his Sutras.

In the thirteenth century, a Buddhist sage, Nichiren Daishonin, concluded that the Lotus Sutra is the definitive teaching of Gautama Buddha. To quote from a Buddhist booklet: 'The Lotus Sutra asserts the inherent dignity and equality of all people and, indeed, of all life. Nichiren Daishonin crystallised the teachings of the Lotus Sutra into a concrete philosophy accessible to all people and established a practice that is simple yet profound and suitable to modern times.'

Much later, in the twentieth century, at a trying time in the history of Japan, Sensei Makiguchi revived Nichiren Buddhism. He was imprisoned for his beliefs and his refusal to give in to state-prescribed religion. He died in prison, but his disciple carried the torch forward to form the Soka Gakai International or SGI.

Today SGI is one of the most popular organisations of lay Buddhism with members increasing worldwide. People meet in homes to chant together, study meetings are held every week and 3 May is celebrated as Founder's Day.

To me personally, without making too much of a fuss about 'conversion', I can practise Nam-Myoho-renge-kyo and feel I am on my way to attaining peace and joy in my life, if not realising my Buddhahood.

The lotus blooms and produces seeds at the same time, and represents the simultaneity of cause and effect. The theory of karma is based on these principles too. But we do have control over our destiny. I am a firm believer now that transformation begins with a simple chant and an even breath. By transforming your own self you have the ability to change not only your own karma but also the karma of your society.

Scientific research has proved that people who meditate live longer, are at much less risk of getting mental illnesses, and have a more peaceful mind that is conducive to creative and rational thinking. It directly affects your endocrinal system, making you a healthier human being.

The primary goal of Nichiren Buddhism is Kosen-rufu or world peace. Once our personal goals are achieved, we must endeavour to create a better world for those who will inherit the Earth from us. In the twenty-first century, we are on the brink of World War III, with hatred, ignorance and greed creating conflicts politically and socially. I cannot think of a better goal than Kosen-rufu. In that sense, Nichiren Buddhism, whether practised as a way of life, or simply respected for its values, is perhaps the timeliest form of Buddhism that addresses all the issues that plague our world.

All goodness is innate in human beings because we belong to the laws that govern Nature. Whether we choose to bring it out through chanting or through a rational understanding of our environment is a personal choice. But we most certainly have come to a point in time where we have to now make that extra effort to dispel our ignorance and prejudices. Otherwise we may not survive as a species or as a planet. In the words of Daishonin: 'When the sky is clear of clouds, the ground is illuminated.'

Mahesh Dattani

Laddus in Both Hands

We are at Tapovan, shivering in our winter clothes. It is at a height of 15,000 feet in the Himalayas, and above it looms the Shivalinga mountain. In the epic, the *Mahabharat*, the Pandavas were supposed to have set out to die there, but only Yudhistira managed to reach the top. The Ganga flows in a trickle into a narrow stream, before she appears at Gaumukh, at 12,000 feet, and roars down to Gangotri. We are exhausted and dizzy with altitude sickness. The gentle presence of Shimla Baba heals us. He offers us dal-roti cooked by him, gives us blankets, and asks us to rest. At dawn, we see him silhouetted against the glowing snow mountain, doing his sadhana. Baba in his loin cloth and bare feet was a vision of serenity. Later we asked him, 'Baba, don't you get bored alone here? Don't you find it annoying to serve people like us who bother you and come in the way of your sadhana?' Baba smiled and said, 'I have laddus in both hands. Doing seva is like having a laddu in one hand. Doing sadhana is the laddu in the other hand. When people come, I am happy I can serve. And when no one is here, I am happy I can do my sadhana.'

This metaphor has been one of the best lessons I have learnt in my life. When I was denied my promotion, I saw it as an opportunity to do my research and writing for which I'd had no time earlier. Every situation one comes across can be seen as a laddu. To me, this is the secret of happiness and equanimity.

Malavika Kapur

The Lesson of the Cow

In the 1930s, I was a student of a village madrasa in UP. There I studied an Urdu Reader in which there was a poem composed by the well-known poet, Ismail Meerathi. It was titled 'Hamari Gaye' (Our Cow). One of the verses spoke of the cow as a special kind of animal. It eats grass and in return gives us milk. In other words, the cow is a 'divine industry', which is able to convert non-milk into milk.

This poem became a part of my memory. It taught me a great lesson. God, the Creator, has made the cow a model for human behaviour in that it gives us a lesson in high morality.

It is said that man is a social animal. But what is society? Society is full of differences. Every day we experience some provocative situation, every day we face some unwanted behaviour from others and suffer from anger and tension because of conflicts arising out of differences with others.

What should we do? The cow is the answer. God has created a model for us to follow in the form of the cow. We have to adopt 'cow culture', we have to develop in our personality what may be called 'the capacity for conversion'; we have to turn negative experiences into positive thinking.

The fact is that everyone enjoys freedom. But everyone is free to misuse his freedom. It is this misuse of freedom that creates problems. As we cannot abolish people's freedom, we have no option but to learn the art of problem management.

According to Islam, the present world is a testing ground. Every man and woman here is being tested. If they have freedom, it is because, without freedom, there can be no test. This freedom is God-given, and as such, no one has the licence to abolish it. Thus we have no option but to follow the cow pattern, that is, to turn negativity into 'positivity'.

Once a man came to the Prophet of Islam, and said: 'O Prophet, give me a piece of "master advice" by which I may be able to manage all the affairs of my life.'

The Prophet replied: 'Don't be angry.'

'Don't be angry,' means learning the art of anger management, learning the art of converting anger into forgiveness, learning the art of converting anger into peacefulness.

Leaving society and going into the jungle or the mountains is a lower form of spirituality. The higher form of spirituality is that which is demonstrated by the cow — we live with people, experience all kinds of unwanted behaviour from others, but try not to react negatively. We have to imitate the cow. Just as the cow converts grass into milk, we have to convert negative thought into positive thought. This is the highest form of spirituality.

Most men and women are battling stress. They ask, what is the way to de-stress themselves. I would suggest that they learn a lesson from the cow. They should adopt the 'cow habit' in their affairs and they will be able to de-stress themselves quite successfully. The cow symbolises an elevated form of lifestyle. Adopt this lifestyle, and you will be able to enjoy a tension-free life.

Maulana Wahiduddin Khan

Home Thoughts

My mother would never move into a new house without going through a 'milk-boiling ceremony'. On an auspicious day, decided according to the Hindu almanac, she would sally forth, armed with a pot and some milk, to the new house. Then she would heat the milk on the stove, always making sure that it boiled over. We would all sip a little of that milk solemnly, for we believed that Lakshmi, the Hindu goddess of prosperity, came on the upsurge of the milk to bless the house.

I have consciously followed this ritual through all my travels as an adult. This, to me, has been a spiritual experience, encouraging our grounding and promoting empathy between the house and me, be it in Chennai or Bangalore, Jakarta or Singapore. Thus is prepared the ground for shared family experiences, which invest our lives with comforting familiarity and warmth, so that the house becomes a home.

Many of the experiences which have meant home to me have involved both my mother and her religion. Often, when I had returned from boarding schools to wherever my parents were at that time, I would wake up in a strange house. But when I smelt those smells associated with my mother's puja in the early morning hours — that special fragrance of incense, sandalwood, and flowers — I knew where I was, and would be comfortingly reassured.

My mother loved using flowers, and knew the significance of each variety in the ritual. She punctuated her chants with elegant flicks of her wrists so that the flowers flew in graceful arcs to land in front of the gods. Wherever she went, she planted bushes or creepers of the white-starred jasmine and the scarlet hibiscus; it was probably her way of anchoring. And when I breathed in the sacred odours which accompanied her rituals of worship, and knew what they meant — that she was sending up her prayers for our well-being through the wafting incense fumes — I knew I was on hallowed ground.

It is therefore a tribute to her that I do not remember the strangeness or the hassles which might have accompanied the transfers — I have moved house a total of twenty-seven times, eleven before marriage and sixteen after — but have a marvellous mosaic of memories of our various homes. My mother's way of confronting my father's career moves smoothed over any distress that might have occurred. Her quiet strength and her matter-of-fact acceptance did not encourage any soul-searching questions about psychological damage or adjustment problems. As a family of six — our parents, three daughters and a son — we just packed up and moved, underwent new experiences, went to new schools, made new friends and got used to different vistas from new windows. Of course, memory's truth is changeable, adding not only fairy gold, but reshaping, eliminating, amplifying, and comparing, creating its own interpretation of events, colourful and variegated, but lucid. It is nature's way of coping with the past and the present, so that the memories lying behind our eyelids are only the enchanting ones, to be recalled at our will and pleasure.

Some magical evenings I well remember, in colonial bungalows in the remote rural districts to which my father was posted as a young police officer, when the electricity went off, as it does even now. I recall the light of the kerosene lantern, the flickering golden-red flames on our childish faces, and my mother teaching us to make chains out of broken glass bangles. She held the shimmering arcs of colour over the candle flame till they became pliable, then curved them gently till the ends touched, and looped the arcs together. Useless rainbow chains we'd hang over our mirrors, but they symbolised the linking of our experiences to provide us with a sense of continuity and stability, and captured the essence of those nights, jasmine-scented, with the atmosphere of an ancient timeless ritual.

Memories are intangible links with the past. But from time immemorial man has invested inanimate objects of earth, clay, wood and metal with significance. And so the various artefacts I possess are scattered around wherever I live, disparate yet coherent, like the landscapes they represent, bringing back fond recollections of the homes I've lived in, and the places I've visited all these years.

There are the photographs of the children at various stages of their lives; the Indonesian landscape paintings, timelessly Asian, with the ubiquitous water-buffalo and the orange-gold flowers of the flame of the forest trees; the brass lamps from my mother, which I reverently place facing the east, and the books of my childhood, well loved and thumbed, all these and more have dotted my homes wherever they have been. So, wherever I am, I am content, living in a present enhanced by memories of the past and hope for strength to handle the future. The grace to be grateful for life's favours and to accept the presence of troughs and swells in life is rooted in my mother's faith in the universe. It has led to my own sense of home, which is within me and permeates the space that I occupy. And for that, I am grateful to her.

Maya Jayapal

Looking for God on Brigade Road

It is under some more than usual stress that one realises how little one has changed from the child one once was. Recently, I was optimistically looking forward to a vision of the Divine at one of the edges of consciousness — either before I drifted into anaesthesia or out of it. Alas. No such sublime experience came my way. But it triggered a memory which is nearly half a century old.

When I first began to enjoy listening to stories from the Bible, I couldn't tell the difference between the Old Testament and the New. What did it matter to me when or where Samuel or Paul had lived? Exciting things seemed to have happened to both of them. My chief interest concerned their direct experience of God. If *they* had experienced this power, why shouldn't I? I felt an overwhelming longing to hear and see this God who remote-controlled things both at home and in school. No food at home before lamp-lightings and prayers, and school was full of nuns who kept saying, 'Praise the Lord', though I sensed that different departments in heaven were being addressed by my mother and my teachers.

If I didn't try, if I didn't let Him know, how would God know that I wanted to see Him?

At age six, the world is waiting to be conquered. I often dodged my brother and ayah, went off by myself and tried saying loudly, 'Here I am!' hoping that, like Samuel, I would hear the Voice. What a story that was and how thrillingly my teacher narrated it in class! The whole class used to chorus, 'Here I am!' So I was fairly sure I could recognise His voice when it reached me. It would be so different and would boom from above. But God proved difficult to contact and the stories about the times he spoke with people were not always pleasant. So after a while I thought it would be a better idea to try and reach Jesus. At least I had a vague idea of what he looked like.

Then, one day, I heard that he had said, 'I am always with you.'

'With his disciples, eh … always?'

'No, with everyone.'

'Us also?'

'Yes, with us also.'

I made up my mind to see Jesus as soon as possible. Perhaps, he was actually somewhere around and, because no one had had the sense to watch out for him, no one had spotted him. I questioned people carefully. Have you seen him? No, of course not. Don't be silly, we can't see him. Your heart has to be pure … all sorts of glib explanations. Well, of course, my heart was pure. I didn't hurt people or animals. In an effort to become even more blameless, I stopped plucking flowers and leaves for fun.

I began watching people. Most of them looked angry or sad or disgruntled, so it couldn't be Christ in disguise. I began to take short walks to the gate by myself. Perhaps he was waiting for me to be alone. Heart pounding, I stepped outside the gate — something I was not supposed to do — and looked

carefully up and down Rest House Road. No. No one at
all. In the evenings, we sometimes took a walk on crowded
Brigade Road. If he wanted to hide, this is where he might
be, but I would spot him in his long robes. The colour of his
hair was a real problem. Some paintings in school showed
dark hair; in some his hair was blond. What a bother that no
one seemed to have got it right, once and for all.

After several days of waiting for God, and hoping to see
at least Jesus, I was both angry and sad. I went to school
with a swollen face. During a lull between classes I decided
I would have it out with the Sister seated at the desk before
the blackboard. When the bell rang at break-time, I went up
to her.

'Is Jesus here in this classroom?'

She looked startled and said, 'Yes dear, of course he is.'

'Then why can't I see him?'

'Well …'

'Can you see him? Have you seen him?'

Her answers were evasive and her smile infuriated me.
I let out a roar of frustration and pain. Many teachers from
other classrooms reached ours and soon the Mother Superior
swished in, a tall, pale woman. She stooped to reach my
level, held my shoulders and asked me seriously what the
problem was.

'I want to see God … or Jesus.'

'Oh-oh-oh,' she said, in an accent very different from the
ones I was used to hearing.

'If *you've* seen God, when will I?'

'My child … uh …'

'Why can't I be like Samuel?' Having attracted so much
attention, I felt I had to be specific and really, now, any route
would do, I wasn't particular.

Sensing a spiritual crisis, Mother Superior came to a
decision. 'Yes of course you will see. You will see them both,

but not when you are so little.' The great adult conspiracy against children.

She lifted me up, carried me off and away to a dim room, sat me down on a piano stool and very slowly took out a small glossy picture of Christ from a big book and gave it to me.

'Till you see, keep this carefully. Then ... give it to someone else.' Was her back to me when she said this? I cannot quite remember.

The tears of a six-year-old who has drawn the attention of adults dry like magic, and I went off very pleased with myself. At the end of the corridor, when I turned to look back, I thought I saw Mother's blue eyes shining unnaturally as she stood at the door watching me, but I couldn't be sure.

Mini Krishnan

Shades of White

We both wore white when we first met, and it became a joke cementing our friendship. I prefer to dress in white for freshness, purity and new beginnings. But I never expected Rajat to share my taste in this. I imagined meeting him against his favourite poetic backdrop of mellow fuchsia and orange sunsets or, perhaps, dark clouds split by lightning. But after a year of exchanging comments on each other's writing through emails, we were destined to meet in the most prosaic way. He was passing through my city on business, so could I meet him over a cup of coffee?

I picked up Rajat's photograph with trembling fingers, taking in the sword-sharp nose, menacing moustache and sinister grin. Was I really going to meet THAT? I mentally replayed every tale I had heard about malignant predators trawling the Internet. Should I tell my friends to keep my family informed, and perhaps call the police, if I didn't return within a reasonable time?

I reminded myself that he was a talented writer who gave me no-nonsense advice and did not expect to be showered with praise. What could happen if I met him for just half an hour in a crowded coffee house? I stroked my white organdie kurta, the one embroidered with pale turquoise and lemon flowers amid spring-green leaves. This dress never failed to bring me luck, and I needed it to meet the swarthy demon in the photograph.

At the appointed time, I arrived at the café and scanned the crowd for Rajat's fierce handlebar moustache and intense eyes. My jaws hardened and the skin on my forehead tightened. Yet I knew in my heart that only a truly good man could write such poetry. I could never write in isolation. I needed, we both needed, an understanding and supportive friend to bounce off our ideas. When inspiration played truant, we prodded each other to bring back those creative ideas. Our exchanges helped us to hone our craft, gain confidence and grow as thinking, sensitive human beings. No, I would not flinch no matter how terrifying he looked.

After leafing through several pages of a book without reading, I saw a tall man rise from his seat and move towards me. 'Excuse me?' He stood wringing his hands, long legs poised for a quick retreat. 'Are you,' he glanced around the coffee house and added in a lowered voice, 'Moni?' The man had clear, honey-coloured skin and no hint of a moustache, but he knew my name. And yes, those eyes matched, with more vibrancy than any photo could capture. It was Rajat.

Rajat's smile warmed and relaxed me like a woollen wrap on a chilly evening. His low, rich voice enticed me out of shyness and wove a snug cocoon separating us from the din of the bustling café.

'Lady in White, indeed,' he said, his words effervescent with muted laughter. 'You look as fragile and vulnerable as my baby sister who is finishing college this year.'

'Indeed!' I drew as much dignity as I could into my five-foot-four-inch frame and looked this man who towered above me, straight in the eye. 'Besides, it's you who misguided me. I expected to meet a bandit from the Chambal ravines.' I twirled my fingers around an imaginary moustache and added, 'But I see the noble Nawab of Awadh.' I eyed his white kurta-pyjama with intricate Lucknow chikan embroidery at the neckline.

He raised his palms and said, 'I surrender. But please, be careful and don't go by appearances alone. Those who fool you into thinking they're cultured nawabs may be the real bandits.'

We talked over cup after cup of steaming coffee, marvelling at how writing had brought us together. If I had not known him through his poems, would I have ever ventured to even speak to this man?

Rajat spoke as if he'd read my thoughts. 'When I write, it isn't only for myself, but because I want to exchange ideas and reach out to others.'

'Yes,' I replied. 'We may be meeting for the first time, but it's as though we've known each other all our lives. There is a good deal of "me" in my stories, just as your poetry tells me so much about the real "you". Yet there is much that is imagined and reaches out beyond the finite "you" or "me".'

'Ultimately, creative art, whether through words, song, paintings or dance, explores the deepest spiritual nuances of life's journey,' Rajat said. 'It is about love and understanding, about connecting and sharing.'

'We may live in Delhi, Bangalore, London or Lagos,' I replied. 'And you might look like a bandit or nawab depending on your mood. And I ...'

'You might remind me of my spoilt brat of a sister,' Rajat added with a grin. 'But the differences are superficial. We write about ideas and emotions which extend beyond man-made boundaries.'

'Yes,' I said. 'We write poems and stories because we must; because the endless delicate details of our shared human bond cannot be cramped into catchy two-line blurbs.'

'To write with honesty,' Rajat said, 'and at the same time to believe in one's insignificance, is all we can do.' His grey eyes flashed with greens and gold as the mood took over us both.

'I shouldn't have felt so suspicious after seeing your photo.'

'Suspicion isn't an entirely bad thing.' His smile eased my misgivings for blurting out a tactless truth. 'Always be suspicious of praise or you might sink into smugness. Look for criticism — there might be more truth in it.'

'Many of us refuse to even try to think for ourselves,' I said. 'We wait for someone else to set trends and tell us what to do. I know writers are not supposed to offer solutions. They ask questions, pose moral dilemmas. But I want to write some day of the gloriousness of the human spirit.'

'It's easy to laugh at others, but what about our own passive role in this chaos? The world is becoming more violent and life more absurd and there are no heroes to look up to. It's tough for any writer to make sense of this world. So what do you say? Shall we make a pact and try to create those heroes?' He offered a raised palm and we exchanged high-fives.

We bantered and laughed on, two lifelong friends meeting for the first time. When our table couldn't hold more empty coffee cups, the waiter smiled and signalled that we could sit without ordering more. And then, it was time to leave.

'I brought something for you,' Rajat said, handing me a parcel. 'Go ahead, open it.'

I removed the pearly white gift wrapping and brought out two crystal prisms. Holding their cool, clear surfaces to the window, I watched white daylight stream through them and split into all the brilliant hues of the spectrum.

'Place the other prism in the line of the spectrum and see what happens,' Rajat said. The colours entered the second prism and became white light again. 'They are like your imagination,' he continued. 'Only an artist can see all the colours and their nuances where others see ordinary white light. And only an artist can see a riot of colours in this chaotic life and focus them into a single, pure white.'

Rajat's prisms have sat on my desk for years as bookends. Whenever the white blankness of a new file challenges me from my computer screen, I turn to my prisms. I watch them draw brilliant reds, greens, and indigo from white light and transform them into clear white again. The light frees my spirit from darkness and distractions. And then, my ideas flow.

Monideepa Sahu

Yoga and Rollerblading

A few months back, I decided to learn rollerblading with my daughter (and all the neighbours' kids). My foray into the sport was anything but smooth. Initially, I spent more time painfully horizontal on the ground rather than up on my feet, and my loud screams and big thuds provided greater entertainment to the kids than the sport itself! After a few lessons, there they were, all those tiny tots who were not even half my size (and that included my daughter!) zooming around gracefully, with a smile on their face and the wind in their hair, while I continued to go hobble, wobble, c-r-a-s-h! I was battered and bruised and even had a black eye that was turning interesting shades of blue, purple and green. But there was no way I was going to give up.

'Are you crazy?' said my friends. 'Your days are packed as it is, and you have more than enough on your plate. What's the big deal about rollerblading, anyway?'

'I want to do it! That's all.'

My near and dear ones shook their heads, and waited for me to come to my senses before I broke a bone or two. I persevered, thought positive thoughts and waited for a breakthrough. Somewhere along the way, what had been merely an impulsive decision to learn rollerblading had morphed into something completely different. Strangely, a simple thing that all the children around me had now mastered had expanded into a pushing-the-boundaries-and-surmounting-challenges experience for me.

Then, one disastrous day, when nothing worked out right, the instructor who had been observing my plight, took me aside and said softly, 'Listen to your skates!' And those cryptic words somehow made sense, and immediately, the whole thing just fell into place.

The skates had a mind of their own and I had a mind of my own, and the whole problem was that they were not aligned at all! Once the instructor had pointed me in the right direction, as a regular practitioner of yoga, I knew what I had to do. After all, we had been taught that yoga is skill in action. So which action? *Any* action, really.

Once you learn yoga it becomes quite easy to throw your attention to any part of your body ... and be that part of the body. So I went to my feet and sort of 'listened' to my skates. I just let go, loosened up and asked them, 'Tell me where you want to go, and let us go together.' And at that moment, my skates seemed totally willing to cooperate with me! And that was how my skates and I became friends forever and we just love rollerblading now.

This is no different from our life. As my yoga master, Krishanji, said one day, 'Every moment has a mind of its own'. And when our little mind aligns itself with each moment, when it is willing to listen to the present moment, life flows smoothly.

Preeti Prabhu

The Great Miracle

'Soon you will see a great miracle,' you whispered as we children watched the little green caterpillars munch away on the leaves you fed them. You had made them a home from an empty shoebox, punctured with little holes on top for ventilation. Sure enough, in a matter of a few days, the caterpillars began to cocoon themselves and we looked on astonished.

'Is this the miracle?' I asked.

'No,' you said, 'wait and watch.'

And then we waited and watched through the holes on top of the box. We waited for days and the suspense was killing.

'When will the miracle happen?' asked Aziz who was six years old.

'Be patient. It can happen any day now.'

And then the caterpillars emerged from their cocoons as butterflies and you set them free. I still remember the first time that happened and I couldn't believe it. 'How did it happen, Ammi?' I asked.

You smiled and said it was a miracle.

Saeed Mirza

It Will Come to Us

Contentment is the first sign of prosperity. I'll narrate an anecdote about this. My grandfather was thought to be very simple-minded and liberal-hearted. He used to give away everything he owned. If someone said, 'Oh, you have a nice watch,' he would say, 'Take it,' and readily give it away. So many times he would come home with just a vest (undershirt), jacket, coat and a shawl, after giving away the rest.

My grandmother was from a royal family. She was devoted to my grandfather and did not complain about this. My grandfather, with his generous nature, gave away his wealth in a few years' time. He gave his three children a good education but nothing else, and he died leaving my grandmother with nothing. She didn't have any skills except that of somehow feeding everybody. Her three children were just teenagers at the time. My grandfather had given away practically everything in the house. People commented, 'What is this? He didn't leave anything to the children.'

My father supported the family and had to walk several miles to work, every day. Life was not easy, but my grandmother never lost her serenity or her smile, not even for a single day! She'd just pray and say, 'Everything is in plenty.' Friends who visited her would remark, 'I saw your grandmother; she is so content and happy.' She would never be upset about anything. If she cooked a meal for two persons, and four came, she would feed them all. She would simply say, 'It will come to us. God is giving us everything.'

Surrender and love are synonymous. Whomsoever you love, you surrender to them. It's not a doing but a state of being, when the mind is free of doubts and troubles. The word 'surrender' is frightening because we have heard it in one context — when an army loses, it surrenders; a defeat is understood to be surrender. Surrender is not submission. Only the brave, the knowledgeable and the wise can surrender.

Surrender is realising that everything belongs to the Divine. 'I' am not in control — that is surrender. This little mind realises that it is not in control; the entire universe runs on its own and it does not matter whether you exist on this planet or not, things will happen. In the same way, you realise that your life is happening and that you are happening in this ocean of consciousness. Your heart beats by itself, your breath moves by itself, sleep comes, you feel good and bad. With this realisation comes a deep relaxation, a feeling of trust and being at home; that is surrender.

Sri Sri Ravi Shankar

Thy Will Be Done

*Surrender is the simple but profound wisdom of yielding
to rather than opposing the flow of life.*

Eckhart Tolle

I first experienced surrender as a sixteen-year-old returning
home to Orissa after my first semester in a Mumbai college.
To complicate matters, my father sent me a telegram on the
penultimate day asking me to change my route to Nagpur. He
would take me onward from there since he was going home
via Nagpur after dropping my mother in Delhi, for my third
sister's confinement. I was frightened by those last-minute
changes, especially since I did not have much spare money. In
fact, I just about had enough money to buy a ticket to Nagpur.
From there on my father would take care of me, I believed,
and set out. The nightmare began when my father's train,
the Grand Trunk Express, drew in and drew out without my
locating him. With mounting fear and horror, I took stock of
my situation. I was stranded far from home without money.
What on earth was I to do?

I remember walking round and round the station bench I had placed my luggage on, my mind examining options furiously. I was sure of one thing. I should not sit down, or else the game was up. I would be lost. For what seemed like a lifetime I walked around in circles, then defeated, sat down and promptly burst into tears. What followed was pure Providence. An elderly Sikh couple, moved by my distress, came over and asked me what the matter was. When I sobbed out my plight, they went and fetched the station master. That saintly man, who must have seen innumerable situations such as this and could very well have been inured to it, sprang to my assistance like a guardian angel. He bought me a ticket to my destination, and even gave me money to buy a meal for the night. He ensured that I got into the right train and sent me on my way.

God bless this man, wherever he may be now. I owe him much. But the interesting thing, which I have never forgotten, is that help came to me only when I did what I thought was unthinkable — I gave up. It might seem that giving up is a far cry from surrender, and so it is when we give up because we couldn't care less, or do not want to put in the effort. When one, however, tries one's every resource and then gives up, it is not really giving up, it is letting go, even if it is not a conscious decision.

That form of unconscious surrender happened a few times in my life. Later, after moving into spirituality, surrender happened at different levels. Many years ago, I participated in an exhibition for *Life Positive* and tried my hand at marketing. Each time a customer walked by without responding to my smile or invitation to hear about *Life Positive,* I felt as if he or she were taking away a piece of my self-esteem. Sales began to flag. Suddenly there swept over me a wonderful sense of well-being and assurance. The outcome ceased to matter, and I was immersed in the moment. Calm flooded into my heart and from that place of surety and certainty, I became an ace salesperson. That sense of letting-go was one aspect of surrender.

At that point I did not yet know that experiences came and went like fireflies in the night and that the spiritual journey was like a spiral staircase, the same insight or experience presenting itself at different times of the journey, each time at a heightened depth and breadth. A couple of years back, surrender visited me once again, this time in a much more complete and conscious way. It came to me that my stuff — thoughts, feelings, actions, reactions — was not really my stuff. It was God's. Instead of taking credit or blame for them, I simply had to pass them on.

That state too, gradually left me. What I feel myself groping towards now is surrender in the real sense of the word. A state in which the ego gratefully relinquishes itself at the feet of the Almighty. Self-will is vanquished and God's will is all. There is nothing one wants as much as to obey the will of God. Self-will and God's will become fused — they are one, not two.

Only in surrender can we know true joy, peace and love. The mind's tumult finally stills — what is there to complain about? All life's problems are offered up trustfully. We recognise that our life is really not our business — it is God's. All we have to do is keep our eyes fixed on the moment. That is all. That is our only task. Everything else is God's problem.

How simple life is!

Suma Varughese

Just Sit Still for Two Minutes

There is something beyond our mind which abides in silence within our mind. It is the supreme mystery beyond thought. Let one's mind and one's subtle body rest upon that and not rest on anything else.
                                        —*Maitri Upanishad*

'Don't leave me and go,' I screamed from the first floor. I rushed down, my foot slipped and I went tumbling, several steps at a time. Half-an-hour and a-deserved-dressing-down-from-my-parents later, I was sitting on the bed with a sprained ankle and disappointment in my heart.

Tucked under a blanket, I was trying to read the comic book in my hand but my eyes were on the door, waiting for my parents to return from the temple. After what seemed like a very long time, they were back, and in my mother's hand, I saw something that brought the smile back to my face. She was holding a tiny bowl made of areca leaves. 'It's your favourite today — kesaribath,' she smiled.

The year was 1986. I was seven years old. My parents had just returned from the eighty-year-old Ganesha temple in Malleswaram, one of the oldest parts of Bangalore. This is a temple I grew up visiting, be it a birthday, or a quick prayer before my exams, a festival, or simply because I was in the neighbourhood. With its lazy air, lazier trees and a set of familiar faces — from the beggars sitting outside to the head priest — this temple became my touchstone for religion for the first eighteen years of my life. The smell of camphor, the way my feet felt on the cold stone steps, the loud echoing of the bell resonating in my ears, the sound of breaking coconuts and the holy water the priest served with a silver spoon — they were all metaphors of 'God's dwelling place'. But the first chord that repeatedly pulled me back to this temple was the prasad, the holy offering which is distributed to devotees in a symbolic sharing of energy from a higher source.

To my seven-year-old mind, though, it was but a delicious sweet, or a dish that one couldn't get anywhere else. So I eagerly repeated my visits to the temple, my mind always on the surprise waiting for me at the exit. Before leaving the temple, it is the normal practice to sit on the steps in silence, for two minutes. As a child, I remember how impatient I would get when I was required to do that. 'Meditate. Think good thoughts,' my father would tell me. All I had wanted to do then was to rush for my share of the prasad.

The years went by, I grew older, and the prasad no longer held as much attraction. The temple visits grew fewer and far between, and for more selfish reasons too. Soon, I was entering the temple only twice a year — on my birthday and just before the annual exams. The rebel in me started to question every ritual … and I got no clear answers.

Several years later, on my way back from Kodaikanal, I was in Madurai to catch the flight to Bangalore. I reached the temple town a little early and decided to wander along its main streets. When I reached the main entrance of the famous Meenakshi temple, I could smell the strong fragrance of incense mixed with the scent of camphor. The temple bells rang loudly and the sound echoed all around me. Stopping in front of the temple, I looked at all the activity there. I was then distracted by the cries of a young girl. 'I want some more,' she was telling her father in Tamil, between sobs. 'But it's over. I'll get you some more outside. Stop crying,' her father tried to pacify her.

'But it's not the same outside,' she howled.

Behind them I saw a family walking with leaf bowls full of kesaribath. I found myself smiling. Instinct then drew me towards the temple. As if led by an external force, I went along. I was entering a temple after many years. The stones, the oil lamps, the incessant ringing of bells, the kumkum in bowls kept in the corners — everything again struck that once familiar chord. But I found myself taking in all the details.

My pace had slowed down, and somehow, the answers seemed to be somewhere around the corner. But this time, it felt different. The reason finally dawned on me when I sat down on the steps before heading out. 'Meditate. Think good thoughts,' my father's words echoed. When I was a child, those words meant that if I sat quiet, I would be rewarded at the end of those two minutes, with prasad. As I grew older, it became a part of the many other temple rituals, the meanings of which I'm still trying to understand.

But that day, as I sat on the temple steps, with the bells ringing and my mind calming down to a soothing pace, it felt as if an inner cleansing was taking place. I was being absolved of all the unnecessary muck inside of me. Two minutes of silence in the right environment is all it takes to centre oneself, to drop all negative thoughts and to feel light once more. And this, I had never really understood in all those years.

It was in Madurai, when I spontaneously left my ego outside and walked around the murti as a devotee, just like the child in me once had, that the real meaning struck home. And this, no book will ever be able to teach. But there was definitely something that helped me along the way — my parents' persistent efforts to make temple visits a habit with me. They had fulfilled their dharma in teaching me the rituals involved during such a visit. I had struggled for a few years, grappling for answers — the whys and wherefores. But that struggle was crucial for growth ... for understanding that we do not need to understand everything. Perhaps, rituals also have the function of making us comfortable with not fully understanding everything.

It took an innocent child's cry for more prasad to make me realise my own spiritual progress. It dawned on me during that visit that the 'two minutes of silence' before heading out of the temple is a way to make us offload the ego, send out positive vibes and wish everyone well. One can do it at a temple, or by simply sitting still anywhere in the world at all.

As I walked out, I did take my share of the kesaribath. It was as delicious as ever. I decided I was definitely going back for more.

Sumaa Tekur

Light on a Hill

In the span
Of a God's
Body conjoined
The Goddess,
In the span
Of time we
Call the flutter
Of an eyelash,
Love was found.
Trees, grass, water
Fell from the sky,
Insects, birds, animals
And all of us whom we describe as human
Gathered
At the feet
Of this ancient hill.
The winds rushed and seeds scattered
The stones were bronzed under sunlight

And waiting becomes
A sign in the soul,
Quieter than absence
More still then dead,
More wilful than living
And nothing is achieved
Except the sound of a hidden waterfall
And a lost stream.

Susan Visvanathan

The Meaning of Life

A young boy left home in search of the Truth. He met many people and became richer in the awareness of his ignorance. Since people went to the forests to meditate, he too went to a thick forest. He did not know how to meditate. For years, his only mantra was screaming at the forest to give him knowledge. He believed that if you are committed, existence will help you.

One day, a monk came to him. He asked, 'What do you want, my son?'

'I want to know what the meaning of life is,' he replied.

'Go to the town. The first three persons that you meet will show you the meaning of life,' the monk replied.

The boy went to the town. The first man he met was engaged in carpentry. The next man he met was engaged in sheet metal work. The third man he met was making strings. Disappointed, he sat on the bank of the river. Suddenly, he heard the sweet strains of violin music. Something mysterious touched him. He had suddenly found the answer he was looking for and he started dancing.

The carpenter was preparing the wood for the violin. The sheet metal worker was preparing metal for the strings and the strings were meant for the violin. Life has everything; all you need is to be able to connect the dots. You need to work out new combinations. And for that you need creative perception.

You have to change the notion that difficulty is pain ... In sports, there is difficulty but there is also joy. In your relationships, when there is difficulty, treat it as joy. Just re-programme your mind.

In prayer, you don't have to do anything; just be available to receive God's grace. Prayer is a deep readiness to receive God's flow. It is passive alertness. Go deep and you discover your original mind ... it is deep passiveness. A greedy mind is richer than a Buddha, but rich with desires and greed; so a Buddha is 'poorer' than you are. And as the Bible says, 'Blessed are the poor for theirs is the kingdom of God.'

When someone asked the Buddha what he attained through his enlightenment, he said, 'I did not gain but I lost. I lost my ignorance, my dogmas, my likes and dislikes, my ambitions.'

You can live in two ways — mechanical or meditative. The meditative way involves your being more aware; that awareness is passive alertness. When you are passively alert, you will realise that you are born free ... you have choices and that is your freedom. When there is no freedom, there are no choices. Be more meditative and you will make the right choices that will help you grow rather than feel trapped.

If you choose wisely, you are in paradise. When you eat, eat meditatively. Totally be in your eating. When you have a bath, be total in having your bath and a different paradise opens up. Next, bring in love energy into whatever you do ... feel your inner being.

With the energy of silence, be 'total' ... and you will be moving heaven.

Swami Sukhabodhananda

4
LIGHTER
MOMENTS

True laughter, that is true prayer ... in nature everything is just waiting for you to laugh. When you laugh the whole of nature laughs with you. It echoes and resounds, and that is really the worth of life. When things go all right, everybody can laugh, but when everything falls apart, if even then you can laugh, that is evolution and growth.

Sri Sri Ravi Shankar

Anchor

Manjula Padmanabhan

When God Answers Our Prayers...

In a small town on the banks of a river, there lived a pious priest. Once, during a storm, the river was in spate, and the town was flooded. People ran around in panic, trying to find ways to get to higher ground as the water rose quickly in all the streets, and began to flow into the houses. When the priest saw what was happening, he said to himself, 'I've served God faithfully all my life and He will surely save me. I shall not flee with the others, but stay right here and wait for Him to rescue me.' So the priest climbed to the roof of the house and prayed, 'O God, I trust in you. Save me!' and waited for Him to do something.

Soon afterwards, a man came by in a boat and offered to take him to safety. But the priest shook his head and said, 'No, no ... don't worry, God will save me.'

Steadily, the water rose higher. Next, a boatload of people came by in a motor boat and urged him to join them. 'No, no ... don't worry, God will save me,' he said again.

Soon the water was up to his shoulders, and still rising. Once more, the people who were passing by in a raft came to his help. But he waved them away and said, 'God will save me. He will never let me down.'

The house was soon submerged in water, and the priest drowned. When he went to heaven, he looked at God and said sadly, 'How could you have done this to me when I trusted you with all my heart, and served you faithfully? Why didn't you do anything to save me?'

'Umm,' said God. 'Who do you think sent those three boats?'

Author Unknown

The Body Temple

I just got back from a ten-day road trip with my wife, this guy, his wife, a common friend, and four or five other people I was meeting for the first time. It was okay. No, really. The usual unusual that is life in the company of few. The scenery was breath-taking. The treks were brutal. The toilet facilities, abysmal. And the company, splendid. No, really. So what did it teach me?

First things first, grin and bear it. Okay, now get this. This is a big thing for me. Writing about it is even bigger. Almost like a spiritual ablution. Yeah, a spiritual ablution is what it is. Hilly-billy aphorism of the moment for memory and total recall: 'You can take a man out of his comfort zone, but you can't take a comfort zone out of a man.'

The other thing I learned about myself on this trip, actually, two other things I learned on this trip were how confused I am. All those I journeyed with, including my wife, are doing what they like doing and have been at it for close to a decade. I, on the other hand, have always felt like I was at the end of my tether, staring down an abyss. Luckily for me, most times, there was something exotic staring back at me. Shh.

Hilly-billy aphorism of the moment for memory and total recall:

'The higher you go, the smaller you get.'

Now that we're back, I'm thinking, how can I draw upon all the tangible and intangible things I may have internalised from my conversations with the hills to deal better with my current reality? The one thing I hear loud and clear above all the spiritual babble gleaned from my time in the hills is this: hit the gym.

Avinash Subramaniam

Sweets and Prayers

My father was posted to the Command Hospital in Bangalore around 1929. Bangalore was then a quiet city of stately parks and leafy avenues inhabited, it seemed, mostly by retired gentry with lovely gardens behind gates that warned the unwary and the wicked to 'Beware of Dogs'! The family moved to a comfortable house on Primrose Road near South Parade, and my two sisters, Lulu and Meenu, and I settled into our new school.

On evenings and holidays, we children would walk to a nearby general store, Venson's, where Mother often shopped. The kindly salesmen there would slip us zebra-striped bullseyes that would be eaten, not greedily, but sucked slowly through as many delicious minutes as possible.

In the Book of Ecclesiastes it is written, 'To every time there is a season, and a time for every purpose under the heaven'. Mother was a strict disciplinarian and, according to her way of thinking, there clearly was a time for study and a time for play. It was during such a time for study, one morning, that she drove off for a meeting in her soft-top red Baby Austen, leaving us with a stern injunction to study. As soon as she departed Lulu said, 'Let's go to Venson's.'

Meenu and I readily nodded assent, and off we trooped on that daring enterprise, tingling with anticipation. Our manager friend at Venson's greeted us warmly and thrust some bullseyes into our not unwilling palms. Our taste buds had scarcely begun to tingle when what did we see through one of the windows but — horror of horrors! — a red Baby Austen drive up and park outside. Panic might have been our undoing. But with great presence of mind, Lulu communicated the extreme urgency and delicacy of the situation to the manager. Appreciating the emergency, he gamely pushed us into his private office in time to greet Mother who was just entering the store. Lulu fell on her knees with a tremulous, 'Let us pray.' And all three of us sinners were soon fervently intoning the Lord's Prayer, particularly the bit about 'forgiving us our trespasses as we forgive them that trespass against us'. There could not have been a more devotional moment in our lives.

The good Lord heard our prayers. The danger passed. The red Baby Austen moved on, and three pairs of legs took off as fast as they could run, to get back to base. Her little angels were immersed in study when Mother returned home! Impressed as I was by the power of prayer that day, I have never been overly religious or believed excessively in organised religion but, presumably like most others, have always turned to prayer in times of trouble. What I did, however, imbibe from my parents and family, and later at school, were moral values, ethical standards and a regard for faith or spirituality rather than mere indulgence in the rituals of organised religion.

B.G. Verghese

Magic Fingers

When I was a little girl, I longed for a violin. Not one of those gleaming ebony and maplewood beauties in the windows of Judson's Musicals. What I coveted was a contraption made from a coconut shell, pieces of wood and some wires! This crude instrument, even though it came with its own 'bow', did not resemble a real violin at all. 'Violin' was what we children called it for want of a better word.

I displayed no musical talent at all at the age of eight, but that did not stop me from wanting to own and 'play' one of those instruments. The door-to-door violin salesman was interesting too. He bore a close resemblance to the kabuliwala in the famous story of the same name and probably came from some remote mountain village across the border. Tall and stately, dressed in flowing robes, he wore a bright orange or, sometimes, a mint green turban on his head. Once in a while, he strode past our house playing a lively version of *Mera jootha hai Japani* or *Chaudvin ka chand*, which were two of the most popular Hindi film songs at the time. Sometimes he played haunting folk melodies, which were probably all about love and loss and heartbreak in places far away.

I begged and pleaded and, at last, my grandmother caved in and beckoned to the violin man. He lowered the basket full of instruments that he carried on his head, and my grandmother opened negotiations. Though they all looked the same she ran her eye over the contents of the basket and chose one of the instruments as though she were an expert. The deal was clinched and I became the proud owner of a 'violin'. The violin seller went on his merry way, pursued by the neighbourhood children, like an oriental Pied Piper.

I sat down on the doorstep and drew the 'bow' across the strings. The sharp squeal that emerged was enough to set the teeth on edge and make one's hair stand up straight. my grandmother retreated in haste to the sanctuary of her kitchen. Days passed. I scraped away at the instrument. What I lacked by way of talent I made up for with tenacity, but I still could not produce a recognisable tune on my 'violin'.

Eventually, my grandmother joined me on the doorstep, which had become my practice room. 'Give it to me, child,' she said. 'Let me try. First we have to play just the notes — sa, re, ga, ma.' I stifled my giggles. My grandmother was no better than I was. It sounded just like cats fighting! After weeks of making no progress at all, she put down the 'violin' in disgust. 'I know what the problem is. He sold us a defective instrument,' she declared at dinner, one night. ''Tis a bad workman who blames his tools,' admonished my father with a twinkle in his eye. My grandmother ignored him.

Never one to give up easily, the very next time the violin man came by, my grandmother was ready. She called him over to our gate. This time she refused to choose an instrument from the basket. She pointed to the one the man had been playing a moment ago. 'Give me *that* one, the one that you are playing,' she said. 'They are all the same, Maaji, you can have mine if you like,' he said cheerfully, and handed it over. My grandmother paid the asking price of three rupees. He extracted another one from the pile, hefted the basket on to his head and walked away, effortlessly playing yet another delightful melody. 'Ha,' said my grandmother triumphantly. 'Now, we shall see.'

To our disappointment, this time around was no better. Tortured screams and high-pitched shrieks were still the only sounds we could produce. We had to admit it. We could not make music. My grandmother looked sadly at the violin. 'But how does *he* do it?' she wondered aloud. 'He must have some magic in his fingers that I don't have. Quite useless I am, to be sure,' she said. I looked down at her gnarled fingers lying defeated in her lap. When she was sad, it was as if the sun had gone behind a cloud. Everything suddenly became grey.

A thought struck me. 'But you *do* have magic in your fingers, Grandma,' I said. 'You made that lace to put on my best white dress; and Ramu the gardener says that the spinach plants that you planted are the ones that are growing the best. Even Father says it's because you have green fingers! And the gulab jamun you made for my birthday,' I continued, warming to my theme, 'no one can make them like that.'

My grandmother brightened visibly. 'Yes, child,' she said. 'God never sends anyone into the world without giving them a gift or two to help them on their way.' An image floated into my mind of cherubic rosy-cheeked babies on white clouds, plump arms wrapped around colourful boxes tied with satin ribbons, like birthday presents. I was about to say so when my grandmother began to murmur in Sanskrit.

'Are you praying Grandma?' I asked.

'Not really,' she said. 'It's some words I just remembered.

'What are they, Grandma?' I asked.

'Well,' she paused, 'they mean: just as there is no letter of the alphabet which cannot be used as a mantra, no root growing in the forest that cannot be used as a medicine, no person is born absolutely useless. He who can identify his abilities and put them to good and proper use is indeed a rare and precious human being.'

My grandmother is no more with us, but I often have cause to remember her words which never fail to cheer me up.

Leela Krishnamohan

Digging for Hell

I was four years old when I joined school. By then, my Muslim parents had instilled in me a sense of respect for all faiths. I used to go to church with my Catholic ayah and enjoyed being blessed with holy water at the door. Visiting temples was not uncommon for us and, at four, I already had a sense of all religions being very much alike.

My first week at school was full of strange experiences. Miss Jackson, an elderly Scotswoman who was head of junior school, had made it clear in the morning assembly that unless we accepted her rather one-sided version of the divine, we were likely to go to hell and pass up the gift of eternal life in the kingdom of heaven.

That was a rather worrying thought for a four-year-old. All her talk of heaven and hell had really bothered me. So while playing in the sandpit at morning break, I turned to William, a blond-haired, blue-eyed English boy who liked playing with sand. (That made him my new best friend.) 'Willy, where is heaven?' I asked.

'In the clouds,' said Willy, with great conviction.

'So where is hell?' I questioned.

'Below the ground,' said Willy, with the sort of wisdom that only four-year-olds possess.

'I want to see it,' I replied. I knew that we wouldn't be able to see heaven because the sky is too high to reach when you are four. But if hell were below the ground, wouldn't we find it if we dug a hole deep enough? If I got to see hell, maybe I would be able to make up my mind on whether or not it was such a bad place to end up. I pictured a red man standing with a little pitchfork just under the ground we stood on. Like most kids that age, my idea of the devil was derived from Loony Toons and Disney.

After much thought and investigation I decided that we would start our expedition to hell from under the wooden playhouse, a lovely little structure in the middle of the playground that had slides and climbing ladders and bars all over it. Under the playhouse was a gap where the two of us could crawl and sit undetected by anyone passing by. Every break and lunchtime we made our way to the playhouse with two plastic spades and a little bucket. The soil was soft and our little hole grew rather rapidly as we sweated away in our tireless effort to find hell.

After a week of digging at morning break, lunch break and after school, we had only discovered that long grass has long roots and mud only gets harder to dig with plastic as you go deeper, but hell was nowhere in sight. On the last day of our digging, we managed to dislodge a rock about the size of a tennis ball. Disappointed by the fact that there was no peep-hole to hell or little red man under this rock, I came to the only logical explanation one can have at four. If you can't see it, it isn't there.

'Willy,' I said with the air of someone who had realised the truth, 'there is no hell. If there was, we would have found it. They must have lied to us.'

In retrospect, I think there was a great revelation in that moment. When I thought about it, I realised much later that you need to question all beliefs, but know there may not be a concrete answer to your questions. And most important of all, it taught me that faith is not tangible, and belief is based on the many things we cannot see.

Shaizia Jifri

Laugh and Grow Wise

Bhagavan Sri Ramana Maharishi, the Sage of Tiruvannamalai, had a fine sense of humour as these incidents show. Once, when the pain in his joints became pronounced, not only his attendants but even some devotees began massaging his legs. A seventy-year-old retired judge also wished to do so. When Bhagavan asked him the reason, he said, 'Let me earn some punya.'

Bhagavan then said, 'All of you please be quiet for some time. I also wish to earn some punya massaging these legs,' and actually began doing so!

♦

A devotee once sought Bhagavan's permission to take to sanyasa as he was no longer able to face the problems of family life. Bhagavan advised him against it, but the devotee persisted saying, 'You came away but you say that we should not.'

Bhagavan replied, 'When I came, I did not seek anyone's permission.'

♦

A number of devotees and disciples would offer food to Bhagavan and insist on his eating it. He had to eat even if he did not want to. He would often say, 'Only I know the problems associated with being a swami. If you are not hungry, you need not eat, but if I didn't eat, nobody else would eat. So I have to eat whether I am hungry or not.'

Once Bhagavan felt that it would be good if he were to go away all by himself so that he could fast at least that day. So he quietly walked towards the forest at the foot of Arunachala. On the way he came across seven women who had come to collect firewood in the forest. One of them had had Bhagavan's darshan earlier, and so could easily recognise him. She immediately offered some eatables to Bhagavan and requested him to partake of them. So did the other women.

Bhagavan had no choice but to partake of the food, and thus had his fill. The women did not leave him with that but insisted that Bhagavan should have his lunch with them. To avoid that, Bhagavan walked deep into the forest, but around lunch time the women appeared there also … Once again the women served him various items of food. Bhagavan was baffled that his own plan of fasting that day had been foiled. After the meal, he began his return journey to the ashram. Strangely enough, Ramaswamy Iyer (an old disciple) was waiting for Bhagavan at a mantapa on the road to offer him some mango juice. Bhagavan had to accept that also, and returned home, saying he would never spend a day fasting again!

Sri Krishna Bhikshu
(Translated by Pingali Surya Sundaram)

5

ON OVERCOMING ADVERSITY

*If I accept the sunshine
and warmth,
Then I must also accept
the thunder and lightning.*

Kahlil Gibran

A Pair of Silver Anklets

Four years after the Bhopal gas tragedy, I found myself in that city on an assignment.

What has been described as the world's worst industrial disaster took place on 3 December 1984 when forty-two tonnes of methyl isocyanate leaked from their steel containers at the Union Carbide factory and released a cloud of deadly gas. It left a legacy of instant and deferred death. The first count was set at 10,000. In the intervening years, that number has doubled and even exceeded it. The factory looms over the city in a corrosive grey mass of cement and steel. It too is dead. But never, it seems, buried.

My brief was, however, with those who had lived. It was a story about the survivors. These were mostly the women, who had to take on the burden of caring for their families after the men had died, or had been left maimed and without a means of supporting themselves. The first thing I learnt from these women was that it was mostly the young children who had died in that first wave of poisoned gas, even as their mothers held them to their breast. There would be those who'd be born with birth defects, and those who would carry the imprint of that night in their blood. The women were carriers of that singular night of horror, and yet, they had to continue with the daily business of keeping themselves and their families alive.

As I walked through the cramped rooms and halls where the rehabilitation work was in progress, all I could do was to stand by each woman, and if possible, listen to her story. As with so many relief operations involving the succour of poor women, they had been taught to expand their skills at stitching. They were being trained to work at the sewing machine — ancient foot-operated treadle machines — to stitch leather accessories and garments for the fashion industry, and to create stuffed leather toys.

Some of the women can only talk in whispers. Others blink their eyes against the light, as if afraid to look out of them again. Their eyes tend to water continuously. Others, like Hazra Bi, don't look up at all as they piece the scraps of leather that will go into the making of shoulder bags. Hazra Bi was eighteen when her husband died, leaving her with two infants under the age of two and a mother-in-law to look after. She had never worked before, but learning the trade has given her the confidence to be a supervisor.

'Her work is the neatest,' say her co-workers. 'She works fast. That is why you cannot talk to her.'

Lakshmi Bai twinkles with life in comparison. She wears a shiny bindi in the middle of her forehead and is forthright and talkative. She used to work in an anganwadi, she tells me. Then her voice trails off. Her two young children, both little boys, died in the tragedy. She cannot bear to be with children any more. She introduces me to her co-workers. Nazneen is a girl with dark rings around her eyes. Her skin is the colour of hibiscus petals that have been soaked for too long in water, grey-white; when she smiles her eyes light up the room. She is all alone, she says. There is no one left in her family. She wants to make the stuffed toys that are fashioned out of goats' skin into deer, tigers and bears. 'I want to make the animals,' she admits, 'if they will teach me how. It looks like fun.' Like some of the other young women, she wears a watchstrap around a thin wrist. The older women wear bangles. And chains around their necks.

One of the brightest girls is Rasheeda. She wears a brilliant yellow, printed salwar-kameez and a gold-coloured watch. She too does not look up, but when Lakshmi Bai whispers to me that Rasheeda was married recently, she says in English, '4 June 1988. Marriage. I am happy again.'

As she presses down on the treadle of her sewing machine, her eyes concentrating on the circular base of an evening bag, I stop to admire her silver anklets. They are in a design particular to the silversmiths of Bhopal. They are made up of tiny whorls of silver rings, with a shiny pendant disc at the centre. Each segment has been linked together to form a garland of loops like a line of tatting.

It is almost lunchtime when I get back to the main office. It is a Spartan place where there are two bare tables with drawers to keep a register of the orders that they have managed to get, and cupboards pasted with photographs of the latest models that the unit has made.

Just as I am about to leave, Lakshmi Bai, the anganwadi worker, is standing before me. She is trying to make a speech. For some reason, she has become speechless. She holds out her hands. There is something wet and glistening from being freshly washed that she holds in her outstretched palms.

'This is for you,' she says. 'It is not a gift but something that we want you to keep. It's from all of us. Rasheeda wanted you to have them.'

Rasheeda is standing next to Lakshmi Bai, smiling mysteriously. When I look down at her feet, her slim ankles are bare.

'Do not forget us,' she says, picking up the shining silver anklets that she has removed and washed before placing them delicately in my hand.

It is a bolt of brightness that I shall always treasure, from the heart of Bhopal.

I've never managed to wear the anklets. As I touch each link, each silver disc catches the light. It is a reminder that even in the darkest night, from the deepest troughs of despair there are moments when the human spirit lifts itself up and throws a bracelet of silver spangles filled with hope.

Geeta Doctor

Taking Flight Again

There is a pattern in all that happens, in the troubles that come our way and in the opportunities that we're granted. Now, when I sit back and think of all that has transpired in my life, I know that there is a pattern-maker somewhere who charts our lives in specific ways, for a purpose. But one thing is certain — there is always a light at the end of the tunnel as I have learnt from a series of apparent 'coincidences' that occurred, after my accident, fifteen years ago.

At noon, on 12 Feb 1995, the last day of the paragliding camp on the outskirts of Mumbai, something went seriously wrong ... and I crash landed. I knew I was in big trouble ... and there I was, among people I had met for the first time just a few days ago. Suddenly, I saw the familiar face of Sam Mall, an old professional associate, whom I had not met in several years. He recognised me and took complete charge of the situation. Sam even borrowed a vehicle from the local MLA (who was campaigning for elections that Sunday), after convincing him about my need for emergency treatment. Did he just happen to be there, or did some divine force have a role in this? Why had Sam suddenly decided to appear at the camp site, at that particular time? There were no logical answers.

By chance, one of the best spine surgeons happened to be at the hospital where I was taken, as he was preparing for a workshop on the spine, commencing there the next day. So I got the best medical treatment, as he operated on me from midnight till 3 a.m. in the morning.

Then, barely two months after the accident, I got a call from a senior management consultant from Chennai, whom I had met briefly at a conference, asking me to lead market research projects for his company in Mumbai and Pune. He called and visited me and before I could explain to him that my rehab took six to eight hours every day, and that it would continue for the next two years, he had convinced me to start working for them! What and *who* made him think of me, and that too at this juncture in my life, when things seemed to be falling apart?

I also started getting offers to teach at various business schools in Mumbai; and I could choose the day and the number of hours. This meant connecting with the world outside and keeping myself updated in my management field. Why was the universe so kind to me when I needed it most?

On 24 June 2000, my sister, Nina, took me for a stroll in the park and, after meeting my friend's young son, I told her, 'It's so good to have a young child in the house.' The same night, while watching TV, she told me to rub her left knee — it was the first and last time she asked me to do that. She expired the next morning. I had lost my parents before my accident in 1985 and 1992, and the sudden loss of my sister was a hard blow. She was only thirty-nine years old, and my anchor, inspiration and beacon. 'You are so fortunate to be surrounded by the best doctors, therapists and caregivers,' she'd said in the days after my accident, refusing to allow me to dwell on what I had lost. My injuries had caused waist down paraplegia and paralysis, including lack of bladder and bowel control. But Nina made me focus on what I had gained — the friendship, support and goodwill of some very fine human beings. In my previous avatar before the accident, as a management consultant and visiting professor at business schools in Mumbai, there would not have been any possibility of coming across such wonderful friends.

That was the beginning of my belief in spirituality. For me, spirituality is our ability to connect with something greater than ourselves, and to be of service in this world. So, in 2001, when my mentor, Dr Atthreya, suggested that we set up an organisation in Nina's memory, to help others, we thought it was a great idea and although my sister was gone, the Nina Foundation was born.

And that was not all. A year later, Dev was born to Rupal and Dhaval (my sister-in-law and younger brother). I saw that Dev had a birthmark in exactly the same spot on the left knee that Nina had asked me to rub the night before she died! Was it a miracle? We believe it definitely was! Eight years into their marriage, Rupal had been to the best doctors and had been told that she would never conceive. During Rupal's difficult pregnancy, even the doctors had been worried. Dev, however, turned out to be a normal, happy, smiling child with all his faculties intact. The divine force had taken care of everything.

In 2003, Prof Dr Uday Salunkhe, the group director of the Welingkar Institute of Management, asked me to join as editor and a full-time faculty of their college. He called on 25 June, Nina's death anniversary! I thought over the proposition and the significance of the date on which the offer had been made, and said yes. This opened up new possibilities — as a researcher, management editor, educationist and mentor, giving me an identity as an educationist. I have been able to develop a decent body of work in the field of disability studies — a hitherto untouched subject in India — and have written research papers in national and international publications. It also enabled me to complete my PhD in a subject hitherto not covered by anyone in the area of healthcare management. A vocation of your liking also improves your health, I realised. The pattern-maker was active!

Several people would dismiss the above as sheer coincidences; but surely when there is faith, belief and positivism, more spiritual connections occur. We should be ready to receive, and willing to experience. Surely, so many coincidences in one's life must certainly be nothing short of a miracle!

Nina would very often tell me:

Think good, and it returns

Think ill and it rebounds too.

So always have pure thoughts, kind gestures,

Believe in the goodness of the people around us,

And life will be easier.

I have learnt to surrender to God and trust that there is a reason for whatever happens to us ... that we need to have faith and belief. And, as the quotation goes:

Don't tell God you have a big problem,

Tell your problem you have a big God.

Dr Ketna L. Mehta

It Always Adds Up!

When you are a journalist, you sometimes land up in really weird places. So there I was, on a rainy October evening in 2006, standing outside a brothel in Chilakaluripeta, in the Guntur district of Andhra Pradesh. All in pursuit of that story which would win me a Pulitzer. Well, not quite. But believe me, a pat from my editor came very close to winning the Pulitzer.

I was writing a report on HIV-infected sex workers, and a source of mine had asked me to visit this former lady-of-the-night, who'd apparently turned things around for several of her kind. More importantly, she was going to give me some juicy quotes.

Our photographer, Anil, and I waited under the tarpaulin shelter of a shop as it poured like it only can when you have some urgent business. I hung my head low as though expecting one of my former schoolteachers to come and give me a firm rap on the knuckles for venturing into this 'bad place'.

Radha Kumari, the former sex worker, was running late for the appointment, and boy, was I jittery! The shopkeeper, who seemed well-informed about HIV and NGO workers, asked me if I was from the Red Cross. Just as I began to nod in order to stem the conversation, Anil piped up to tell him that I was a 'national' reporter and was waiting for Radha.

Radha ... Where was she? Several NGO workers had vouched that she was the right contact and that colourful tales would ensue if I spent even an hour with her. Well, it had been over an hour. And my patience had worn pretty thin as the rain drops grew thicker.

Suddenly, there appeared this lovely girl, who looked like she was in her early twenties. She was riding a rickety Luna, which she parked against the wall of the shop and walked up to me, her eyes shining bright. 'Madhavi?' she asked, flashing a confident smile. 'Shall we go inside?'

Inside turned out to be a small office right above the shop. It had basic furniture, a cane sofa with some worn-out cushions, two yellow plastic chairs, a table. On the walls were several posters of the inspirational variety with the sort of lines Magic Johnson would perhaps have spouted. The 'house' was at the opposite end. Mercifully, it appeared devoid of action tonight.

Radha removed a flask from her bag, and poured out some tea for us. 'I think you need this,' she said, continuing to smile.

Anil took his mug and made himself as invisible as possible because Radha was clear that a photo-shoot was not happening. I waited, cursing my wet clothes and shoes and life in general, which seemed pretty soggy as of now. What was I doing, I wondered. I was thirty-two years old and, of late, was beginning to question my choice of career. The thrill of writing these 'human interest' reports had waned. I had turned a journalist at twenty-one and was what one would term, only moderately successful. Most of my friends and classmates were in jobs that took them to places like Germany,

Italy, France, South Africa ... while I had never been abroad. And I dreaded their emails which asked, 'What are you doing this weekend?'

Well, it was a Saturday and there I was sitting with a former sex worker ... the 'former' part was pretty questionable, I felt. My weekend seemed awful.

Radha began talking in a clear voice, throwing in plenty of English alongside her Telugu. She told me she was thirty-three, although she just did not look it. And that she had been forced into the flesh trade at the age of fourteen by a cousin, with the full consent of her poverty-stricken parents, who were labourers.

Radha had worked in Guntur all the time. In all the years that went by, Radha never gave up on her studies and her 'caretaker' had allowed her to study 'till Intermediate', though privately.

About two years ago though, she had started coming down with frequent coughs, colds, fever and skin allergies. A random test at an NGO health camp changed Radha's world overnight. She was HIV-positive. 'I know I don't look like I have the virus,' she said, smiling at my shock. 'That's because I take care of myself and am on Anti Retro Viral therapy.'

Radha soon found herself out of her profession, but the local NGO that tested her asked her to join them. Her job: to counsel fellow sex workers to quit the profession, or at least get clients to use condoms. In return, the NGO would take care of her treatment and pay her a monthly salary of Rs 2,000.

'So that's what I do now ... go around, telling my friends that they should not fall prey to the virus like I did,' Radha said. As I looked around the room, I saw this poster of a young boy licking an ice candy. 'Life's like an ice-cream. Enjoy it before it melts,' it declared. Radha, who was following my eyes, said laughingly, 'Now enjoy your tea before it goes cold.' As I smiled for perhaps the first time, she continued, 'It's true, Madhavi. We have to make the most of our lives. To tell you the truth, I have begun to savour every moment more, ever since I discovered I have HIV.'

'That's not possible,' my expression said.

'Yes it is,' she answered in response to my silent pessimism. 'I believe in Lord Ganesha, the remover of obstacles, and I feel that he dares me every day to cross another hurdle. That's how I live life. Jumping over hurdles with as much strength as I can muster.'

Radha told me that she had also begun taking yoga classes of late, and that it helped her to cope with her disease. To my own astonishment, I found myself telling her about my disillusionment with everything in general. Me, Ms Stiff Upper Lip, discussing life's little woes with a woman who shared nothing in common with me, or so I presumed.

Radha listened earnestly without interrupting even once. When I stopped, she looked directly at me and said, 'I can understand. All of us question our lives. But even the richest or most successful or famous person in this world has his or her share of lows. Joys, sorrows, no matter how we quantify them, add up to the same number. The pluses and minuses of every human being in this world are the same, believe me. Name one person who does not have problems.'

I was mesmerised by this simple philosophy. This and Radha's honest devotion to Lord Ganesha really impressed me. My mind went back to this glass showcase in my living room at Hyderabad where my husband and I display some of the Ganesha icons we have collected. I would periodically dust these and playfully rub the Lord's belly because my mother had once told me that it would bring me luck. I had, however, conveniently forgotten the other things she'd told me about him. He is one God who, in his lovable manner, enlightens his devotees about the various facets of life. His instruments are an axe, which tells us to cut down on our worldly attachments, a rope, that's meant to carry devotees to the path of truth, and a laddu that he wants us to have when we devote our being to a spiritual awakening. Those lessons came rushing back. And with a jolt, I remembered the most important lesson of all — Ganesha was the Lord of new beginnings.

Perhaps, it was a message from the Lord that a whole new universe was waiting for me, if only I would open the door. My cynical mind had shut out the simple joys of life. If a terminally ill, former sex worker who was my age could approach life so positively, what was stopping me? I smiled wryly, thinking my life had soured because I had not 'embraced' the universe.

Radha later gave me the statistics and other nuggets I required for my story. But as we stepped out of the cubbyhole office (and I say 'office' with great respect now), her words rang in my mind: 'Life's pluses and minuses. They all add up to the same figure for everyone.'

I waved goodbye to Radha and headed to my hotel in Guntur. As I sat with my laptop to write and then mail my story across to the head office, I idly checked the other e-mails. 'How's your weekend going,' asked a friend who lives in Florida. This time, I had no hesitation. 'Never seen a better weekend,' I wrote back and dialled room service to order a strawberry ice-cream.

Madhavi Tata

A Flaming Lesson

It was 8 June 1942 — the year the Quit India Movement began. We lived in Rawalpindi (in today's Pakistan), where my father worked in the Military Accounts Department. My mother had to manage the six of us — five girls and a boy, between the ages of seven and eighteen. I was the youngest.

Our parents had brought us up with a fair amount of 'religion' in our lives. Every day, we chanted shlokas and took part in the puja: simple things that were common to the Hindu households of the day. But it took a trip up a mountain to really pull us together and make us believe in a higher force. The experience was so unexpected and terrifying, that it humbled us and taught us about having faith in ourselves and in something greater than we could ever imagine.

My third sister was suffering from constant bouts of malaria and the doctor's recommendation was that she be taken to a hill station, as the salubrious climate would help her get better. So a trip to Abbottabad, a few hours away from Rawalpindi, seemed like just the right medicine. For us children, it was a bonanza. As the plains of Rawalpindi were unbearably hot, we were often confined indoors and not allowed to go out to play. What better way to spend the vacation than in a hill station we had not seen. The great outdoors beckoned.

We had an old green Hillman, those days. Cars, then, seemed more roomy than they are now. In any case, my mother was good at creating space out of nothing. Bedsheets and pillows were arranged to create cushiony seats for us on the floor board at the back. Three adults — my parents and eldest sister who had a baby with her at the time — and the five of us, climbed into the car. In addition we had a young Jeeves who helped my parents with many chores. Our Jeeves was an all-rounder — he cooked, told us stories (frightening or funny, depending on his mood) and was small enough to squeeze into the front seat with my brother. My father took the wheel, as he so often did. The back seat became a Ladies' Special (save for my little nephew). We left after lunch, hoping to reach Abbottabad by sundown.

As we drove on, stopping only to buy some strong rope to tie the luggage on the carrier at the top, a bit of smoke spewed from the floor of the car on the driver's side. Manian (aka Jeeves) got out to investigate what had caused this. Not finding anything wrong, he told my father we could proceed. My father started the car and drove very slowly, by way of abundant caution. We covered a great deal of ground even at that speed — in another half hour we would reach our destination, or so we thought.

It had suddenly become very dark, and there was so much smoke in the car now that my father declared it would be impossible to drive any further. He stopped on the left side of that mountain road, which was terrifying as it overlooked a sheer drop and any slip would have meant sure death. On the other side, the mountain rose high — even that was quite frightening. There was no traffic. In fact, there was no one for miles around.

We children stood shivering by the side of the cold mountain road. The night sky was full of stars — very clear in the inky darkness. I was scared and hungry and, possibly, so were all the others — but we didn't breathe a word about that. I know we all prayed to Him to keep us safe. With the overactive imagination of children, we were sure that the mountain dacoits we kept reading about would come and ambush us, kill our parents, and kidnap us. I longed for adventure, but was also scared of the unknown. I did not know what it was I wanted, but I prayed hard.

Manian quickly got down and ran to look below the car, and shouted 'Saar, thi ...' meaning 'fire'. In a jiffy we all got down. My sick sister was quickly whisked away to the other side of the road, by my mother. We do not know to this day where we kids summoned the strength to tug at the strong ropes we had used to tie the luggage, and dislodge as much of our belongings as possible. My thinnest sister (we joked about it later) was the one who unloaded the maximum number of pieces. We had only a few minutes to grab what we could, and then my mother shouted to us to get away from the car. As we rushed to the mountainside sans slippers and shawls, the car caught fire and was engulfed in tall flames.

It was a mercy the petrol tank didn't explode — that would surely have meant a different ending for us. And the most eerie thing was that the horn started blowing, loud and clear, on that deserted mountain road. There was not a soul other than us to hear it. The cold of the mountain air was merciless and, helpless and vulnerable, we simply huddled together without a word. We knew that our parents were thankful we were all safe. Looking back, I realise that we have never been closer to each other emotionally and physically than at that time. Can this sense of bonding ever happen again, I wonder, now that we've all grown up! How precious indeed those moments were in spite of the harrowing circumstances!

I still remember a quietly exchanged glance among us all as we thanked Him for a providential escape.

Manian went into overdrive. He was heartbroken that all our things, which he had so painstakingly packed, including a lot of eats, had gone up in flames. Out of earshot of our father, he whispered darkly that we would probably end up dead on that cold mountain. Some of us younger children began wondering what the end would be like. For we were far away from help of any kind. Our father comforted us saying that this too would pass, and that night was followed by day. He made the most of a bad situation by saying that we would be shown the way.

We had no means of contacting our hosts at Abbottabad, and they must have wondered why we had not arrived. (No cell phones — no phones even, along the way.) After what seemed like eons, a mud lorry came and we stopped it. Its sudden appearance through the misty darkness seemed a miracle, almost as if in answer to our prayers. The driver and his assistant were shocked to see a burning car on one side of the road, and on the other, its one-time occupants, staring hopelessly at it. We thought of them as our guardian angels, and sure enough, they turned out to be so.

They loaded us into the back of the mud lorry and took us up the last few miles to Abbottabad. My sister and mother, as well as my little nephew, were made to sit in the front seat by the driver, and the rest of us had to jump in at the back of the lorry, and stand wherever there was space near the mud that was heaped in it. When at last we reached Abbottabad, well past midnight, and told our hosts — the kindest Sardarji family I have ever met — what had happened, they lavished their concern and affection on all of us, and made us feel on top of the world. What a blessing, they said. It was an unbelievable miracle that all the family had been saved. In a matter of moments, we might have been enveloped in the flames. Or worse, only some of us might have escaped.

During the next few days, we did mundane things like buying clothes and the basic necessities, for the car and everything in it had been destroyed. Our father did not have a vacation — he was tied up with sorting out the insurance and related matters, assisted by our host.

For days thereafter, the burning car, the mountains and the sheer drop on the side, haunted us as we struggled to collect the threads of routine. We thought about the warmth and affection of our dear hosts — truly a wonderful blessing. The accident and the image of the burning car made us more thankful for everything we had. No doubt it saddened us that many of our parents' hard-earned possessions had literally gone up in flames. But it helped make us see that nothing can be taken for granted; that the 'secure turf' on which we are standing can be pulled away suddenly; that when disaster strikes, we need to be tough, think fast, and believe in ourselves and in that Guiding Hand; and then, surely, miracles will happen!

Padma Ramachandran

Victim by Remote Control

A couple of years ago, two days before New Year's eve, a policeman came home with a court summons. It was so unexpected that it felt unreal. Not taking it too seriously, I joked around with the constable. Later, I read the crumpled piece of paper. It said I had to appear in a Kolhapur court within the week, in a case of fraud! Kolhapur is hundreds of kilometres away from Chennai. I had to get there somehow to answer for a crime I knew nothing about.

I hurried to the neighbourhood police station. The sub-inspector said, 'Must be mistaken identity, try and prove your innocence.' But the case had been registered. I had to be present at the Kolhapur court on the date mentioned.

In desperation, I called my closest friend who lived in Mumbai. He in turn consulted his lawyer friend who had an office in Kolhapur. 'Let me get in touch with the party's lawyer, I'll call you back,' he said. 'We'll have a better idea of what we're dealing with, then.'

I spent anxious moments waiting for his call. I hadn't a clue as to what was happening. Who was this 'party'? Why was

I being targeted? Why should I go all the way to Kolhapur when I'd done nothing wrong?

I had bleak visions of being imprisoned.

No, I had to fight back and prove my innocence. But I didn't know how to fight. Or whom to fight!

The lawyer called back after several hours with a strange story. The complainant was a small firm in Kolhapur that rented out heavy-duty machines for road-building. They'd been contacted by a contractor from Chennai some months ago. After hiring one of their machines for a project, the contractor had not paid for it. The Kolhapur firm faced a huge loss. The Chennai client wouldn't answer their calls, he didn't reply to emails or letters, and his office seemed to have shut down abruptly — in short, he'd absconded.

They then checked the Chennai telephone directory and found a person with the same first name as their client — me! And by some mad coincidence, the client's office was situated in the same locality as my previous house. It was a conspiracy of unfortunate circumstances.

I had long conversations with the Mumbai lawyer. He had long conversations with the 'party's' lawyer. Nothing happened. Finally, my wife suggested a solution. 'What they'll need is proof of your identity,' she said. 'Why not send them samples of your writing and work details to prove you're not their absconding client?'

I wrote and handed over a declaration to the sub-inspector at the station. He said sceptically, 'Mmm — same name, address — doesn't look too good!'

There was absolutely no time to lose. We had only half a day to communicate with Kolhapur. The following day was a Sunday. My details had to be faxed right away. But there was a power cut in my neighbourhood. For a moment I thought: the conspiracy's gaining ground! Precious time was draining away. I told my driver, 'Go anywhere you like, but please fax this immediately.' The fax was sent. But since the summons had been issued, it was still necessary to appear in court!

Only my wife knew of the crisis in my life. I didn't tell anyone else at home. She and I spent anxious moments discussing the pros and cons. Finally, as always, I placed my trust in Shri Padmanabha, our family deity, and rested my case.

The court hearing was inevitable. Accepting the fact, I grew calmer. I drew courage from prayer, from my wife who was always beside me, calming and counselling, and my friend in Mumbai.

That night, the lawyer called with good news. 'Problem's over,' he said. I held the phone in my hand and stared at my wife. 'You don't have to go,' he continued. 'We've tied up things this side. Just explain to the police there and see they're satisfied that you had nothing to do with the case.'

It came as a great relief. The knot of tension was beginning to unravel. I made an appointment to meet a senior police officer who'd also been my senior in college. Meanwhile, there was a flurry of activity at home. Clothes were being taken out and ironed in preparation for New Year's eve. My sons were especially excited about wearing their suits.

Monday was a hot day. I met the officer after a long wait in the sun. He assured me that I didn't have to worry. By the time I returned home it was late afternoon. I was red-faced and feverish, and in no condition for the evening's party. My children were disappointed, but once they learnt the reason, they agreed there was more to celebrate than the coming New Year. They were glad to celebrate it at home.

◆

The crisis had passed peacefully, leaving only a slightly bitter taste in the mouth. And, yes, a rather interesting memory that could now be shared with friends. I thanked

God. But my blood boiled each time I thought of the Kolhapur firm. They'd caused me such torment! How could they crucify me on the basis of a flimsy directory listing? What if I hadn't acted quickly enough? What if I'd been forced to serve time? How casually they'd destroyed my peace of mind!

As I considered their crime, they grew from a small firm in Kolhapur to a gang of evil criminals! They'd picked me out and victimised me through remote control! There was no way I was going to forgive them! My friends urged me to file for damages. I will, I will, I told them, and the weeks passed. The Kolhapur villains were never out of my mind for long, and they were growing ghastlier by the day.

♦

A couple of months later, I was woken up early one morning. 'You have visitors,' my wife said. 'It's those people from Kolhapur. The ones who filed the case against you.' They had come to my house! I was livid.

There were two men waiting for me. One was middle-aged. The other appeared to be in his early thirties. They stood up as I entered, greeting me with folded hands. The younger one had such a woebegone expression that I was taken aback. The older man told me that his nephew had come all the way from Kolhapur to see me.

So there was one of the villains! As I sat down and listened to the uncle, I studied them both. They were small town people, quaintly polite and steeped in old-world culture. Their clothes were shabby. The villain seemed unable to look me in the face.

I thought of all that I'd struggled with during those last two months. I wanted to pour out my bitterness, but I couldn't. They looked gentle and harmless! I said, 'Do you know I could have filed for damages?'

The younger man looked up hesitantly. Then he began
to speak in a mixture of English and Hindi. He spoke as if
emptying his mind, and his words were jerky and full of
emotion.

He came from a family of five brothers, he said. They
were farmers, but their father had become sick and was no
longer able to work the land. The brothers then took over
and decided to go into business. It was difficult. They had no
skills, and weren't exactly prospering. They needed money
for the children's education and the medical expenses of their
parents, and to keep the business afloat. On top of all that,
they'd taken loans, which were due for repayment.

The Chennai work had come as a bonanza. The job was
completed, but when they tried to contact the client (the
man with my name!) he hemmed and hawed and did his
disappearing act. The family was devastated. They had no
idea what to do. It was a lawyer friend who suggested the
phone directory. 'Best to catch him at home,' he told them.
'At least get a commitment. And if he doesn't give you that,
then file a case.'

'We called your number several times,' the young man said
gloomily. 'A lady answered and said the name was correct,
but there was no company. My elder brother became angry.
He said we should take legal action.'

My wife cut in. 'I remember that call! I wondered why they
kept asking the same thing over and over again.'

'I'm only trying to explain what happened,' the young man
said. He looked tired and helpless. 'We can never justify what
we did. All I'm asking is, please consider me as a younger
brother. Forgive me and my family. They are waiting to
know what you'll say. We didn't intentionally harm you. It
was our ignorance and our desperation. We have nothing
left now. But if you don't forgive us we'll have no peace, not
even when we die.'

There was a deep silence in the room. Then something made me reach over and take his hand. 'Everything will work out well,' I told him. 'Tell your father and your brothers that we'll be praying for you. If we ever come to Kolhapur we'll certainly visit you. And you know that our doors are always open for you. Don't worry. Have faith in God. He guided us. He'll certainly guide you.' I could see his tears and my wife's approval as I spoke.

We gave them fruits from our garden and saw them off. My wife smiled. 'How quickly you changed!'

'Everything changed!' I replied. 'I thought badly of them from all that distance. Then they came close, and my perspective changed!'

'I'm glad,' my wife said softly.

Shreekumar Varma

Miracles Still Happen

In 1974, I was invited to hold a dance workshop during the International Youth Festival at Bayreuth, in what was then West Germany. That was where Richard Wagner wrote his famous operas, and every year the Wagner Festival is held there. I was in Bayreuth to teach bharatanatyam to young people from all over the world. My German fiancé, Dr. Lechner was also with me.

Over the weekend, we used to go to the nearest city, Nuremburg, which has beautiful monuments and museums. We had close friends there, painters, sculptors and lovers of good music and wine. The weekend when my life turned upside-down began like any other. We had rented a Volkswagen Beetle and driven away as usual for a weekend with our friends. As we were driving back to Bayreuth after dinner on Sunday, sometime past midnight, suddenly a deer crossed the road.

My fiancé braked hard to avoid it and disaster struck. The Beetle went spinning and somersaulted three times. Then the door was flung open. I was thrown fifteen feet away like a parcel, and passed out (the Beetle had no seatbelts those days). Fortunately, we were seen by the driver of another car, who immediately called the police. There was not much traffic on the autobahn, which passed through dense woods. Bayreuth was just forty kilometres away from the tri-country border of East Germany, West Germany and Czechoslovakia, and not many people ventured in that direction, especially at night.

Soon, an ambulance arrived from Pegnitz the nearest town. Someone sprinkled water on my face and I surfaced for a few brief moments before sliding into oblivion. When I regained consciousness again, I was in hospital. The pain was unbearable ... excruciating. Four ribs on the left side and my collarbone were shattered, I had all sorts of neurological problems and, worst of all, was the damage to my spine — my twelfth vertebra was smashed to smithereens. I spent two days stretched out on a foam mattress while the doctors debated. Messages began pouring in — Prime Minister Indira Gandhi's telegram was the first to arrive with her good wishes for my recovery.

There were only two options — one was to insert a steel rod in my back, the other was to put me in a plaster cast. The patient had to choose the course of action. The doctors made it clear that they were in favour of the steel rod. I wanted to ask so many questions and get all the answers before I made my decision, but the pain made it impossible for me to speak. I had only one thought in my mind. I had to dance again no matter what, and something — call it intuition or divine intervention or what you will — told me that if I opted for the steel rod my dancing days would be over. By nodding slightly and making signs with my eyes, I made them understand that the plaster cast was what I wanted.

The next morning, I was taken to the 'torture chamber' as I came to think of it. Those days orthopaedic treatment was in a rather primitive state. For the plaster cast, I had to be suspended between two tables — my head on one table, knee downwards on the other and the rest of me hung in limbo like a cloth bag. And they had to pat layers and layers of plaster and gauze on me. I was determined not to scream even if I had to bite my tongue. Hours later, from neck to hip, I was in plaster — four kilos of it.

After fourteen days we decided to leave for Montreal, where my fiancé had a job. I was taken by ambulance to Frankfurt airport and told to wait in a clinic, somewhere below the departure lounge. My fiancé and I were not aware that the airlines people had forgotten to switch on the intercom. When it was almost time for the Montreal flight to take off and we had still not heard any announcements, my fiancé went to find out what was happening.

By the time things were sorted out and I was taken on a stretcher to the aircraft, the rest of the passengers had boarded and the aircraft doors were shut. After much gesticulation and talking to the captain on walkie-talkies, the ground staff had bad news for us. The captain, who was standing at the door of the aircraft, refused to take such a serious 'case' on board as he had not been told about it earlier, and proper arrangements had not been made.

One of the male nurses carrying my stretcher told me, 'Darling, if you want to get on that flight, you have to walk up those steps to the aircraft with a smile on your face.'

There was no aerobridge those days. Forty-nine excruciating steps. I somehow climbed them all, smiled and said, 'Good afternoon,' to the stunned captain and walked into the aircraft.

Spirituality is not only the act of connecting with a higher power that is somewhere out there, but also evoking the higher power — atma bala or atma shakti — within us. When we do, miracles happen although we don't know how.

My odyssey, which began with the agony of those forty-nine steps, continued as I sat through the trans-Atlantic flight, gritting my teeth, negotiated Montreal airport in a wheelchair (as a stretcher was not available), and ended when we reached the apartment where I was at last able to lie down in bed. I wept and wept and wept and passed out with the pain.

Over the next few days, with four kilos of cast on my torso, a 'rucksack' holding my shoulders back to allow my ribs and collar-bone to heal, and a throat that could not produce even a squeak, my head began to buzz constantly with questions. Would I be able to dance again? Would I even walk? What was the point in staying alive if I couldn't dance?

Then Dr Pierre Gravel stepped in and gave me a new lease of life. Gravel, a French Canadian, was one of the top ten chiropractors in the world. He had seen one of my dance programmes and when he heard about my accident, he left his summer-vacation chalet and rushed to my side. He even brought his X-ray machine home, spoke to the German doctors who had treated me, studied my X-rays from Germany ... he just took over. Who sent him and why and how?

It took him a fortnight to talk to people and study my case. Then, he came home and pronounced his verdict: 'Sonal, I'm afraid ...' and I began to howl. 'Sonal, listen to me! I'm afraid, you will be able to dance again.'

I was laughing and crying at the same time. The German doctors had said I would walk in two years, maybe, but that I would not dance again, ever.

Nothing else would matter if I couldn't. It had been my calling, my passion since the age of six or seven. So would I really be able to dance?

'Why not? Just follow my instructions.'

From then on I put all my energies into recovering. At the end of four-and-a-half months, without any preamble, the doctor asked my fiancé to bring me to his clinic. He cut away the cast and I had my first bath in months. Shampoo, soap, bath salts, the works ... oh, it felt marvellous. There was my fiancé, my doctor and his fiancé, all helping me. Later they plied me with Cognac and snacks, and even made me watch Walt Disney movies (including the *Three Little Pigs!*) to cheer me up and get my mind off the doom and gloom of the previous months.

The first day I tried to dance again my doctor advised me, 'Start by doing exactly what you did the first day you started learning.' So I started at the beginning like a novice. Imagine my horror when I couldn't manage even the very first steps. Each part of my body seemed to have an agenda of its own and none of them coincided with what I had in mind. When I willed my limbs to lift, move or bend in a certain way, they took off on their own trip or simply refused to move. Again and again, I cried out to myself, 'Is this me? Is this my body? What's going on?' It was disheartening, heartbreaking, and oh, the pain ... but I just focused on my goal and persisted. I started with two-minute sessions, increased it to five minutes, then ten.... Oh-so-slowly, my body began to respond and eleven months later, contrary to the general medical opinion, my doctor felt I was ready to go back to India alone, to dance.

And dance I did. I performed in Delhi, Bangalore, Bombay. Letters and telegrams came pouring in from people in all walks of life, including the prime minister, strangers on the street, friends, students, well-wishers. I was overwhelmed by the goodwill and encouragement showered on me.

My doctor summoned me back after two months and took several X-rays. He looked at them, again and again, as if he couldn't believe his eyes and then said, 'Sonal, you've made medical history! As a dancer, you made demands on your body and it responded.' Between the eleventh and thirteenth vertebrae, a new bone had grown like a bridge in place of the twelfth vertebra that had been smashed. It was a miracle.

I realised that in a single moment you could become lowlier than a worm or rise to great heights if you have faith in yourself and in the divine. Even when you think there is no choice, there is always a choice. Had I not gone with my instinct but allowed the doctors to cut me open and put in a steel rod, who knows what would have happened. If you make demands on yourself and pay attention to your gut feeling you never go wrong.

♦

When I dance I become a spiritual being. I don't believe one can 'practise' spirituality. It's a state of being. It's there around you; you just have to be aware of it and absorb it. Surrender yourself to the forces without questioning. Let your inner being bask in a state of complete silence. Then you'll learn to enjoy inner peace.

Every moment of my life has been beautiful in its own way. Even the harrowing times that I went through were precious … because of the problems that I had to overcome, I was able to show others the way, and learnt to help them. God has a mission for every one of us and I have been walking a chosen path or, rather, the path has chosen me. Mukti is here and now, and we need to develop an awareness of our mission and pursue it with total dedication and commitment in such a way that others also benefit. It was heartening that many people who listened to my story found the courage to deal with their own misfortunes. After all, in one's life, it is only sharing and giving that matters.

Dr. Sonal Mansingh

The Miracle of the Flying Leap

As I waited outside my publisher's eighth-floor office to see him, I was strangely calm, except for the fact that I was clutching a piece of paper rather tightly. It was my resignation letter. I could not believe that I was actually sundering ties with an organisation that had been home for the last five-and-a-half years. I dared not think of what lay ahead of me — because all I could see was a blank horizon.

It had been a strange but sublime set of events that had brought me to this juncture. Just one year after I took over as editor of a lifestyle magazine, I had been gifted with a powerful spiritual awakening. It happened through the break-up of a relationship. The person told me two things that impacted me powerfully. 'You have not made me happy,' was one. The other was, 'Relationships are meant to be beautiful. Ours has not been.' The idea of happiness and beautiful relationships seized my imagination. I longed to know what it was like to make another person happy and what a beautiful relationship was like. Then and there, I vowed that I would make this person happy outside the relationship, if not within.

That, however, was not easy for he was provoking me to extreme anger and jealousy. Despairingly, I asked myself how I would ever make him happy if I continued being engulfed in negative feelings.

What followed was a pure act of grace. For I suddenly discerned that if I really wanted this person's happiness, whatever he said or did should be okay with me. No sooner did I have that thought than all my negative feelings just slid down like water and I was clothed in peace. In my determination to make the person happy, I had somehow managed to tear the veil of ego that divided us from each other, and landed in oneness!

It was the most magical moment of my life. I felt invulnerable — as if I could cope with anything that others threw at me. After all, wasn't it their happiness that mattered? I soon fashioned it into a mantra. 'It's their happiness that counts and not mine.' No sooner would I say those words than the ego veil would part and I would experience the other's needs and wants as palpably as my own. It was my own 'Open Sesame' into the enlightened state. In the next one month, the whole jigsaw puzzle of life fitted into place. I recognised that we were so constructed as to attain true happiness only by making others happy, which means there was a constructor — ergo, God.

I also recognised that one can only attain that state through constant ongoing growth. I re-evaluated my priorities and put growth above conventional goals like money, fame, power, and so on. At the same time, I continued my editorship of the magazine because, although I had understood that what I wanted more than anything else in the world was to help heal the world of its misery, I also instinctively understood that I had to go through with this job, and not simply chuck it away and gallop after my goal. Wisdom lay in going step by step.

For the next three years, I continued with the job and hugely enjoyed the task of developing my skills as editor, people manager and writer. All the while though, I struggled to find a correlation between my values and those of the magazine. For a while, I flirted with the idea of marrying high living with high thinking. What put paid to that notion was the liberalisation era. Lifestyle magazines like the one I edited felt the full blast of the onrush of foreign brands as they burst through the floodgates, round about 1994. At first I had been excited at the thought of liberalisation because I thought it would provoke us to excellence, but it became increasingly clear that open markets had unleashed a maelstrom of greed. I watched as people began to spend more and more lavishly on objects that they did not need, and which the media seduced them to possess. Our traditionally austere and thrifty nation began to flaunt money and covet it increasingly. I realised with horror that the market concept of more and more goods would completely destroy the environment.

I woke up to the sorry truth that liberalisation had brought in more problems than it had solved and that I did not want to support it in any way. That left only one option for me. I had to leave the job.

When I told my publisher that I planned to leave, he nobly suggested that I start a magazine for him more in line with my values, but after a few months, we decided it was not feasible financially.

Which brings me to why I was standing outside my publisher's office, resignation letter in hand. I had decided that I did not want to be part of the mainstream world because all of them were catering to the consumerist market in order to get advertisements. What did that leave me? Freelancing. To my surprise that option ignited possibilities in my head, although any journalist knows that freelancing only means free to starve. But, for me, intuition operates through unleashing possibilities and I unfailingly follow its cues, so freelancing it was.

As the day wore on, my enthusiasm flagged and fear gripped my guts. I had little money put by, and I had a mother to support. I was also in a state that left me with little energy or initiative. How on earth was I going to freelance for a living? Doubts played havoc with my mind and tore at my self-confidence. It was with a shrinking heart that I went home that night and proceeded to tell my mother that, as of now, I belonged to the vast army of the unemployed. I remember how she started up from the bed she was reclining on, horror on her face. 'What!' she exclaimed. Miserably, I tried to tell her why I could no longer work at the magazine, when suddenly the buzz of the telephone interrupted our talk. It was about 10 p.m., and I wondered who would call me at that relatively late hour.

'Hello, Suma,' said a voice on the phone. The caller turned out to be Parveen Chopra, a Delhi journalist who had been commissioned by Penguin to do a book on the New Age in India. Hearing that I was planning to come out with a magazine on spirituality, he had come to meet me. That had been four months ago, and we had had no contact since.

And then he proceeded to unfold the biggest miracle of my life. 'I am starting a New Age magazine in India and I am looking for a Mumbai correspondent.' The words spread out under me like a safety net. I was saved! I had been given a job in the only kind of magazine I could have borne to join. I would not have to starve.

It was the timing that staggered me. I had not even had to spend one sleepless night. God, my loving Creator, my guide and my support, had simply stepped in and banked my flying leap of faith by catching me in His arms. Blurting out a fervent 'thank you' to Parveen, I rushed to my mother. 'Amma,' I cried, close to tears, 'I have a job. I have a job.' The poor thing had to suffer a reverse shock for the second time that night. But all was well!

I went to bed that night so filled with joy and gratitude that I could not sleep for a long time. I took deep shuddering breaths of relief as I reflected on all that this meant. It came to me then that if you do the right thing for the right reason you are taken care of. I had not left the magazine in a fit of emotional reaction. I had borne almost a year of near nausea at the prospect of writing about yet another model or beauty queen, and quit only when the inner voice had shown me that there could be no possible reconciliation between my values and that of the magazine.

The miracle of the flying leap has been a huge source of strength to me in the intervening years. The sense of being looked after has only deepened with time. And it gave me the courage to take risks when I needed to. And by the way, the magazine I joined is *Life Positive*, which I edit today, a good fourteen years since I first took shelter under its wings.

Suma Varughese

Being Veerappan's Daughter

Mother, grandmother, friends, newspapers, strangers ... they say different things about him: 'he didn't smoke or drink', 'he respected women', 'dreaded dacoit', 'murderer', 'sandalwood-smuggler', 'forest brigand Veerappan'. He was my father, and all I know is that with me he was gentle and caring, and I loved him.

My first memory of him goes back to the time when I was three. He came home once and took me on his lap, and I looked at his handlebar moustache and thought he was a policeman — there were many of them around, where I was growing up.

I was brought up by my maternal grandmother, in Nerupoor (north-east Tamil Nadu) and my world began and ended with her. I had not seen my mother till I was four or five, at least, I didn't remember her. One day, my grandmother took me to the jail, showed me a woman and said, 'This is your mother.' I was shocked! I did not want to believe this and ran away from her.

The village where I grew up was idyllic, with streams and mountains and open fields. Everyone showered affection on me and treated me well, sometimes better than they did their own children because they respected my father. I took it all for granted. I would take things from any shop, and no one seemed to mind. My grandmother would often find me sleeping soundly in some neighbour's home, after a good meal.

As I grew older, things began to change. My mother was out of jail, but was constantly harassed by the police and we were hardly ever left in peace, although we had spent very little time together as a family. In fact, I met my father only twice and it felt odd and confusing for he was a stranger — and everyone told me he was my father! The first time, I sat rigidly on his lap. And then, I saw him again on my eighth birthday.

The relatives I was staying with told me that we would be going to the temple. But instead, we stopped on the outskirts of a jungle, and my father came to meet us. We had a wonderful time those few days. We slept under the stars, cooked in the open and washed ourselves in streams. We were constantly on the move and my father carried me on his shoulders. He was kind, and I loved him and was crying when I left him behind.

I never saw him again.

When I joined school, only my headmaster knew who my father was. I was a good athlete and won prizes in the district and state-level championships. I was to enter the nationals, too. Then, one day, a newspaper revealed my identity. After that, parents, teachers, even students were afraid of me. Till then, I was the sports captain, but had to give it up and could not even compete again. We changed schools five times in six years.

One day — I was fourteen at the time — I was called from the school assembly. Some of my relatives were waiting outside, and they told me that my father was dead. I did not believe them: people had said that so many times before. But my relatives who had come to see me were crying. 'He's gone, child! It's true.'

I was really angry with them. What a thing to joke about, when I had been hoping, praying, that he would be safe, that I would see him soon! That we would be together like my friends who all lived with their father and mother and grandparents.

By then, everyone was talking about it — teachers, students, staff. And I fainted.

◆

My mother was arrested. How could she be punished for living with my father for three months? Why does it have to be so difficult for me, I wonder, when other girls my age have it easy? Then I remind myself that I must be brave and remain hopeful. I pray, I think of my mother. She has always told me, 'No matter what, we must make some difference in the world before we leave it.' And I will, I will! I am not bitter. I know God works in His own way, and things will change for the better, one day. In fact, I want to change the administration from within and I'm preparing for the Indian Administrative Service examinations. And yes, I choose to believe in second chances, in people, and in God.

Vidhya Rani
(As told to Asha Menon)

6

ON DEATH AND DYING

The Self cannot be pierced by weapons or burned by fire; water cannot wet it, nor can the wind dry it. The Self cannot be pierced or burned, made wet or dry. It is everlasting and infinite, standing on the motionless foundations of eternity. The Self is unmanifested, beyond all thought, beyond all change. Knowing this, you should not grieve.

Bhagavad Gita II 23-25

When God Takes Something

Recently, I read, 'When God takes something from your grasp, he's not punishing you but merely opening your hands to receive something better.' And the quotation goes on to say, 'The will of God will never take you where the Grace of God will not protect you.' In my own life, I have experienced the truth in these words.

Like most people, I thought God would continue to favour me with a wonderful family. Out of the blue, I had to cope with the death of my husband and a year later, that of my twenty-five-year-old son. Though two very dear people were taken away from me, God also gave me the resilience to find inner resources that helped me come out stronger. He also granted me the loving support of my daughter and her family.

I have realised that we get in touch with our inner strength, not when everything is going well for us, but when we are pushed to deal with difficult situations.

Vipassana meditation, which I attended after the death of my husband, helped me immensely. I realised it is not what is happening in the outside world that decides our state of happiness, but how we respond to that event. I came to terms with the reality of life — all of us have to die one day and the only thing we are unsure of is when, where and how we will die. Once we accept the inevitability of death, we learn to focus on meaningful relationships, nurture them and invest in them. We realise it is no use feeling guilty after a person dies, and instead it is best that we use all our energy into making meaningful relationships work.

We also internalise that our stay on this earth is short and, whatever be our position, our role is dispensable and our impact inconsequential. This realisation keeps our ego in check. Instead of being interested only in wealth and titles we also focus on inner peace and equanimity and reach out to the people around us.

Death, one of the most difficult things to come to terms with, also gives us the inner courage to face any other adversity in life. What at first appeared as a cruel blow, turned into a rewarding experience of being in touch with my inner strength, and choosing a more meaningful life.

Anu Aga

Who Wants to Be a Millionaire?

We walked together, my husband and I, tuned to the rhythm of silence in the cool dawn. I loved those brisk, silent early morning walks, on the sand along the beach. And I loved Sundays better than other days because my husband, a very busy surgeon, did not have to rush to work early as he did on weekdays; and leisurely, we could take in the dawning of a new day.

That Sunday morning, we returned home happy and content after watching the sunrise. In a while, my husband left for work — and, a little later, his body was brought back. He had left with a smile, not knowing he would never return home. And I had seen him off, not knowing I would never see him alive again. What followed afterwards was like a dream. Days rolled by. The sun rose every morning as usual, covered with an orange veil. But the dawn no longer appeared beautiful to me. I hated those silent early mornings. I hated Sundays.

People poured in continuously during the next few weeks — people who had known him, people who knew me. Every one of them said, 'Oh! You have always had so much faith in God. How could this happen to you?' Or, 'Your husband was such a lovely person and such a good doctor. Why did he have to go so young?' And things like that.

Suddenly, one day, I heard a different note. It was from my teacher, who had taught me to make sentences from the letters of the spiritual alphabet I had gathered from childhood. He had been abroad, and had written after hearing about the tragedy: 'Uncertainty is the name of the game of life, and nothing can prove it more convincingly than what has happened now. Find strength in your understanding of life, God and yourself.' This was my initiation. This was my mantropadesa. I realised I had not been chosen as special in His creation to escape the law of nature, but I was surely one of the 'chosen' in that I had been fortunate to have a teacher, who brought a different perspective to life. While others tried to help me camouflage my pain with 'painkillers', he made me think that I should go in for 'surgery', rather than treat the symptoms.

The very first sentence I'd heard when I entered his class for the first time was 'Here and Now, not Then and There'. Years ago, I used to attend his classes, though not regularly. So whatever little had sunk in, had obviously remained as a seed with the potential to grow into a tree later.

He would always say, 'Sit down quietly.' I used to wonder how sitting down would make one grow but, nevertheless, I did it ritually, morning and evening, day after day. I continue to do it. When the sudden demise of my husband hit me like a thunderbolt, I found myself gathering strength during those still, stationary hours, to take me through all the running around through the day, sorting out things without getting exhausted mentally. I realised I was able to cope with all the external sounds around me without going deaf, only because of the cushioning of the Silence from beneath. I sat quietly, every day, contemplating my 'mantra': 'What is my understanding of life? What is God? Where is He or where is not He? What is my strength and how can I find it?' The whole exercise was about coming to terms with myself.

I found myself standing under the shade of the 'plant', which had taken life from the 'seed' planted long ago by my teacher. I was convinced this was the only 'shade' that could protect me, and that I had to put in all my efforts to make sure the plant would become a tree to offer me shelter always — in all ways. So I started counting the rosary of the mind. I had to find the 'template' that is the 'constant'. I knew I had to return 'home', if I did not want to get lost.

When my teacher sent me the condolence note, I did not understand that it was a signed cheque worth millions. Having deposited it in my mind bank, after years of sitting down quietly counting the beads of my mind, today I find the cheque has been realised, credited to my account, and is earning enormous interest. I love not just the silent early mornings, but also every moment of each new day. I feel like a millionaire. Fortunately, there is no ceiling on the number of cheques issued and every one of us is assured of the jackpot if we know what to do. So you decide — do you want to be a 'millionaire'?

Anuradha Sivasundar

Shaking Out the Terror

But we have this treasure in jars of clay to show that this all-surpassing power is from God and not from us. We are hard pressed on every side, but not crushed; perplexed, but not in despair; persecuted, but not abandoned; struck down, but not destroyed.

—The Bible, 2 Corinthians 7-9

On 11 July 2006, I took the 5.50 Churchgate slow to Borivali. I was tired, and clambered in only after the rest of the crowd had hurried in, hoping to get a place to sit. Some of us took our usual place near the door, plugged in our earphones, and made little conversation. The everyday hustle-bustle of the glorious Mumbai local train had taught us how to find our space.

On this day, as usual, our compartment was brimming with many oversized, middle-aged women. As the train picked up speed, the wind gathered momentum, and so did our spirits. We were a little less haggard, and a little more relaxed.

In the seats behind us, there was a birthday celebration. A cake was ceremoniously cut, a song was belted out, and hugs were passed around. The journey then resumed its usual flow, with the usual slew of people nudging their way in and out of the train.

My friend, Alisha, alighted at Bandra station. I made a quick call to my driving instructor, cancelling my driving lesson. I was looking forward to a long, languid evening in the swimming pool. And then, a cup of coffee and warm conversation with a friend or two. In anticipation, I moved closer to the exit, listening to music. Little did I know how my plans were about to change.

Moments later, I heard a terrifyingly loud sound. A sound that will stay with me, perhaps, forever. And then, I watched the woman in front of me, crumble and fall to the floor. We had to grab her to stop her from falling to the tracks below. The train came to a sudden halt. Chaos prevailed. A slew of announcements echoed through the train. Co-passengers began helping us off the train. I looked around me. Women were crying. Men looked horrified.

Then, I turned my eyes to the site of the disaster. The general first class compartment, with its roof torn to bits. Its insides flung open. Its broken windows, laced with flesh, blood and gore. A mere compartment away from my own. The singular image of a bunch of people, in the wrong compartment at the wrong time, pushing for their lives.

I looked away. It struck me later, that if I had died, perhaps it would have been an ideal moment to go. A moment of bliss, a mundane moment, a moment of musical delight. For at the exact moment when I heard the loud sound, I had been listening to my favourite, Sting's *Fields of Gold*.

There were voices screaming for water, ambulance sirens.... I eventually pushed my way past the throngs, hurried along the tracks and managed to get a rickshaw that took me and a couple of frightened women home. It took three hours, for a journey that is normally half an hour. I didn't get in touch with anyone until later, and by then my body was shaking. It never really did stop, until much later at night.

I came home, and saw on TV the full impact of all that had happened. It was only then that I realised the blast was not a random occurrence. It was a doctored, structured, deadly terrorist attack. The Mumbai Train Bomb Blast that would mark 11 July forever in our city's memory.

I heard many tales of the people who lent a helping hand in the hours that followed. And, I heard of the resilient Mumbaikar. The Mumbaikar who took the 6.34 Churchgate–Borivali local the very next day. Then, I was angry. What was this gibberish about the 'resilient' Mumbaikar? As if we have a choice. As if the fanatics who subverted their religion, played political games, and dictated the course of our lives gave us a choice. We still have our livelihood to earn, our colleges to go to. And we still have to use the Mumbai local train.

In the beginning, it was hard to shake out the fear. It was hard to shake out the deathly silence. But then, I began to salute the train. I began to salute the lifeline of many a Mumbaikar. Most of all, I began to salute our ability to handle fear. For that fear could have crippled our city, and crushed its spirit.

I too took the train a day later — and have been doing so every day in the three years that have passed, even as I did today. And, I keep learning and remembering how to survive fear. It took a deadly terror attack to shake out the terror!

There will be adversities, but there will be joy. I have learnt how to keep on believing. And, how to embrace the joy, despite the odds.

Gayatri Makhijani

Their Lives or Ours?

We were part of the Indian contingent that had been sent to Sri Lanka on a special mission to destroy a terrorist stronghold in one of the key places there. This region and some of the adjoining areas had already seen terrible, often unwarranted, destruction. Houses had been burnt, livestock destroyed, and human beings blown to bits. The smoldering embers, the smell of gun powder combined with the stench of animal carcasses and decaying human bodies was unbearable. We, however, had no choice but to get used to it and move on.

As we advanced towards the terrorist stronghold, in the stillness of the night we heard some faint noises emanating from a prominent structure in the vicinity. We froze, for at the moment, the line between life and death seemed very thin. Quickly we took stock of the situation, and our immediate assessment was not reassuring: it was evidently an advance position assumed by the terrorists to stall or delay us and signal an early warning of our presence. We immediately made plans to neutralise the structure, and blow it sky high. With our hearts in our mouth, a few of us reluctantly inched forward to get a closer look at the building. It turned out to be a small temple with a courtyard and a few rooms within the compound. We got back to a safer position and made a detailed and rather audacious plan to blow it up along with its occupants.

No one likes to destroy a place of worship, but there didn't seem to be any other option. It was their lives or ours. We divided ourselves into several groups to carry out our plan of action. My men were extremely buoyant, and the decision had been backed by everyone. But at that point, quite suddenly, something began to gnaw at my mind. Whether it was an inner voice or guidance from somewhere beyond me, I do not know even now. But then, on that eventful night, the call was so clear and insistent that I believe they were the same. Whatever it was, all I know is that the voice could not be stilled with logic. 'You need to take another look, a closer look.' It was not the practical thing to do, but what was it that impelled me to do it anyway, I wonder. Along with a few of my trusted lieutenants, I ventured towards the temple. The stillness of the night, the cold sweat, the pounding of hearts, the deep, uneasy breaths that we drew — everything seemed to put more and more fear into our minds. We halted very close to one of the rooms, and I heard very distinctly the sound of children crying, and the rest of our group heard it too. The terrorists, we were now sure, had taken children as hostages. So what were we supposed to do next?

After thinking about it for a while, we made announcements calling on those who were holed up inside the temple complex to come out and surrender. Otherwise, they would be blown up. In fact, we made numerous announcements at intervals, but not a soul stirred. Our patience was fast running out, I instructed two of my men to kick open the door of one of the rooms. With great caution, they carried out this task. From this room emerged old men, women, children and their pets.

They were shell-shocked, seeing us in our combat gear, and the expression on their faces gave us the impression that they had seen the god of death in person.

They started weeping and crying aloud in the courtyard. Those who were in the other rooms of the temple complex were also brought out and they too began to weep and wail. This went on for quite some time. We were able to communicate in the local dialects with some of the elderly men who informed us that they had taken shelter in the temple complex along with their families, and a few earthly belongings, out of fear of the armed forces moving in the area and the terrorists. They'd had no food or fresh water for quite some time, and were in an extremely miserable state.

We offered them the little cooked food and water that we carried with us, but initially, their fear and pride prevented them from accepting anything. In a while, the little children reached out for the food and the others slowly followed. We assured them that they would be safe and that no harm would come their way from our forces. Slowly but surely, the anxiety, fear, and hatred from their faces changed to wry smiles and thankfulness. In the end, they even promised to pray for us, and blessed us as well! We went our way, and returned successfully from our mission, quite unscathed, maybe because of the good wishes of the people, and the grace of the Almighty, whose timely intervention, or that inner voice — call it what you will — had saved us from doing the unthinkable. Otherwise, the blood of those innocent people on our hands and the destruction of a holy place of worship would have haunted us for the rest of our lives.

Major A.J. Kuryan

7

ON CARING AND SHARING

The veil of ignorance clouds our vision and deludes us to regard others as aliens.

Nirankari Baba Hardev Singh Ji

Don't Worry, Jesus

And Jesus said, 'Verily I say unto you, Except ye be converted, and become as little children, ye shall not enter into the kingdom of heaven.'
— *The Holy Bible, Mathew 18:3*

'Blood, blood on the hands, blood on the feet, blood on the heart.'

I swung around terrified. What was my grandson, three-year-old Joshua up to?

I had been distracted for just a few minutes watching a baptismal procession come out of the church at Andheri. But a few minutes was enough time for disaster to befall a young child in unfamiliar territory.

I turned, expecting to see him covered in blood, and there he was, gazing in terror at a huge crucifix near a grotto. The foot of the cross was on a level with his eyes and the artist had spared nothing in his attempt to depict the gory death on Mount Calvary as realistically as possible.

'Look Ammama (Grandma),' cried Joshua, a look of horror on his face. 'Blood on the hands, blood on the face, blood everywhere.'

It was not the first time he was encountering Christ on the cross. He had seen Jesus nailed to the cross many times before. But it had always been a silvered figure, aesthetically pleasing; no graphic depiction of blood and gore; in short, easy on the eyes and mind. In his imagination, he probably saw the Son of God swinging from the wooden beams, doing pull-ups for pleasure and exercise.

But now it had all changed. He was confronted with a reality too terrifying and harsh for his young mind.

As I ran towards him, he added in the voice of one who knew and understood the pain of being unjustly accused, 'I didn't do it, Ammama.'

'Of course you didn't,' I hastened to say. 'I know that.'

'Then who did?' he asked, trying to comprehend such cruelty. 'Then who did this to Jesus?'

'Some wicked people,' I said vaguely, hoping he would be satisfied with the answer.

'But why?' he persisted, just as I had feared he would.

I took refuge in silence.

With all my years of experience and wisdom as mother, teacher and now grandma, I had no real answer to this question.

Still troubled, but reaching out instinctively to someone in distress, Joshua called out to the figure on the cross, 'Don't worry, Jesus. Joshua will take the phone and call 1- 0 - 0, and the police will come and save you.'

My heart ached at the innocence that led him to have such infinite faith in the efficacy of just one phone call to the police.

Then he ran into the church to fetch his cousin Shanaia, about eighteen months older and wiser than his three years.

Soon he was back and the two stood there gazing mournfully at the cross.

'Why is Jesus wearing only his chaddi?' Joshua wanted to know, his observant eye taking in new details each time he looked up.

Shanaia tried explaining, as best she could, the tumultuous events that had taken place more than two thousand years ago. 'He was wearing clothes,' she said, 'but the wicked people snatched them away.'

Spontaneously, three-year-old Joshua responded again in the fullness of his heart. 'Jesus,' he cried. 'Don't worry. Joshua will eat lots of food, grow up quickly, work hard, and buy you new clothes.'

My heart was moved by the childlike innocence that the world would soon destroy, the capacity for compassion that we adults have lost, and the implicit belief that you can make a difference.

The point was not whether or not the police would respond to this crime against humanity, but that a child could see and experience suffering that we had become inured to and that he was prepared, not just to call for appropriate action and then stand back, watch and criticise, but be a part of that redemptive process.

I often ask myself what we need to make the world a better place: a place where man does not inflict untold misery and pain in the name of law or justice; a place where we are not blind to the misery of others and deaf to their cries for help.

The answer came to me as I listened to these two little children at the foot of the cross.

As an adult, I had knelt so many times before the same crucifix in prayer, alive to its religious significance and dead to its human implications. I needed a child's innocence and spontaneity to respond instinctively to those in pain. I needed their ability to experience the suffering of others. I needed their courage to act and not wash my hands of responsibility or wait for the cock to crow twice.

Annie Chandy Mathew

The Purpose of Life

I believe that the purpose of life is to be happy. Therefore, it is important to discover what will bring about the greatest degree of happiness.

I have found that inner tranquillity comes from the development of love and compassion. The more we care for the happiness of others, the greater our own sense of well-being becomes. Cultivating a close, warm-hearted feeling for others automatically puts the mind at ease. This helps remove whatever fears or insecurities we may have and gives us the strength to cope with any obstacles we encounter. It is the ultimate source of success in life.

The need for love lies at the very foundation of human existence. It results from the profound interdependence we all share with one another. It is because our own human existence is so dependent on the help of others that our need for love lies at the very foundation of our existence. Therefore we need a genuine sense of responsibility and a sincere concern for the welfare of others.

How Can We Start?

We should begin by removing the greatest hindrances to compassion: anger and hatred. As we all know, these are extremely powerful emotions and they can overwhelm our entire mind. Nevertheless, they can be controlled. If, however, they are not, these negative emotions will plague us — with no extra effort on their part! — and impede our quest for the happiness of a loving mind.

I must emphasise again that merely thinking that compassion and reason and patience are good will not be enough to develop them. We must wait for difficulties to arise and then attempt to practise them.

And who creates such opportunities? Not our friends, of course, but our *enemies*. They are the ones who give us the most trouble. So if we truly wish to learn, we should consider enemies to be our best teacher! We should feel grateful to our enemies, for it is they who can best help us develop a tranquil mind! Also, it is often the case in both personal and public life, that with a change in circumstances, enemies become friends.

So anger and hatred are *always* harmful, and unless we train our minds and work to reduce their negative force, they will continue to disturb us and disrupt our attempts to develop a calm mind. Anger and hatred are our real enemies. These are the forces we most need to confront and defeat, not the temporary enemies who appear intermittently throughout life.

Compassion and the World

In conclusion, I would like briefly to expand my thoughts beyond the topic of this short piece and make a wider point: individual happiness can contribute in a profound and effective way to the overall improvement of our entire human community.

Because we all share an identical need for love, it is possible to feel that anybody we meet, in whatever circumstances, is a brother or sister. No matter how new the face or how different the dress and behaviour, there is no significant division between us and other people. It is foolish to dwell on external differences, because our basic natures are the same.

Ultimately, humanity is one and this small planet is our only home. If we are to protect this home of ours, each of us needs to experience a vivid sense of universal altruism. It is only this feeling that can remove the self-centred motives that cause people to deceive and misuse one another.

I believe that at every level of society the key to a happier and more successful world is the growth of compassion. We do not need to become religious, nor do we need to believe in an ideology. All that is necessary is for each of us to develop our good human qualities.

Tenzin Gyatso, the Fourteenth Dalai Lama

Yatra

I had long dreamt of doing the Char Dham Yatra in the Himalayas, and in May, when we started our yatra, spirits were indeed high. It was a sixteen-day trip, and by the time we reached Kedarnath, we had already been travelling for the past ten days, and energy levels were beginning to ebb.

On the eve of our Kedar trek we were staying in a guesthouse in Gupt Kashi, and hearing tales (from weary pilgrims coming back from Kedar), of bitter cold winds, temperatures dropping to minus two degrees, and heavy rains, and my anxiety spiked. The three-kilometre-long traffic jam the next morning did not augur well either. But since I was determined to walk all the way up to the temple, I took a stout stick and started the climb. I was probably the slowest climber that day as I found it very taxing — I took ten hours to do that fourteen-kilometre trek, which most others do in five; but at the end of it, though tired, I felt exhilarated. For one, I had walked in the midst of horses that were both going up and coming down, without either becoming petrified or hysterical with fear — and there were ten times as many horses as there were people walking. I understood that people (the elderly, as well as the young and able), who were going up either by the dolis or the khandis were providing the local populace with much-needed earnings, which would see them safely through the winter months, when they had no other means of livelihood.

I understood the power of love from a middle-aged Telugu couple who were walking very slowly, hand in hand, and were barefoot; the woman was obviously very exhausted, but the man kept her spirits up by narrating various mythological tales and parables, interspersed with the words, 'only a little longer, and we will be there'. As I walked past them, I saw that the woman was blind, but I did not feel sorry for her because she had the one thing that many others yearn for and do not get — love.

It was on that pilgrimage, when I saw some very old folk literally crawling up, bereft of physical strength but pushing themselves forward on the sheer momentum that faith gives them, that I also understood the meaning of the phrase, 'believe and you can'.

A little further, as I sat huffing and puffing on a rock, my mind misted with fatigue and wondering if I could make it before nightfall, a young yogi going past me called out, 'Don't sit, don't rest, God has given you the strength to come this far. Come on, He will give you the power to run the rest of the way!' and he quickly walked out of my sight. Though I laughed, I felt truly energised, and started walking with a new vigour and a spring in my step. The towering snow-clad mountain, the crystal clear air, the sweet water from the mountain rivulets and the glorious Alaknanda rushing way below in the deep valley, came back into sharp focus. I felt blessed and strong as I started walking again in the yellow light of the evening sun. Now I knew that it is attitude that matters. If you are positive and have the right attitude, then you almost will the events to happen the way you want.

In the last leg of my climb, though I had taken a long time to get there, I was aware of many blessings: that I was fit enough to climb; that I had the power of sight to see the mighty Himalayas and the snow glinting in the light of the setting sun; and that I could hear the river rushing down the valley — and that I had the heart to acknowledge the countless blessings.

When I finally reached the guesthouse in Kedarnath, the relief and joy of my brothers and the other members of the family who had reached earlier, on horseback, was evident in the riotous welcome I received, and I knew that the greatest blessing was to be loved.

I had accomplished more than a mere physical trek; the kilometres I had traversed in terms of 'soul time' were many more than I had done on foot.

Karuna Sivasailam

The Sufi

He had a small bicycle-repair shop on the way to the tomb of a famous saint. Though many pilgrims had once trudged up that path, the area was now desolate. The town had developed in another direction, while the way to the tomb remained the narrow dirt track that it had always been. Besides, there were grander monuments on the other side that claimed the small trickle of tourists that still visited this dusty town.

My friend had told me that I must visit this little-known darga because, as he put it, 'You'll find something unusual and unforgettable there.' Though I am not particularly religious or superstitious, I was curious: 'Why not?' I said to myself. 'Let me give it a try.'

I guess I must have miscalculated the intensity of the heat because, by the time I was halfway to the tomb, I began to feel tired and dizzy. It was about noon. My throat was parched, and I was drenched in sweat. I thought I should rest somewhere. Just then I sighted the cycle-repair shop under what I could see was the only tree around.

As attractive as the shade under the tree was, the large earthenware pot on its sandy base, with a wet, white cloth clinging to it, was what caught my attention. Without worrying much about the cleanliness of the glass, I eagerly quaffed the cool, incredibly refreshing water, with its mild earth scent, which my host offered me. As I sat down, I took a good look at him.

He was about fifty-five, with a greying beard, a weather-beaten, kindly face and a white skullcap on his closely cropped head. His eyes were his most remarkable feature — deep and intense, burning like coals in his head. I thanked him politely for the water and eyed the meagre tools of his trade, neatly arranged around him: an air pump, a hammer, an old, battered tube of rubber solution, old tyres and tubes, scissors, and so on. I couldn't help asking, 'Bade Mian, do you get enough business out here? After all, how many people travel this way any more?'

He said, 'Everything is fine, by the grace of God. Allah ka fazal hai. Why ... haven't you come today? Every day someone like you comes. And I am a humble servant of the saint,' he said, pointing to the tomb. 'As long as he's there, I am here to serve those who come to visit him. On days when no one comes, I am still content.'

I said, 'Tell me, what's so special about your saint? You know he hardly has any following today. Even his tomb isn't properly maintained.'

He sighed, 'Today everyone looks only at the externals. No one is interested in the inner reality. Even the religious leaders have reduced God to what is written in this book or that. You see, my saint believed in the religion of the heart, not the religion of the book.' Then, after a pause, he added, 'Or, let me put it another way, the book was transferred to his heart; it was there that the Beloved writ his message of love and brotherhood. And thereafter, he lived the book.'

We remained quiet and the moment seemed to stretch infinitely. I became oblivious of the heat and the dust. A soft breeze rustled through the tree under which we sat. In the distance, some bird called plaintively, once then once again.

The tomb of the saint was very plain, almost austere. There was no cash box nearby to collect money from the devout. I remained there only for a few minutes, yet felt that my visit had been worthwhile. Because the cycle-repair man had answered my questions almost completely. It seemed that, for a moment, I had grasped the difference between the essence of religion and its trappings.

Makarand Paranjape

Do Unto Others

Sarah was a first-time visitor to India and was touring the country, while Meera was a middle-aged woman who had joined our tour group when it started from Delhi. The special attraction of the tour was the Valley of Flowers in the Himalayas, en route to Badrinath. Meera was a retired schoolteacher, and this trip was the result of many months of saving. Apart from teaching, her entire life had been devoted to bringing up her younger brothers and sisters on her small income. Now that they were independent, she was at last doing what she had always dreamed of — travelling.

Meera's life had been spent doing things that were necessary. Yet her eyes twinkled with joy and she smiled all the time. At the beginning of the tour, Meera and Sarah had had adjacent seats and made strange companions. Much to her surprise, Sarah discovered that Meera was knowledgeable about many things. And she was exceedingly friendly. Sarah thought she was lonely and probably needed people, or that she wanted something from them.

On the short treks to various shrines, some travelled on ponies or mules, some in litters carried by porters, and those who were fit walked. At such high altitudes, it was not easy to walk on the rough-hewn tracks. One such trek was to Gangaria en route to the Valley of Flowers and Hemkund. Meera walked slowly and steadily. When she stopped for tea, she discovered that Sarah had fallen behind, and the rest of the party was way ahead. She retraced her steps and found Sarah, who looked ill. Meera stopped a couple of mules, made her sit on one of them and took the other. Sarah muttered, 'No need … I can manage,' but was almost falling off the mule as she spoke.

Meera said, 'Don't worry, child.'

Sarah grumbled, 'I am not a child, I am a grown woman. I can manage.' All the same she hung on to the mule.

The next day, Sarah was fit enough to go on the trek to Hemkund. Before they started out, Mr Rao, an elderly man, had trouble breathing, but did not want to be left behind on his own. Meera said soothingly, 'Mr Rao, don't worry, I will stay back with you.'

By now, Sarah knew how much Meera enjoyed the treks. She whispered to her, 'Why do you have to stay back, he is no relative of yours. Even if he is, how can you forgo your visit to Hemkund?'

'He is afraid and alone. I cannot leave him like that.'

By the evening, Mr Rao's condition had worsened. It was decided that he should be carried down to the plains and taken in a taxi to Hardwar. Mr Rao held on to Meera's hand and kept saying, 'Please don't leave me.' Meera chose to stay with him, and Sarah thought it was strange that with forty people in the group, including the doctor, only Meera felt obliged to do so.

That night after dinner, Sarah asked Meera, 'Why are you doing this? What will happen if the old man gets worse?'

'I helped you when you were sick. Did you even once wonder why I stayed back to help you?' Meera said softly.

Sarah said, 'You need not have. I did not ask you to ... I could have managed.'

'If you recall, the rest of the group had gone ahead, it was getting late and in the mountains, it rains early in the evenings, and you could have been stranded. Most of the teashops had closed. How would you have managed?'

'I could have hired a mule myself.'

'Why didn't you? Why were you sitting in a corner of the tea stall and shivering?'

Sarah had no answer. She had been sick, dizzy, confused. She could not have hired a mule. It had taken all of Meera's persuasive skills to do so, as the owner knew that the mules were exhausted after a long day.

Sarah held Meera's hands. 'I am sorry, and you are right. I am truly grateful. I don't know what would have happened to me if you had not stopped by and helped me.' For once in her life, Sarah had thanked someone.

Meera said gently, 'What is it that makes you feel the world owes you everything?'

Sarah thought for a moment. 'I am young, and I have to have everything before I get old. I hate old age. It's terrible.'

'I am old but I'm happy. I may not look young but I feel very young.'

Sarah said musingly. 'Tell me how you do it. I have not seen anyone like you. You're constantly giving, and yet you are happy. Now, you're even planning to leave the tour midway to take the old man to Hardwar. How can you be like this?'

'It's a long story.'

'I want to hear it! I really want to know.'

'My parents died when I was young,' Meera began her story. 'No one bothered about my schooling. I had to fend for myself, and look after my younger brothers and sisters. No one thought of my future. If I wanted to be someone, I had to do whatever was needed. I went to school, and took care of the cooking. Then I got myself a degree and became a teacher. By that time my brother-in-law went blind and lost his job. With their three young children, they had nowhere to go. I prayed for divine support and took care of them. Now they are doing well and they are all grateful to me. And my conscience is clear for I have not failed in my duty. Did I lose anything because of this? Absolutely nothing. You are truly independent when you help others without expecting anything in return. If you want others to do things for you, you are a slave of your needs. At a spiritual level, we are all connected. We are all a part of the whole. So when we help another person, we are only helping ourselves.

'In this world, the more you owe others, the farther you move from salvation. I had a cousin who died young. He was very dear to me. My cousin always helped others. It was my good fortune that I knew him and, one day, I hope to be like him. Selfishness is hard to shake off, but once it is done, life becomes comfortable and easy.'

'Does unselfishness come to you when you are old?'

Meera said, 'Some are eternally old and some are eternally young. I don't think people can change unless they want to. One can remain selfish even when one becomes old. Others like my cousin were generous, compassionate and giving even when young. The person who gives but expects nothing is young. The one who gives nothing and expects everything is burdened with debt and is old.

'Is it possible to change and become truly young?'

Meera said, 'Yes, if you wish to do so.'

'Will you please write to me when you go back?' Sarah wrote down her address and gave it to Meera. 'I will write to you only when I am able to change.'

'You have already set the process in motion,' murmured Meera.

A month later, Sarah was back home, very subdued after her trip to India, yet more at peace with herself. One day, when she returned to her apartment, she found a letter for her from India, which put things in the right perspective for her:

Dear Sarah,

I do not like loose ends, so I thought I'd tell you what happened after I left Gangaria with Mr Rao. The tour operator sent his assistant, a young man, with me. By the time we reached Hardwar, Mr Rao passed away. Several people advised me to cremate the body on the banks of the Ganga and resume my tour. They said it was foolhardy to even think of transporting the body all the way to Bangalore, which is where his family lived. I sat on the banks of the river and prayed for divine guidance. There I was, a single woman with a young boy and a dead body — what was I to do? I was not able to contact his family over the telephone, so I sent a telegram, but what was I to do with the body? If I'd cremated it in Hardwar, nobody would have blamed me, but what about his wife and children? They were being deprived of a last look at him and a chance to carry out the appropriate rites. I could not do it — how would I have felt had it been my father? In a flash I knew what I had to do. For some reason, I had set out on the tour with a large amount of money though I had no need for it. Perhaps this was the reason! I was able to bring the body to Bangalore, by air, and hand it over to the family, who wept with gratitude. It was not my doing. I was made to do it by a divine force.

Yours,
Meera

Sarah read the letter again. And then sat down to write a long, heartfelt reply.

Malavika Kapur

Remembering Alicia

I first met Alicia while I was volunteering at a heart camp. Alicia was completely isolated from the rest of the children, but she sat playing contentedly with her beads. Her veins protruded through her pale skin and her arms and legs were no bigger than a toddler's. Her seven-year-old face was flushed with excitement as her delicate fingers fiddled with the beads of her latest art project. She didn't seem to care or notice that all the other children were playing tag, or fishing, or going for boat rides.

'I see you've met Alicia,' one of the volunteers remarked on my third day of volunteering.

'Yes, she's so interesting to watch, but why is she here?' I asked, knowing full well that all the kids at the heart camp had some heart disorder or the other.

'Alicia was born with a weak heart, and the older she gets the harder it'll be for her heart to keep pumping blood. That's why we make sure she conserves her energy and doesn't exert herself too much.'

'There is a cure, right? I mean, can't she just go for a heart transplant, or something?' I asked, the hope in my voice betraying everything I felt inside. It seemed so stupid that a 'small heart' should prove fatal, especially given the advances in technology in recent years.

'It's not that simple. Heart transplants are in such high demand ... we just have to pray that Alicia enjoys what little time she has left.' I could sense the hopelessness in the volunteer's voice, but I had one other question left.

'Does Alicia know?' I asked, but I didn't need to see the volunteer's nod to discern that Alicia did know.

After that I would watch with increased interest as Alicia's pile of jewellery grew larger and larger. And, every day, I watched as she distributed the necklaces and bracelets she made to the adult volunteers and the other children. I don't know why I was so intrigued by the little girl who had an obsession for jewellery, but eventually I introduced myself to her. Sometimes, we would sit in silence, making jewellery, and other days we would talk about our families, hobbies, and friends. But finally, I asked her the question that had been lurking in my mind since the day I laid eyes on her.

'Alicia, why do you give away all the pretty things you make?' I asked casually.

'Because I want to,' she said simply.

'Oh?'

'And because my mom says it doesn't matter if you live a lot or if you live a little, just as long as people remember that you lived. I love people and I love making jewellery for them. And now, when they wear my necklaces they'll remember me,' she added. Such simple logic! I thought about the millions of people who had lived but never left their mark, because they had not loved or thought enough of others to do something for them. And then I thought of Alicia, who in her own way, was leaving her mark on the world, because her world embraced everyone. We all belonged there, even strangers like me.

I have no doubt that I will learn countless things in college from countless professors, but perhaps the most important lesson was taught to me by a little eight-year-old girl who had a penchant for making jewellery.

Priyanka Seshadri

The Merciful One

Upagupta, the disciple of Buddha, lay asleep in the dust by the city wall of Mathura.

Lamps were all out, doors were all shut, and stars were all hidden by the murky sky of August.

Whose feet were those tinkling with anklets, touching his breast of a sudden?

He woke up startled, and the light from a woman's lamp struck his forgiving eyes.

It was the dancing girl, starred with jewels, clouded with a pale-blue mantle, drunk with the wine of her youth.

She lowered her lamp and saw the young face, austerely beautiful.

'Forgive me, young ascetic,' said the woman, 'graciously come to my house. The dusty earth is not a fit bed for you.'

The ascetic answered, 'Woman, go your way; when the time is ripe, I will come to you.'

Suddenly the black night showed its teeth in a flash of lightning. The storm growled from the corner of the sky, and the woman trembled in fear.

◆

The branches of the wayside trees were aching with blossom. Gay notes of the flute came floating in the warm spring air from afar. The citizens had gone to the woods, to the festival of flowers.

From the mid-sky gazed the full moon on the shadows of the silent town. The young ascetic was walking in the lonely street, while overhead the lovesick koels urged from the mango branches their sleepless plaint.

Upagupta passed through the city gates, and stood at the base of the rampart. What woman lay in the shadow of the wall at his feet, struck with the black pestilence, her body spotted with sores, and hurriedly driven away from the town?

The ascetic sat by her side, taking her head on his knees, and moistened her lips with water and smeared her body with balm.

'Who are you, merciful one?' asked the woman.

'The time, at last, has come to visit you, and I am here,' replied the young ascetic.

Rabindranath Tagore

Vivekananda Every Day

The location: the over-bridge at the Tirunelveli railway junction. On the walkway, amidst the clatter of passing footsteps and the noise and bustle of the busy station, is a small makeshift 'shop' selling vegetables. It is Selvam's shop, and Selvam himself is so nondescript and unassuming that you might easily pass by without even looking at him, unless you wish to buy vegetables. Then, as you stoop to select half a kilo of brinjals or beans, your glance might, perhaps, fall on something utterly unexpected ... Arre, what's this? Displayed prominently amidst the heaps of tomatoes and onions and potatoes, is something one does not normally associate with a vegetable shop — a medium-sized board with a few lines written neatly on it.

If you ask Selvam about it, he will explain that it is one of Swami Vivekananda's sayings ... that he writes a new one on the board, every day. Wisdom and vegetables? If you are intrigued enough to probe further, he will tell you his extraordinary story, very matter-of-factly, and with no frills.

Selvam was a young boy when he received an unusual gift from one of his customers. It was a book — a Tamil

translation of the teachings of Swami Vivekananda. Selvam
had been to school only till the third class, and books
had played a very small role in his life until then. But he
somehow felt drawn to the book he had been given. Selvam
studied it with concentration and was so inspired by Swami
Vivekananda's message that he went back to it whenever he
had a few minutes to spare. It was as if Swamiji had spoken
to him directly, and there were any number of occasions
when he was troubled and found spiritual guidance in his
words. Selvam wished everyone could benefit from Swamiji's
message just as he had, but he had no money to buy books
and distribute them. In any case, most of the people he knew
had no time to read books. So he wondered what he could do
and, all of a sudden, a very simple solution flashed across his
mind. Selvam began to write down short messages from the
book on a board, which he then displayed in his shop.

Although he works hard and keeps long hours, Selvam
(who is now forty-one) spends half an hour every morning,
to select the thought for the day from Swami Vivekananda's
teachings. His customers are drawn to the brief, meaningful
messages he writes on the board, and read them before
proceeding to buy vegetables. Selvam is happy that he has
found a way of passing on the words of wisdom that worked
wonders in his own life. What does he want from all this? He
hopes that his humble service will similarly help and guide
many others in their time of need.

Author Unknown
(Transcreated by A.N. Ramachandran)

Once Upon a Time

Today belongs to us, yesterday was, tomorrow will be. Every day is bursting with opportunities for us to do and to serve, to act and to express, to love and to live. We must make use of these chances and diligently live our life rich, truthful and useful for others at all times.

Swami Chinmayananda

Dhruv Mahendra's journey started the day life threw a brick at her: her sixty-three-year-old mother passed away, and she had died in penury and pain. Dhruv's mother had been a pious person, a loving mother. Dhruv's parents had relocated in 1947 from Karachi, in undivided India, leaving behind all their material possessions including a 500-acre rice paddy. Dhruv's mind was in turmoil — did her mother's struggle in life not count for anything? Did she have to endure a painful death too? Her mother had given generously to charities despite her own dire circumstances, and given up creature comforts to provide basic education for her children. Why had she not even had the reward of a painless death? Why did bad things happen to good people?

It was Swami Chinmayananda who explained the theory of karmic debt to Dhruv: the action of today becomes the destiny of tomorrow. The good and the bad you get in this life are the result of the good or the bad you have done in your past lives. He also said that even when life seems to be an uphill struggle, believe that you are not being punished, you are being taught a lesson, which you need to learn in order to evolve spiritually. And slowly, Dhruv learnt to overcome her resentment and transform her life.

◆

It's no wonder that Dhruv's view of spirituality is a rather practical one. She believes that to be spiritual one does not have to go and live in an ashram, or conduct elaborate rituals. One merely has to be a good human being. In Dhruv's book, a good human being is one who does seva for the less fortunate. Seva is not just feeding the hungry or giving alms to the needy. Although that too is welcome, not all of us may have the means to do so. But surely all of us have some gift — a skill, an ability or knowledge that we can share with people to uplift them spiritually. Dhruv chose to share the gift of story-telling, and through stories she reminds us all of the values we ought to live by. All of seventy-nine now, she began her second innings as story-teller Granny Dhruv, just two years ago.

While earlier Dhruv had spent her afternoons playing cards, she now visits the local blind schools to read out books. Wherever she goes she shares her thoughts and views on life by illustrating them with stories. It isn't that she rehearses the stories beforehand; they just spring to her mind — a boon from Ma Saraswati, she says. The rich repertoire of folk tales she had heard from her mother, the folk tales she had collected from travels in India and abroad have all been reworked to suit modern times, with characters morphing into contemporary heroes. Impressed with the impact Granny Dhruv has on her audience, academic institutions, management academies and top notch corporates have invited her to address their executives.

Dhruv's mantra and guiding force in life are these lines from H.W. Longfellow's 'Psalm of Life':

Lives of great men all remind us, we can make our lives sublime,
And, departing, leave behind us, footprints on the sands of time.

Here is a story that Granny Dhruv often likes to begin her 'stories with values' sessions with.

The hero of the story is an income tax commissioner, and the scene is the just concluded birthday party of his five-year-old son. As the young boy eagerly unwraps his numerous presents, one tiny gift-wrapped box reveals a dazzling diamond ring. Shrieking with delight, the wife of the IT commissioner picks it up, declaring that she will wear it to her next kitty party. The commissioner swiftly cuts short her fantasy saying that accepting an expensive gift can only mean accepting the obligation to do an unacceptable favour. 'I would rather keep my honesty and integrity and return this ring.'

While getting into bed that night, the child asks his father, Dad you've never told me how you celebrated your birthdays in childhood. Did you have parties like mine? 'Yes, I did once ...' said his father and recounted the story of his birthday party.

'My father was a school teacher and he believed in simple living and high thinking. One day he was invited by the headmaster of his school for his son's birthday party and he took me along for the party. I was totally mesmerised with what I saw: tables heavy with exotic food, shiny boxes of gift-wrapped presents, dazzling lights and people in the finest clothes. I was left speechless then, but for days after that, I talked of nothing but the birthday party. Somehow, I persuaded my mother to hold a party on my next birthday.

'On my next birthday I got up early, had my bath and wore new clothes. Then my father handed me a huge bowl of groundnuts and another small bowl with it. He told me to sit on the pavement outside my house and offer a small bowlful to passers-by who looked like they would take these alms. "They will bless you with all their heart," he said.

'In the meanwhile, the neighbourhood women had come over to our house to help my mother with preparing a grand feast. When I had given away all the nuts from the big bowl, my father asked me to help him load huge pots of food into a cart and we went to the poorest neighbourhood in our village. We distributed the food to the pleasantly surprised villagers. "They will bless you with their heart," father said.

'All this was fine, but I still waited with bated breath for the grand party in the evening. And there wasn't one. I was heartbroken. Mother tried to tell father that, perhaps, next year we should have a party for me, but I still remember my father's reply: what I have given my son today are values. These values will guide him towards becoming a great human being, far better than the valuables he would have got as birthday gifts. My mother tried her best to coax me into acceptance, but I just cried myself to sleep.

'A few years later, my father passed away, leaving us with very little to live on. My mother sold her gold to pay for my education. Yet, miraculously, I did well and even passed my IAS exam. I believe it was the blessings of the poor that carried me along in the trying times.'

The next morning, as usual, the income tax commissioner set out for work, and his son too got into the car to be dropped off at his school. But on the way, the boy asked the driver to stop the car. He got out with his bag and was gone for a while. When he returned, his father looked up from the newspaper he was reading, with a puzzled expression. 'You know, Dad, we pass this poor people's basti every day and I see the children playing in the mud. I brought along some of my birthday gifts to share with them, hoping they will bless me with all their heart,' explained the boy.

The income tax commissioner hugged his son tight. He understood what his father had meant about passing on values, not just valuables.

Have your candle and cake on your birthdays by all means, says Granny Dhruv, but also visit the orphanages or slums with your kids so that they may learn values and share their valuables.

Sandhya Rajayer

The Red Rice Granary

I was born and brought up in a village in Karnataka's Haveri district, called Shiggaon. My grandfather was a retired school teacher and my grandmother, Krishtakka, had never gone to school. Both of them hardly travelled and had never stepped out of Karnataka. Yet they were hardworking people, who did their work wholeheartedly without expecting anything from anybody. Their photographs never appeared in any paper, nor did they go up on stage to receive prizes for the work they did. They lived like fragrant flowers in the forest, hardly noticed by the outside world.

In the village we had paddy fields and we used to store the paddy in granaries. There were two granaries. One was in the front and the other at the back of our house. The better quality rice, which was white, was always stored in the front granary, and the inferior rice, which was somewhat thick and red, was stored in the granary at the back.

Those days, there was no communal divide in the village. People from different communities lived together in peace. Many would come to our house to ask for alms. There were Muslim fakirs, Hindu dasaiahs who roamed the countryside singing devotional songs, Yellamma jogathis who appeared holding the image of Goddess Yellamma over their heads, poor students and invalids.

We never had too much cash in the house and the only help my grandfather could give these people was in the form of rice. People who receive help do not talk much. They would receive the rice, smile and raise their right hand to bless us. Irrespective of their religion, the blessing was always, 'May God bless you!' My grandfather always looked happy after giving them alms.

I was a little girl then and not too tall. Since the entrance to the front granary was low, it was difficult for grown-ups to enter. So I would be given a small bucket and sent inside. There I used to fill the bucket with rice and give it to them. They would tell me how many measures they wanted.

In the evening, my grandmother used to cook for everybody. At that time she would send me to the granary at the back of the house where the red rice was stored. I would again fill up the bucket with as much rice as she wanted and bring it back for her to cook our dinner.

This went on for many years. When I was a little older, I asked my grandparents a question that had been bothering me for long.

'Why should we eat the red rice every night when it is not so good, and give these poor people the better quality rice?'

My grandmother Krishtakka smiled and told me something I will never forget. 'Child, whenever you want to give something to somebody, give the best in you, never the second best. That is what I learned from life. God is not there in the temple, mosque or church. He is with the people. If you serve them with whatever you have, you have served God.'

My grandfather answered my question in a different way. 'Our ancestors have taught us in the Vedas that one should:

Donate with kind words.

Donate with happiness.

Donate with sincerity.

Donate only to the needy.

Donate without expectation because it is not a gift. It is a duty.

Donate with your wife's consent.

Donate to other people without making your dependents helpless.

Donate without caring for caste, creed and religion.

Donate so that the receiver prospers.'

This lesson from my grandparents that I learnt as a little girl, has stayed with me ever since. If at all I help anyone today, it is because of the teachings of those simple souls. I did not learn them in any school or college.

Sudha Murty

Speaking in Many Tongues

We live in a sentient universe that speaks in many tongues, human as well as non-human.

I grew up in a Chennai where leafy avenues of copper-pod trees burst into yellow flames during summer, and people used the space around their houses to exercise their green thumb. I celebrated the ending of a taxing higher secondary examination by paying a visit to the local horticultural society. My father, who accompanied me that day, suggested I pick up a cannonball sapling and plant it in the backyard. 'The Nagalinga flowers are both beautiful and exotic-looking, my child! They resemble a serpent's hood guarding a Siva linga and the fragrance is so heady that you can smell it miles away. Why don't you buy this little fellow who will one day become a huge, strapping tree and give us flowers for the daily puja?'

The scrawny sapling with five or six leaves housed in a small pot did not seem very promising. I, however, carried it home and planted it in the backyard, which was dominated by coconut trees. It grew taller without any fuss, dropping its leaves twice a year and putting out fresh glossy ones almost immediately. Friends and family warned us about having the tree in the house:

'They attract snakes!'

'You should watch out, and the fruits are really like cannon balls. They could land with a nasty thump on your head if you are standing too close!'

'They are meant to be planted in public gardens and temples and not in houses!'

But I never really worried about all this. I dreamed about the hooded red flowers and the fragrance whose appeal was rated along with ylang ylang.

Sixteen years passed, and so did the contours of many things. The quiet neighbourhood in which we lived morphed into one of the busy, upmarket areas of Chennai. The house and the garden were becoming too expensive to be managed, and so my parents decided to move out.

My heart sank because I knew that in no time, the real-estate sharks would be at our doorstep. Our elegant little house would be pulled down and all the trees ruthlessly axed to make way for another multi-storey apartment. The Nagalinga tree was paramount in my mind. It had grown to a good height of twelve feet or so, but showed no sign of flowering. 'The trunk has to thicken and the roots have to spread far and wide! At least twenty to thirty feet sideways into the ground!' my father pointed out. 'That is when you will have a cascade of flowers!'

My tree could hardly boast of a wide girth. The coconut palm, its neighbour, was more robust. All this filled me with great sadness. I would hug the tree for some time every day and feel the energy rippling through its strong bark. 'Why don't you flower? I am going away and may never get to see you again!' I would say this over and over again to the tree, running my fingers over its trunk and leaves. I am sure that the family of crows, which lived on the uppermost branches, was amused by this one-sided conversation.

We managed to find a good buyer for the house in six months. There was so much to do by way of packing and clearing that I forgot to dream about the flowers. But I would still hug the tree whenever I went to the backyard with a watering hose.

It was a bright May morning. There were just two more weeks left for us to vacate the house. I was woken up by my mother at an unusually early hour on a Sunday. She was ecstatic! 'The Nagalinga has flowered. Go take a look!'

I rushed into the backyard and found a perfectly formed sprig of fragrant pink flowers extending from the young trunk. The hood, the linga and the fragrance were as perfect as I had imagined. I had tears running down my cheeks as I hugged the tree by way of thanksgiving.

That day, I came into the experiential realisation of my favourite lines by Nikos Kazantzakis: 'I said to the almond tree, "Speak to me of God," and the almond tree blossomed.'

The insight came to me as an unwavering conviction that we are members of a larger community comprising both human and non-human beings. In this integral dance of life, everyone wants to communicate and also respond. The greatest responsibility we have as human beings is to listen and respond to the non-human messages which come to us from all directions.

As an endnote, I would like to add that the Nagalinga tree (along with the others in my garden) was spared the axe. The new owner of the house beamingly reported that the tree produces perfumed blossoms in superabundance, and he shares them with the other residents of the street.

Swarnalatha Rangarajan

A Single Candle

Six months back I was in Jaipur on official work. It was my first trip to the city, and I knew no one there. On the very day of my arrival, I met with an accident as I was crossing the road. A scooter, coming from the wrong side, zoomed into my path without any warning. I was knocked down and the man made good his escape before people could catch him.

Several hands helped me up, and a kind man took me to a nearby hospital. There I was X-rayed and examined before the doctor diagnosed multiple fractures and several superficial wounds. My mobile was lost during the accident. I felt lonely and helpless as I lay on the hospital bed, with my leg in a cast. My face was swollen and blue, my limbs lacerated at several places. Unable to move, I requested the nurse on duty to call my family. The earliest my spouse could arrive was the next day.

Without anyone to share the pain I was preparing to spend the longest night in my life, on the hospital bed, when a kind-faced woman walked up to me and asked, 'Does it hurt?'

That was all I needed. It was as though a dam had burst. The tears of frustration and loneliness I had been trying to hold back flowed unhindered down my cheeks. She held my hand and allowed me to cry.

It was a while before I could speak. 'Thank you,' I said in an embarrassed voice. 'Thank you for being so kind.'

'What are you thanking me for?' she asked. 'You looked so sad and lonely that I just walked up to you and sat here for a while. You would do the same for me if I were in your position.'

I learnt that her daughter was in the hospital, being treated for burn injuries. The young woman had little chance of surviving, and here was this woman trying to spread a little warmth and sunshine in others' lives.

If the roles were reversed, I wondered if I would do what she was doing. The thought filled me with guilt as I realised I was so caught up in the race of life that finding time for others was no longer a priority — although each time I'd asked for help, my prayers had been answered. God had sent someone to help me out. They were his representatives on earth; people with bright and shining souls who paused to share the burden of another human being. This has happened again and again, too frequently for me to ignore.

So, while in the hospital, I mulled over the lesson of love that the simple woman had taught me. All those years I had let my head rule my life; my priorities had been skewed, I realised. If only we could live by our heart rather than our head, there would be less suffering in the world. After all, being able to share someone's misfortunes is a blessing in itself.

My mother was not an overly religious person. Though we went to temples, there was not much ritualistic worship at home. During my childhood I had often heard my mother say, 'God lives in people and in your heart. Don't seek him in temples. Do your bit for people and expand your heart to encompass compassion. That is the best religion.'

It has taken me many years to understand the meaning of her words, but this incident brought home the true gist of her principle. They changed my perceptions about spirituality.

Tanushree Podder

An Uncommon Guru

In the small town where I grew up, most families were like ours — middle-class, where our fathers mostly held government jobs and owned a two-wheeler. Our vacations were spent with out-of-town relatives, and our occasional indulgence was a masala dosa in a small joint. Adults were always worried about making ends meet. Every child went to the same mediocre school, and played on the streets afterwards. Then one morning, a family who broke our middle-class stereotype moved into the neighborhood. An older couple with a thirtyish son. They drank their tea in porcelain cups and drove around in a car. Their lifestyle was very puzzling, since none of them even seemed to work. We eventually learnt that they owned a coffee estate and did not need to work very hard. Despite all this wealth and sophistication, there was a very attractive kindness and simplicity about them, especially their handsome son, Ajay. He smiled warmly at us, though we created quite a ruckus in front of their house, and even broke one of their windows.

Ajay offered to make a basketball court for us in the empty plot next to their house. None of us were accustomed to the concept of random acts of kindness. We thought that maybe he wanted to play with us, and went along quite gleefully with the idea. He helped us clean the plot and bought and erected a pole with a basket. Even gifted us a basketball. Taught us how to play the game. Once we got into the groove, he made himself scarce, and got busy with his serious-looking books. His kindness did not end with this: he picked plastic off the streets, helped the elderly with their taxes and banking, nursed wounded birds, and so forth.

Though every kid in the neighborhood played the sport initially, most girls soon lost interest in it. I was one of the few girls who continued to play basketball. Eventually, I was the only girl left in the team of ten boys, more or less my age. I had always been drawn more to what was considered a boy's world. Sweaty sports and motorised toys had always appealed to me more than dolls and make-up. Basketball became the highlight of the day for me. I fitted in perfectly with the boys and never suspected that this phase would ever end. But reality is a harsh mistress. Boys have a simple rule — as long as you run as fast and hit and throw as hard as they do, you are one of them. I matched their strength and stamina until we all turned ten, in about a year since the basketball mania had gripped us. Then, most of the boys suddenly seemed significantly stronger, and I became the weak link in the team. My misery was slowly building, since I was never picked by the team leaders but was thrust into the team that was short of players. I was not only made to sit out most games, but was given tasks that no player wanted: that of cleaning the court, keeping scores, and safeguarding the ball at night. I began to feel more and more unwanted. In the end, I gave up the sport that meant everything to me.

I went into a shell, licked my wounds, felt bitter and sulked. I wanted to move on, but my heart was still not on girly pursuits. I read a little and sat around a lot, doing nothing. A few days into this self-created martyrdom, I saw Ajay walk by my house. To my surprise, he stopped to have a chat with me. After a brief exchange of pleasantries, he asked me why I had stopped playing. I hesitated for a bit but told him the truth: I was treated as an errand girl and nobody really cared to have me as a team-mate. He then asked me what made me happier — sitting at home or playing as an also-ran? I pondered for a while but the answer was clear. I felt better when I was playing.

'Look, I understand that it is terrible being rejected,' he said. 'But think about this. The team wants someone to do the tasks you were assigned. In return, you get to play a few games. Life does not work out exactly the way we want. But if we accept our limitations, make ourselves useful to others, and refuse to let our ego get the better of us, we will be happier as also the people around us.' He then asked me if I had ever stopped to think of the meaning of the school prayer.

'No,' I shook my head shyly.

He then recited the prayer and explained its meaning: 'A tree yields fruits, a cow produces milk and a river flows, all for the benefit of others. This body is only to serve others.' It was probably not a life-altering speech for a young child, but this, coming from someone who walked the talk, must have struck a chord in me, since I went back to playing. I cleaned, fetched water, kept the ball, and ran all the errands without grumbling. I was surprised to find that the team accepted me far more readily than they had done before. Over time, I realised that no task, when useful to others, is lowly.

Decades have passed, but Ajay's words have often helped me tide over life's crises. When the going gets tough, instead of dwelling on why things went wrong, I now stop to find ways of changing myself.

Vanishree Mahesh

8

A MATTER OF PERSPECTIVE

Let noble thoughts come to us from every side.

Rig Veda I-89-1

What Possesses Us?

Experiences on their own cannot teach us; it is we who must learn. This is the story of three seemingly unrelated 'episodes' from my college days in Pune. The episodes were separated by a few weeks, but I learnt a connected set of lessons from them.

It was about 11.30 at night on a perfectly ordinary day. Typically, every evening, this was the time we'd walk down from our hostel to the restaurant outside the college gate, for a last cup of sweet, thick chai before the restaurant pulled down its shutters at midnight.

Often, we'd be accompanied by a channawala, who'd taken to selling his stuff in the hostel compound. He'd come to the hostel at about ten o'clock and park himself and his basket of roasted peanuts, channa, and so on, in the open quadrangle of the hostel, and sell his wares in one-rupee paper cones to the students. The hostelites weren't exactly queuing up to buy his stuff, and often, I'd sit with him, chatting about life in his village — a small place in Marathwada — his two kids who were back home and studying in the local school, and his loneliness in the big city. Even when there was no one chatting with him, he would sit around until we started off for our 'nightcap' chai, then walk with us to the gate, and from there, carry on to his anonymous home.

One night, as I was locking the door to my room, he asked me, in Hindi, what seemed like a strange question: 'Tell me, why are you locking your room?'

'Arre, there's a transistor radio in the room … I have my clothes, my books. If I leave the room unlocked, things could get stolen.'

He paused and said this: 'No babuji. People don't use locks to keep thieves out — after all, if he wanted, a thief could break a lock and steal things. People lock rooms so that a person who is not a thief is not tempted to become one.'

I had learnt an important lesson about possessions. And their ability to tempt one.

I often think of this as I tell someone not to leave money lying around. Or not to keep wallets full of money in office drawers. I learnt that it's difficult enough for anyone to be good, and that I should accept human beings for what they are, without putting them through unwitting and unnecessary agni parikshas to 'prove' their goodness.

A few days later, I was sorting through a whole lot of stuff that had piled up around my hostel room — the kind of bric-a-brac people accumulate without reason, and then need a very good reason to sort out! In my case, it was the fact that I was going to change my hostel room.

I was putting things into two somewhat chaotic, but noticeably separate piles; it was clear that one of the piles was keep-this-stuff, and the other was a why-the-heck-did-I-get-this-stuff-in-the-first-place lot.

I was still sorting things when one of my best friends walked in, and picked up something from the where-the-heck pile. He said, 'Hey, if you're throwing away all this stuff can

I have this thing?' (It was obviously something trivial and I can't even remember what it was.)

But a strange thing happened to me. The moment he said he wanted it, I said, 'No, actually, I haven't decided if I'm getting rid of it.' He must have been taken aback, but all he said was, 'Oh … I didn't realise that,' chatted for a few minutes and walked away.

A sick, nagging feeling lay heavy in me all day. I felt ashamed that here was something that I did not want, but the moment someone else wanted it, I didn't want to let it go! Why? I felt that I had let myself, my friend and our friendship down. I was miserable throughout the day. Until I took the thing to him later that evening. He was large-hearted enough to accept it without saying anything.

I had learnt another thing about possessions. I had learnt that, often, we want things not as 'users', for whom they have a real value, but as 'hoarders', for whom a thing only has value because someone else wants it.

The third episode took place again in the hostel quadrangle. As usual, the channawala was around. He smiled at me as I locked my room, and as we started walking, said this to me: 'Saab, there must be so much fear in your heart, no?'

I asked him why he felt that. He replied, with a curious mixture of wistfulness and an inexplicable contentment in his voice, 'Saab, only those people need locks who are afraid of loss. I have nothing that I am afraid of losing. Yes, I sometimes feel bad that I don't have any valuables. But then I'm free from the fear that accompanies you.'

I realised he was right, I had yet again learnt something from a simple man: in possessing things, you also risk becoming possessed by them.

In just a matter of weeks I had learnt that possessions are not just what you have. They can be temptations. Your attachment to them reveals what you are. And that attachment to them tethers us to fear.

As I have thought about these experiences over the years, I've learnt more. I learnt that it's okay to be human. And that one's better self lives right next to one's 'base' self. I also learnt that liberation is not just the freedom to be, but also freedom from....

Are these particularly new or revelatory? Perhaps not. But I also discovered that learning is internalising what you always knew. And it is a worth a lot to be just a good human.

Life went on. I moved and started working. Years later, I came across this verse, which roughly translated means:

O foolish one, give up your craving for accumulating wealth;
Contemplate reality without passion, and
Be content with whatever wealth you have obtained through
Your honest efforts.

The verse is from the *Bhaja Govindam* by Sri Shankaracharya; but I had heard the same thoughts before from my channawala friend of my college days! Perhaps it is true that sages do walk amongst us, though we may not always recognise them as such!

Anand Halve

A Village Pooram

Mountains of bananas, hillocks of paddy, yards of jasmine, rows of glinting glass bangles, shimmery satin ribbons in rainbow hues, trinkets, toys. The call of the vendors. The mouthwatering aroma of murukku. The beat of the drums. The stamp of feet. The acrid smell of gunpowder. The heat. The dust. This is the lure of the pooram. And, it is to feed this memory that I go home, again and again, to the pooram at the Muthassi-kavu.

In the old house we wait anxiously. A heap of paddy in a para, and a lit bronze lamp is kept ready. As the distant throb of drums comes closer, the children scamper down the mango trees and rush to hide behind the adults. The gate creaks open and the Thira and Poothan saunter in with jangling and clanging that would awaken even the dead. I feel the familiar sense of dread wash over me as the grotesque masks come closer. These are the faces nightmares are made of. The Thira and Poothan are symbolic representations of the goddess who visits each home to chase away the evil spirits and bless the family.

The drummers begin to beat their chendas, cymbals clash and the Thira and Poothan begin to dance. With the vigour of supernatural beings, they twist and turn, gyrate and twirl, raising clouds of dust with their swirling feet. When they stop abruptly, there is an eerie silence. Until once again the drums come alive with a pagan rhythm. In the olden days, measures of paddy were given as an offering of thanks, today it is money. The Poothan tucks the cask into the sash at his waist and turns to go to the next house to announce the coming of the pooram.

In reality, the pooram began almost a month ago when the pooram-mula (pole) was sunk into the ground. On the second of the month, at midnight, the Cherumans (the caste that tills the soil and harvests the produce) bring freshly harvested paddy tops woven around a bamboo pole, along with a red flag, chanting: 'Here is your offering, Amma, this is for you. And once again we give you your dues like we have always done in the past.'

Only when the paddy is brought into the temple and the red flag hoisted at the entrance of the temple is the pooram officially declared on. Then on it is thirty days of non-stop excitement.

The pooram ground sees the blossoming of many art forms — be it classical, folk or contemporary. From kathakali to Carnatic vocal concerts to mimicry to ballet, which is the local term for a musical involving many costumes, songs and dancing with a thin plot line woven to hold it all together. Artists are invited from all parts of Kerala and each year the temple committee tries to out-vie the previous committee's performance.

We walk towards the pooram ground. The road is filled with people to-ing and fro-ing from the temple. It is late in the afternoon, and the grim Anangan mountains seem to frown down from the horizon. The pooram ground, in contrast, is a riot of colour. Moplah girls with their almost fluorescent veils bring alive the brown land. A Moplah girl comes running towards us with a fluff of cotton candy for my son. And as we watch, she takes him to a vendor specialising in glittering windmills. One of the nicest features of the pooram in a small temple is the communal harmony it creates. Never mind what God you believe in, at the pooram ground every one belongs to one fraternity.

It is the day of the kaala-vela. One of the typical sights of a north Kerala temple pooram is the kaala (oxen). Made of straw, built around a bamboo frame, and dressed ostentatiously with sequins, mirrors and brilliant colours, each pair is created to outshine the rest. More than twenty-five to thirty kaalas come from the various villages and wait at the kaala parambu (oxen ground). We walk around each pair, examining its exquisite handiwork. When we stop to admire one pair, the group responsible for it preens in delight. For the moment they have scored a victory over the rest.

Later in the evening, we watch the veluchappad throw rice at the kaalas and lead them into the temple grounds. When each pair has paid homage to the Goddess, it retreats moving in reverse so as not to offend the Goddess by exhibiting its backside.

And then starts the pyrotechnics. Rows of iron cylinders are kept on the ground filled with gunpowder. And as one is lit, the spark from it sets the other one off. The explosions rock the ground, fill your ears and rock within your heart. And by the time you recover from it, the drums begin their thunderous music.

While much has been said and written about the grandeur on display and the pageantry of the Trichur Pooram, it is the pooram of his or her own temple that a Malayali relates to. For while the former does a great deal to enhance tourist traffic to Kerala, nothing can match the pooram of your village or town. The quaintness of rituals, the time-honoured traditions, the flavour of its festivities and most of all the feeling of having come home.

For once each of us is lost in individual worlds. The older folk remember poorams from the past and as always compare this one to those in their memories now further enriched by age. This is a pooram that is almost two hundred years old. It even merits a mention in William Logan's Malabar Manual, dated 1887.

As for me, I feel a deep sense of peace. A tranquillity born of the knowledge that I am on familiar ground. For once I have all the answers to who I am. That is the blessing the pooram bestows upon the faithful.

Anita Nair

Growing up with Mrs P

It is an autumn afternoon in Shillong, and my entire family is huddled together on a large, cold bathroom floor. I have begun to weep and my five-year-old sister, so far merely solemn, receives the signal and joins in whole-heartedly. Dozens of men, brandishing sickles, knives, meat cleavers and other impromptu weapons, are swarming through the garden that runs around our house.

The year is 1979. I am seven years old and we live in a house on a little ridge set back from the street. The orange trees have glossy leaves and there is a single, stunted pomegranate tree that my grandmother says is haunted. At night the dusty skylights look opaque, coated with a bottle-green darkness the colour of the orange leaves. These skylights at night somehow insert themselves into my grandfather's stories. They are the perch from which characters are observed by God or the Devil as the case may be.

◆

October means Durga puja. At pandals in the neighbourhood, we have merely managed to glimpse Durga's face. She is

largely hidden from our two-feet-high eye-levels by the
excited movement of adult bodies. This is our first year in
the house above the busy street. Over time we shall come to
recognise these signs of a changing season — Durga, unfazed,
her make-up still gleaming, will preside over men dancing in
the rear of trucks; quilts will smell of mothballs till months of
use makes them smell of old cotton and sunshine again.

And then, Trouble. A procession in protest against
'outsiders' or dhkars is going on rampage. *The Shillong
Times* issues of early November will record statistics about
the Trouble: 'No. of arsons — 9 houses gutted, attempts to
set fire to 40, one taxi burnt'; a teacher's dead body will be
recovered from a gorge; and on 17 November 1979, 'house
owners apparently acting at the behest of a militant section'
will be reported as 'pleading helplessness' at having to 'ask
their non-tribal tenants to vacate their houses immediately
— in some cases, within a few hours'.

The rioting spreads to our neighbourhood. We draw our
curtains and talk in whispers. My grandfather peers through
a chink in the dining room curtains and motions to us to
come and look. Three men in checked shawls are setting fire
to the shop opposite our house called Laboratory Aids, run
by a large, genial Punjabi businessman. I have never quite
figured out what this shop sells, and now I imagine those
obscure objects of smoked glass and polished metal melting
into each other, their mystery lost to me forever. What will
become of A La Carté, the Chinese restaurant with dim red
cabins where we have, on occasion, glimpsed couples flirting
clandestinely?

Then hordes of men are in our garden and we have locked
ourselves in the bathroom: children sobbing, grandparents
panicky, parents tight-lipped. Our Khasi landlady, Mrs P,
lives next door. She has asked us to come over to her house
if we ever feel threatened in any way. The bathroom door

is closest to the gate that leads across a tarred compound to safety. Mrs P had, perhaps, been thinking of a bullying knock on the front door, a stone chucked onto our corrugated tin roof, an ominously large gathering in the football field near our house — anything that made us feel ill at ease. But we are besieged. The men are running amok in the garden, banging on doors and shouting abuses in Khasi. Opening the bathroom door to run to safety on the other side is out of the question.

◆

My siblings and I hung out with Mrs P's grandchildren, insinuating ourselves into their lives with the quiet persistence of children. Their many-limbed family is strangely organised — missing fathers and husbands, odd relations who potter around the garden or live in villages outside the city, brothers and sisters at perpetual war with each other. The house itself is full of alcoves and anterooms to hide children at play. The family cooks on a wood fire and coal fires burn in the house, throughout the winter. Somebody is always poking at a fire or warming her behind at one.

Mrs P wears a vivid silk jainsem when she goes out, to match the colour of the diamonds at the tip of her dangling gold earrings. She might take us to a wedding with her, a posse of some scornful and some shy children all bundled into tartan shawls from her chest of drawers. The church is packed. We don't sing the hymns from the Khasi hymnbooks with their delicate translucent pages edged with red ink because we would be embarrassed or can never find the right page. The bride is always too far for us to be able to distinguish her face. We fidget and giggle while Mrs P scolds us in heated whispers and is immediately composed again, intently following the proceedings, her scold no more than a mime of a scold and we no more than miming obedience.

Afterwards, 'taking' tea in the bride's house, I will begin on my early experiments with kwai. The twist of lime paste on the fresh leaf and the soft potent nut will send its hot surge through me and make my head spin dangerously. Riding back home in the taxi, the *kwai's* cosy after-effect will fend off the knife-edged cold of the winter evening.

When my mother cooks for Mrs P, we feel that our presence in the big house acquires greater legitimacy. She sits propped up with pillows in her vast four-poster bed, recovering from yet another bout of illness, and we march in solemnly, each bearing a covered steel bowl of something. We hang around watching her devour the food. She loves rich north Indian food — keema matar swimming in golden mustard oil, aloo parathas, stuffed kababs, thick kadi, cloyingly sweet gajar halwa. Seeing her eat with silent concentration, her hold over things weakened by illness, is always vaguely disturbing. We are secretly pleased about her passion for our mother's cooking but also realise that she is not perfect, she can be bribed. She gives us brittle butter biscuits in return. We sit at the edge of her bed, our laps full of crumbs, while she rounds up the meal with her favourite utterance: 'I haff no money'. This she says without any regard for context.

Nevertheless, she does behave like the inevitably rich. When she airs the handsome black Austin her husband has left her, it is always an impressive sight. The old lady — stern, friendly, distracted, greedy, kind, her face behind the butterfly-shaped glasses the colour of sunlight on snow, driving the hunchbacked car in circles in the compound, without a twinge of irony. Then there are the rents she collects from her many different tenants — us, Bihari grocers, Assamese sweet shop owners, Nepali firemen. There is the big house, elegantly old. There are trips to see less affluent relatives in rural Shillong that we accompany her on, bundled into the red and blue and green tartan shawls. Somebody will always be lounging in a doorway as we come into hard mud compounds. Mrs P will gruffly produce warm bread from the folds of her shawl; a few tightly folded notes might change hands.

◆

That autumn evening in 1979, as we huddle in our bathroom — a family forced to reckon with its foreignness — we hear the hooting and thumping sounds from the garden begin to melt away. We cannot see her, but Mrs P is suddenly out there, reasoning with the mob. Leave them alone, they aren't dhkars, she shouts. They're my people. Everybody knows it isn't the truth, and yet the rioters succumb to the act of grace inherent in that lie. Or, perhaps, they let us go because of who she is: the widow of a Civil Service officer, an aristocratic matriarch who thinks nothing of ticking off an armed mob as if they are truant schoolboys.

In the years to come, our parents will lose connection with the north Indian world they came from, spending their long winter vacations in Shillong, not going back except in memory. And even though we shall never again come as close to the Trouble as on that evening, its shadow will seep into the rest of our lives — the thrill of closed schools; the fear of being hurt; the sad calm of curfew evenings; the awkwardness of being hated.

What will lighten the weight of growing up in Shillong but not of it is the knowledge of how Mrs P saved our lives — with a certain nonchalance, without the expectation of gratitude, with a deep confidence in her own humanity and — remarkably — the mob's.

Anjum Hasan

Seeking the Almighty

Our reformers have taught that prayer should be a way to imbibe humility, a way to reflect, to learn about oneself. And engaging in service is the way to know oneself....

That has been the way of reformers in India. And these reformers have actually worked revolutions — while others have just talked revolution. This way of looking at things was brought home to me some years ago by one of the most innovative and effective reformers India has had in the last half-century: Shri Pandurang Shastri Athawale.

Shri Pandurang Shastri has led farmers to set up vrikshamandirs. Temples with no walls and domes, temples of trees alone. Land is secured by the village itself. Everyone nurtures the saplings. Each family in the village takes its turn by rotation to take care of the trees, to keep the temple and its land clean.

In the amrutalayam mandirs which have been set up in tribal areas by Shastriji's movement, there is scarcely a wall. There are two- or three-foot-high brick pillars. From these rise arches of bamboo, and over them and across them stretches a canopy of creepers. Each couple in the village are pujaris by

A MATTER OF PERSPECTIVE

turn, for a week. They wake up early, bathe, make their way to the temple, clean the courtyard, light the oil lamps, and create an atmosphere in which everyone who comes there feels welcome and at peace.

Transformation accrues of its own. All families contribute plants and creepers, all work together to tend them. Such distinctions as there might be are thereby eroded. In the amritalayam mandirs, since every couple takes turns at being pujaris, people learn that function is important, not birth. In the week they are pujaris, the couple forswear liquor as much as lies — temperance is thus imbibed, and the habit of sticking to the truth. A vrikshamandir caters to twenty-odd villages. Every day, by rotation, different villages send persons to be pujaris for the day. They work together as a team, as priests tending the temple of trees, caring for the soil, weeding — they sit and labour and eat and pray and sing hymns together. Animosities between villages, and distances between castes are dissolved in the pool of devotional labour and working together.

Shastriji's idiom — like that of Swami Vivekananda, of Gandhiji — is religious. 'There is much we can learn from the trees,' he teaches the people. 'Trees are marvellous entities. They send their roots deep into the soil and seek sustenance there. Trees are charity manifest — they teach, by their own example to give generously. Like the Lord Shiva, they inhale poisonous gases and exhale life-giving oxygen. They give fruit to those who throw stones at them; their roots are used for medicinal purposes, their flowers and leaves are used in worship; their fruits satisfy our hunger; and their dark cool shade invites the weary traveller to rest. Trees do not expect anything in return for the service they render us. They do not expect even thanks from us; it is their very nature to be unchanging in their generosity and compassion. Truly, therefore, there is much we can learn from the trees ... Your

temple of trees nestles in the loving bosom of Mother Earth.
It has neither doors nor windows; it has only the abundance
of your devotion. When you enter this temple do so with a
sense of worship. While watering the trees, feel the presence
of God. This is your spiritual discipline and your way of life.
God exists inside the temple and outside the temple too.'

The least of the advantages is that this idiom goes straight
to the heart of the people. The more important point is that
the teaching builds on the life of the people, it starts with a
deep respect for what the people already know and do: the
teachings lead them to see the deep meaning in what they do,
as a matter of course. There is another point that enhances
these. The secret lies in what the followers are urged to put
to use. Tribals know how to nurture trees and creepers, and
that skill is what they are urged to contribute — they see that
skill is special, that it is capable of divine work. This is a key
concept in Shastriji's Swadhyaya movement.

Ever so often when we feel particularly holy, or grateful, or
guilty, or fearful, we make a donation to a temple. But Shastriji
teaches us to give tan (body), man (mind), dhan (wealth) — in
that order, one's time and energy, one's mind and devotion
and, only then, money. Those who know of the Swadhyaya
movement are moved by the remarkable transformation
which it has brought about in the lives of lakhs of people.
And when they approach Shastriji with donations of money,
they are politely told that donations cannot be accepted till
they have given of their time, and their particular skills. An
accountant must first help look after the accounts of one of the
projects, an engineer must first help recharge the well...

The special skill of fishermen is in catching fish, in
making and repairing boats. This skill, this work has been
transformed into dharma-work. By contributing their labour
and earnings, fishing communities have bought a motor-
boat each — the matsyagandha, the 'Floating Temple'. It is

cared for as a temple should be, and fishermen take turns to man the boat for the day. Earnings from the catch of the matsyagandha belong to the community as a whole. They are used to help those who are in need within the community, to buy medicines for the sick, to help those without jobs set themselves up, and to acquire civic amenities. Communities of farmers have been led in the same way, to transform barren land into the wealth of the community.

Fasts, festivals, pilgrimages have been similarly transformed. Where the movement has taken hold, on Balipratipada day (the New Year day by the Hindu calendar), all men, women and children from a village visit the neighbouring village. At the outskirts of that village, they draw lots to determine the house at which they shall have lunch; and the hospitality is returned by the first village, in the same way. The consequences follow as a matter of course: the feeling of community is strengthened, the taboos of caste, and disparity of income are overcome, and families develop bonds with one another.

◆

In the Saurashtra region, the hostility between the Mers — mainly agriculturists — and the Kharwas — mainly fisher folk — had been legendary. All efforts to keep them from assaulting each other had failed. No specific issue was the cause. When the age-old enmity was put to Shastriji, he focused on changing the atmosphere, the 'air and water' so to say. Swadhyayees began visiting each community. Both communities developed trust in them. Eventually, both appealed to Shastriji to bring them together.

Shastriji did not seal that consummation by drawing up a contract. He told them to organise a Satyanarain puja. From each community, 1008 couples were made to sit alternately — a Kharwa couple, a Mer couple, a Kharwa couple, and so on

— with each couple performing the puja. And to avoid any but the minimum expense, Shastriji simplified the puja so that it could be performed with just a few flowers, water and rice. When the puja had been completed by such large numbers of people from each community, who had intermingled with one another, and with Satyanarain as their witness, the leaders of both communities forswore hostility to each other....

As will be evident such experiments of our reformers are a result of deep reflection and insight. They are innovative ideas. They are ideas which build on notions and practices which lie embedded deep in the psyche of our people. And, as we see, they are ideas that work.

Arun Shourie

Bashir

*Oh Bullah, let us go some place
where the world is blind,
Where no one recognises our caste,
where no one bothers us.*

— *Sufi mystic Baba Bullah Shah*

In my grandmother's hometown Layallpur (present-day Faisalabad in Pakistan), all communities used to live in utmost harmony. Yet age-old caste restrictions would come into play often, and each community adhered to certain unwritten laws.

My grandmother's brother, Dr Jaswant Sethi, often tried to break free from some of these social shackles. One day, he told his friends that they would all sit in the kitchen with his grandma and have lunch. His friend, Bashir Ahmed, immediately protested, 'Why play with an older person's sentiments. I will sit outside the kitchen.'

'No,' said Jaswant. 'We will all sit inside. Believe me, she will not have an inkling of whether a Bashir or an Abbas is eating with her.'

'I have a better idea. Let's bet on it!' suggested another friend. The deal was struck and, that afternoon, Jaswant and his friends went home for lunch after college.

'I still think we shouldn't hurt her feelings,' said Bashir, but no one paid any attention to him.

'We are starved!' said Jaswant on entering the kitchen. 'And today we'll all partake of our meal with you, inside the kitchen. We want to see what magic potion you use, which makes the food so delicious.'

'Come, all of you sit with me,' smiled his grandmother, looking up from the tandoor she was readying for the rotis.

All of them sat crossed-legged in a row, and then Jaswant began the round of introductions. 'This is Dharamvir, Kishen, Gurdeep ...' and pointing to Bashir he said, 'and that's Hari ... Hari Kumar.' Bashir greeted her a little hesitantly.

His grandmother began serving them, and within minutes they were lavishing praises on her culinary skills. She revelled in them, and continued to offer further helpings from the pans. To everyone's surprise she was extra generous with Bashir, loading his rotis with ghee and offering him large servings. For dessert there was kheer richly garnished with raisins and other dry fruits. And, expectedly, Bashir got a handsome portion.

When the meal was over, the boys thanked her and promised to be back again. Jaswant was smiling from ear to ear as he was sure he had won his bet.

As they were walking towards the exit, his grandmother called out to Jaswant. 'Puttar (son), to me it makes no difference whether a Ram or Rahim, Hari or Jasleen sits and dines with me. We are all God's children.'

Everyone stood perplexed. She continued, 'Next time you bring a friend along, don't change his name. Each name is beautiful. Each is God's creation.'

Jaswant and his friends looked at her in disbelief. 'I can't believe this,' said an astonished Jaswant.

'It's true,' said Bashir, overcome with emotion, tears welling up in his eyes, as he touched her feet.

'How did you know?' asked Jaswant.

'Age,' replied his eighty-two-year-old grandmother with a twinkle in her eyes. 'My Lord up there makes the inner vision stronger as one grows old.'

Brinda Suri

That Wispy Connection

I begin with an empty page, the familiar challenge of extra-bright blankness. Like most writers, I've succumbed to this challenge many a time. There are days when the words tumble over each other, and sentences seem like dirty laundry.

When I first became a writer, the empty page always made me feel inadequate, as if I'd lost the living organism's instinctive ability to create. And then, I found that wispy connection.

It happened at pre-dawn. I had been struggling for hours with a character, trying to mould her into an obedient shape. Suddenly, without warning, she rebelled and assumed control of my fingers. She told me exactly how she felt and why, and went on to dictate her dialogue. Immediately, I heard another voice, that of my male protagonist, responding to her state of mind and leading the situation in an unintended direction. For the next couple of hours, I typed furiously. The thicket spoke to me, the bedroom spoke to me, a minor character shouted his two-paise from across chapters. Finally, I heard the reverberating boom of the story itself — it was demanding a clearer personality.

In the midst of all this, a part of me was a dispassionate observer, trying to make sense of this ethereal connection I felt. I had tapped into a universal train of thought … that much was evident. But how had it happened? And would it keep happening?

The answer evolved over time, over several such serendipitous sessions. I felt the connection whenever I had faith, and whenever I let myself go. That was the key. You can become a parent without understanding the biochemistry of DNA. And you can write without reaching the wellspring of all art and literature.

Today, my personal life has imploded and I'm left holding fragments of past relationships. Things are getting redefined, undefined. I think I've survived all this, in part, due to that wispy connection. Perhaps by drawing from that invisible connection, I feel a little less lonely, a little less aimless. If I were in a flippant mood, I'd say that I regularly converse with God.

Eshwar Sundaresan

Cancer? It's Okay, I'm Stronger!

There is nothing that wastes the body like worry, and one who has any faith in God should be ashamed to worry about anything whatsoever.

—*Mahatma Gandhi*

What can you say about a twenty-three-year-old woman who loves painting and believes the world is her canvas? Who believes she thrives not just on oxygen, but on dancing, laughing and loving. Who has a twinkle in her eye, an infectious giggle. And cancer. This is Nishita's story and I'm going to let her tell it, her way.

The biopsy results were in. It was cancer. Although I had known that there was a possibility that it could be that, nothing prepares one for the final verdict, for the 'C' confirmation. Wasn't cancer something that happened to some third party — someone one hardly knew? Wasn't it something that didn't — couldn't — happen to a health-conscious twenty-three-year-old? When Dad told me the diagnosis, I cried. Then the tears stopped on their own accord, and when I ran the sentence, 'I have cancer,' through my mind, I suddenly realised that there wasn't a trace of fear. Shock, yes, but somehow, I felt I was stronger than the cancer.

There was no time for self-pity, anxiety and anticipation — it was time for action. I went with my family to Dr Advani, the oncologist at Jaslok Hospital, and with that began a unique phase in my life.

Tests after tests, tests after tests. Tests become a part of the routine once you are diagnosed with cancer. I admit that I didn't look forward to all those injections, all those scans but, at the same time, it wasn't something that made me nervous or threatened me in any way. I accepted the fact that I had cancer, and now the next concern was to find out what stage it was at, whether it had spread to the internal organs. I had heard my family and friends speak of religion, but only one idea had been deeply ingrained in my mind, ever since I could remember: 'God will never give me that which I cannot handle. If I am faced with a certain situation, it's because God thinks I can handle it. It's God's way of making me stronger, of making me climb a higher rung of self-belief. Hmm, so God thinks I can handle cancer — I will prove Him right!'

In the meantime, my days were filled with tests. And more tests. Stage II A — the cancer had spread only to the breast and neck. A sigh of relief passed through me. It could have been much worse. Since I had two lumps on my neck and one beneath my rib cage, no surgery was possible and chemotherapy was the only solution. Since my veins were too thin and the doctor believed that if I took the strong chemotherapy medicines intravenously my nerves would become black and painful, a rubber port was surgically put into my neck. Yes, it was not easy to get used to having the thing inside me, but now it's so much a part of me, I forget about its existence.

The chemo sessions started. I had to be in the hospital at 7 a.m., and on a good day would be out by 2 p.m. My brother would accompany me, and his ditzy comments would make me laugh. I cried once, though. The nurse jabbed the needle in the wrong place and I was shaken by unbearable pain, she then pulled the needle out and jabbed me again. This was probably my first experience ever of excruciating pain, and yes, it's bad. But you know what — it's not that bad. I realised then, that actual pain is less 'painful' than imagined pain. When we think of pain, it seems unbearable; when we go through it, we realise that heck, it's not so bad. Am I making sense?

One realises the importance of hair, when one has no hair. Jokes apart, wigs can be a huge hassle, especially because I was determined to continue my life as always. I went to work, partied till 4 a.m. on a beach in Goa on New Year's Day, and attended hazaar weddings. The one at Breach Candy was particularly interesting. While I had to fight the breeze to ensure that the hair remained on my head and not the floor, a particularly nosey friend eyed me suspiciously and kept mentioning how my hair looked different. In retrospect, it was amusing. I would see her approaching and run in the other direction, but since I have always been a very straightforward person, this hide-and-seek did get to me a little. In fact, the only times that I remember crying during the treatment were when I had to lie. If I'd had it my way, I would not have been secretive about it. But since ours is a well-known family in Mumbai, I was told that it would be better to keep it under wraps or people would start gossiping about me. And I saw the point in that as I sure didn't want to be the object of such attention.

Only about ten people who were extremely close to me knew about it. The rest wondered why I suddenly looked a little thinner, and why there was 'something different' about my hair and eyebrows! I, however, knew that these little irritants would pass. The most important thing was to constantly choose life, conjure the image of a beautiful future, and hold on firmly to the belief that this had come into my life because I could handle it. All through those days, I felt closer to God than I ever had before. In the nights, when everyone would be asleep and I was feeling too sick to sleep, God would keep me company. It seemed like from within, He was speaking to me, soothing me and telling me, 'This has come to you, so that you can become even better, stronger. This has come to you so that you can become an inspiration some day, to others suffering from cancer.' His words would act as a lullaby and in time, I would fall asleep.

It is now a year since I was diagnosed with cancer. In my hands, I am holding my test reports. It is all clear — not a trace of the cancer anywhere. I don't know what the future holds, and yes, I probably am susceptible to a recurrence. I, however, have started looking at life like a game of chess. God makes a move, I make my counter move. God brought cancer to me; I decided to fight it out and live even more happily than before. I don't know what God's next move will be, but then, who does? What I do know is that if I play the game well enough, God will let me win. After all, in my victory, is His victory. In so many ways I have started seeing God as a parent — someone who keeps challenging me to grow and, at the same time, watches me through the corner of His eye and ensures that I don't hurt myself. I know that if I could handle a rubber tube in my neck, thirty-six injections in six months, my lungs functioning at thirty per cent of their normal capacity at the time of the last chemo, I can handle everything that He sends me. For now, what matters is expanding my business. And watching my hair grow thicker than ever before. And travelling to countries unexplored. And dancing till my feet ache. And, more than anything else, living as if living is all that matters.

Nishita
(As told to Megha Bajaj)

To or *Through* the Messiah?

In my eighth summer, I walked up to my class teacher's desk to collect a prize for reading and spelling. My prize was a book, a slim volume titled *Illustrated Stories from the Bible*.

In newly independent India, there wasn't a single full-colour magazine; and well-produced children's books were only for the very rich. So my prize-book, the work of American missionaries, was doubly precious. How well I remember the deep maroon of the cover that framed a reproduction of a famous painting of Christ entering Jerusalem, and that distinct scent a new book exudes! Luckily the book slid neatly into my school bag and I placed it between my notebooks and carried it carefully home to my twin. After tea we sat on the floor and looked at all the pictures. Since there were no pictures of horses or cowboys in the book, my brother soon lost interest and wandered off.

As I read story after story, some of which were already familiar, and stared at all the pictures, Jesus became more and more real to me. He was in very ordinary-looking clothes, he wasn't carrying weapons, there was no trace of jewellery or flowers on him, he looked like the other people in the pictures, he had hands and feet, and even a beard.

I dreaded the last page. Would he be bleeding on the cross? Luckily not. He was at a table with all his friends and appeared to be enjoying a meal. I hadn't yet heard the story connected with the picture of the Last Supper.

At that time, I was in III-A and felt I was no longer a child but someone who observed things, combed my hair without my mother's help, walked to school by myself in buckled shoes — not lace-ups — and took small decisions.

One such decision was how to end the daily class-prayer. My school believed in democracy, so every single child in class got a chance to read a short class-prayer quite apart from the one at the daily school assembly. It always ended with words that anyone who has studied in a Christian school will recognise: 'Through Jesus Christ our Lord. Amen.'

When it was my turn, I said, 'To Jesus Christ our Lord. Amen.'

There was a great silence and my teacher, Mrs Bettina Grant, said, 'It's *through* child. Not *to*. Haven't you been listening?'

'Yes, I know that's what everyone says. But I want to go *to* Jesus, not *through* Him to someone else.'

'But that's not how we are supposed to say it.'

'What's wrong with saying I want to go *to* Jesus?'

By this time a thrill had run through the class because no one with any sense argued with Mrs Grant. This was also something dangerous to argue about and how delicious that it was a non-Christian. Everyone looked forward to a dramatic punishment.

Mrs Grant rose and pressed a bell to summon the junior school captain. I was sent off with her to the Principal, an American no one was afraid of because she was incapable of being unkind. Nevertheless, when I was led into the office and had to stand listening to a narration of my rebellion, my courage vaporised.

Miss Johnson stood up and towered over both of us as she looked at me, her grey eyes expressionless. Then she wrote something on a piece of paper, gave it to the JS captain and sent us off. When we returned to class, whatever Mrs Grant read on the notepaper made her look very thoughtful.

'Go to your place,' she said to me. There was to be no punishment to fit the crime.

What had Miss Johnson written to defuse the situation? How had I escaped without being reprimanded?

Years later my father showed me that same note. At some time, perhaps on Parents' Day, Mrs Grant had given it to him. It said very simply in ink long faded, 'Matt. 19, verse 14' followed by the signature, 'Frances Johnson'.

It was undated but I recognised the note Mrs Grant had looked at silently many years ago, and though I'd read the Gospels several times, I didn't know them by heart. So my hands shook as I opened the Bible to check the reference.

'Let the little children come to me and do not hinder them ...'

Mini Krishnan

Mahadeva

As bees suck nectar from many a flower
And make their honey one, so that no drop
Can say, 'I am from this flower or that,'
All creatures, though one, know not they are that One.
There is nothing that does not come from Him.
Of everything He is the inmost Self.
He is the truth; He is the Self supreme.

                                       —*Chandogya Upanishad*

His name is Mahadeva. A thin, dark man — so dark that it is almost indistinguishable where his skin ends and his thick, curly, deeply black hair and beard begin. And in that darkness live two huge eyes that mostly never look directly at you, or if they do, hastily scuttle away with their startling whiteness, as if not to offend or defile you by the 'untouchability' of a direct stare. Mahadeva cleans our road and the outside of our houses of all manner of dirt, debris, waste: animal and vegetable, but mostly man-made.

Every morning, the gentle, rhythmic *swish-grritchh* of the stick-fronds of the broom scratching the dust heralds Mahadeva's arrival. A few months ago, a rat fell into the open water tank at the back of our house and drowned. I found it floating on the surface of the water in the morning, a tiny little grey-brown thing that I almost mistook for a bit of coconut tree debris that often falls into the tank. Naturally, I didn't remove it — this job was meant to be done by people like Mahadeva.

I called out to him over the *swish-grritch* of his broom.

'Amma,' he answered and came and stood at a quiet, respectful distance away from me, head bent.

'There is a dead rat in the water tank. Will you remove it?' The question was a rhetorical one, a command really because it was unthinkable that he'd say no.

Mahadeva removed the rat, efficiently and quietly, and I tipped him ten rupees. Tip, was it? Or the wages of untouchability? Maybe, even conscience money, as if to say — look, I know it's your job and you have to do it anyway, but I'm saying that I'm sorry you were born to do it and grateful that I'm not. Silly thoughts that I brushed away like the flies that would have gathered around the rat if I had left it there long enough.

There are some days when Mahadeva doesn't turn up. After getting over the irritation of having to dispose of my own trash, I am willing to grant that the job satisfaction of harvesting garbage, day in and day out, can't possibly make someone bounce out of bed with a cheery song on his lips. No matter how many leftover packets of lime rice and pickle and the occasional hand-me-down pair of jeans he gets. But I preferred to put it down to the usual tardiness of his kind — lazy good-for-nothings who just did not have the motivation to rise above the circumstances in which they were born, I thought sanctimoniously.

My conviction was reinforced when I discovered the real reason for Mahadeva's frequent French leave. Mahadeva drank. Like a fish. Early one evening, I stood at my gate looking worriedly at the figure of a man lying across the street.

'That's Mahadeva,' the neighbour's maid told me cheerily.

'Is he ill?'

'No, just drunk,' she said, smiling even more cheerily, as if to say, 'It's a natural state of being for Mahadeva.'

'Shouldn't we do something?' I asked.

'Give him some buttermilk, Amma,' she said.

Buttermilk, I thought incredulously.

'Yes,' she said, 'nothing like a bartan of buttermilk to wake up a drunk.'

'I'm learning all the time,' I muttered to myself as I filled an empty jam jar with buttermilk, quickly and gingerly placed it near Mahadeva's head, then rushed away to stand at a safe distance and holler at him to drink it and go home. He did, but only after staggering to his feet in post-buttermilk sobriety and swearing profusely passionate, slurred promises of how he'd never touch another drop, and may he fall down dead if he did.

Mahadeva hasn't stopped drinking. And he hasn't fallen down dead either. His binges are funded by his garbage-collecting consultancy fees and whatever he earns from other jobs — trimming an overgrown hibiscus or pomegranate, clearing the roof of dead neem leaves.... Mahadeva is a very good worker, doing the job with a sincerity and a single-mindedness that you wouldn't have expected — well, of someone like him. And actually, in all fairness to him, I've never seen Mahadeva drunk on the job.

A few weeks ago, his son came to our gate one evening. A small boy of some eleven years with his father's eyes, except that they had not yet learnt the untouchable's downcast, apologetic look, and stared directly at me with a child's clear, shining, uncluttered gaze. He was clutching a small pile of what looked like playing cards in his hand. He gave one to me — again putting it directly into my hand, not keeping it reverentially on the gatepost for me to pick up, as his father would have done. His fingers touched my skin, equal to equal.

'My sister is getting married,' he said in a low, expressionless monotone. 'My father said to tell you to please come for the wedding.'

I realised that what he had put into my hand was a wedding invitation. My mother asked me to give the boy some money. I did, speaking to him in a loud, slow voice as if is he were mentally retarded or deaf or both, telling him to go straight home and give it to his father, and not to lose it. He looked at me — again that clear, direct gaze — and said, again expressionlessly, 'I'll give it to my mother because my father will drink it away.' I nodded and this time it was I who shifted my gaze away and down, a trifle shamefacedly.

As the boy walked away into the deepening darkness, Mummy and I examined the card. It was a pretty little card, printed in unusual, delicate golden-yellow picked out in a peach and brown filigree design. On the flap of the card was a neatly etched drawing of … now who else would grace Mahadeva's daughter's wedding card but his namesake. Lord Shiva. Mahadeva. Maheshwara. Nataraja. The Cosmic Dancer. Being garlanded by his divine consort, Parvati. The four corners of the card were smeared with neat smudges of sacred, auspicious turmeric.

Inside, the chaste, high-class Kannada said, 'Srimati Neelamma and Sri Mahadeva invite you to grace the occasion of the wedding of their eldest daughter, Chiranjeevi Sowbhagyawati Sowbhagya with Chiranjeevi Murugesh and beg you to participate in the vivaha mahotsava and bless the young couple'.

Nowhere in the card was there anything which, in any way, indicated that this was the wedding card of the daughter of a man who cleaned people's dirt for a living ... a man who was not like us, but one on the ragged fringes of society. There was no mark, no sign by which people would know the difference between the wedding card of his daughter and that of people like us. It was almost as if one part of me was saying, 'What right had he, a poor, unlettered, uncultured untouchable to elegance and good taste? For that matter, where the hell did he get to "learn" it?'

I still have that card on my desk. To remind me that at the deepest level, we are all the same ... that who you are has nothing to do with where and to whom you are born, and what you do for a living. It has only to do with who you choose to feel like inside yourself. In that little card, there was more dignity, more self-respect, more class and more self-worth than in all of the wedding cards that I had ever received. Cards that probably cost more than Mahadeva earns in a year, inviting me to the weddings of the daughters of people who are way 'above' him.

The wedding is over and Mahadeva is back on the job. *Swish-grritch* goes his broom every morning. But somehow, it's not the same any more. Every time I look at him, every time I pass him my pail of garbage, I am reminded and humbled by a little golden-yellow card on my table. And I wish that I had the capacity to make so much out of so little.

Ratna Rajaiah

The Face of God

I am not a staunch believer in formal religion. I pray whenever I feel like. That means, unlike most Muslims, I do not do the namaaz five times a day. More than formal prayer, for me, work is worship. When I show truthfulness, commitment and genuineness towards my work, my friends, colleagues, and members of my family, I am being spiritual.

When I pray it is to my late parents. I feel their presence. I can see them on either side of my shoulders. People say that when you pray to God, you can sense He is close to you. But when I pray I can feel the presence of my parents. I am able to connect to them. I ask them to show me the right path and to give me the strength to do good work.

Over the years I have changed a lot. When I was young I was an atheist. I would analyse and reason out everything. I am a science graduate and that was what physics taught me. One day, however, I went to see a seer in south Kerala. I went with the notion that I would be able to negate whatever he said. The seer asked me to touch a letter of the alphabet in the Koran. I decided beforehand which letter I would touch.

Then I closed my eyes and zeroed in on the letter, or thought I had. But, unknowingly, I had touched another letter.

The seer told me that I am a man who plays with the energy that comes out of the throat.

I said, 'Sound?' And the holy man nodded.

Then he said, 'Your skill lies in your fingers.' So, indirectly, he had told me I was a sound engineer. Incidents like this have made me realise that I cannot apply the rules of logic and reason to all aspects of life. There are many things which cannot be explained.

I feel now that there is something enigmatic at the core of life; something which we cannot comprehend. God is an intangible universal force, but we can sense it. When people ask me, 'What is your image of God?' I say, 'Imagine you are sitting under a tree and looking up at the sunlight streaming down through the leaves. For me, that is the face of God.'

Resul Pookutty
(As told to Shevlin Sebastian)

Where is this 'GOD' person?

The Scorpio hurtles down the deserted highway in Maharashtra at high speed. It is the 'time of the horns' as the Zulus call it in South Africa. The time of the day when the sun isn't visible quite yet but the sky is turning pale. The horns of the cattle are the only things visible in the herd. Night slowly gives way to day but not yet, not just yet.

I look out at the lush greenery hurtling by on either side of the road. Forests scent up the crisp, cool morning air and the voices of birds can be heard over the roar of the engine, surprisingly, even at that speed. It is the start of another magical day in ageless India and it is going to be a scorcher. Not a cloud colours the sky. I have experienced many such moments in my travels across all the states of this great country of ours, and yet these moments never fail to leave their imprint on my mind. The beauty of this country never ceases to captivate and surprise even a seasoned traveller like myself.

What hits you first is the contrast highways offer in this country. Empty, deserted, almost haunted stretches of highway suddenly turn into throbbing arteries choked with people and traffic as soon as the sun's first rays fall. The quintessential milkman, tousled hair giving away his rushed morning routine, the morning joggers, their jaws clenched with determination, the uniformed school children, laughing and playing like so many birds enlivening the morning with their fresh anticipation of another day — all a part of the highway in no time. It is easy to forget that just a few minutes ago this looked like a road where no one ventured, and then, suddenly, from nowhere comes this multitude. It's almost like magic. It is magic. It's definitely magical.

They say we have more gods in our country than anywhere else on the planet. One look at the traffic moving along and everybody, mostly, getting to where they are going just sort of proves it beyond doubt, in my mind. How could our traffic move at all unless the divine hand nudged it along a bit, every now and then? It just could not. God is closer than we could believe, and these mornings just bring that into focus for me.

Every morning, a vast majority of people turn their attention to God, at least for a moment if not more. The vermilion tikka on the foreheads of the devout, the temple bells at the morning aarti, the cry of the muezzin calling the faithful to prayer, the shabads in the vicinity of the gurdwaras, the packed Sunday masses at the churches, the thousands going to, or coming from pilgrimages, all prove, even today, that God plays an important role in our lives and our country. The divine is an accepted part of our lives and, sometimes, out of choice, but mostly out of habitual ritual, he is invoked by a billion thoughts. That collective consciousness fills our mornings with wonder. There is always something fresh and magical about every dawn in this country unlike anything I have ever known anywhere else. India springs to sudden life every morning. Thank God.

About two years and 40,000 kilometres on the highways of India have shown me the true fabric of our nation in so many of its contrasts that I now, finally, have a small amount of understanding as to what drives us all. It's making a living, of course. But in India that is not all it is. God is present in the many small miracles we take for granted.

I was once stuck in one of Delhi's polluted, traffic-jammed, water-logged streets. Everybody was abusing everyone, including me ... till I decided to do something totally unexpected. I smiled, then got out of the car, stood in the rain, and waved to a few people 'jammed' in traffic with me. Initially, they looked flabbergasted, then smiles and waves began to ripple through the crowd, and the traffic jam turned into a rather pleasant hour-long chat by the roadside. Believe it or not, a gentleman even offered me a cup of tea from the thermos in his car. Hmm ... makes me wonder what we've all been doing wrong. So this is dedicated to Mr Malhotra, the deliverer of hot tea to a soaked, smiling man by the roadside, whom he did not know, and will probably never meet again. Thank you, sir. You were a godsend. I would wait in that jam again for a chance to share that cup of tea with you and our fellow drivers: Ramesh, who turned out to be a good singer and treated us to an impromptu performance right there, Usha Aunty with that lovely smile, and oh, so many others. All in all, a pleasant group to be jammed with in traffic, in the rain. Well, smiles are probably one way God shows us He exists. Offer one to the next person you meet, and you will see the world is already a little better. God knows what you will think of next!

Rocky Singh

Man, God and Religion

As the Himalayas are the source of the River Ganga, Israel is the source of three monotheist religions — Judaism, Christianity and Islam. For a first-hand view of their coexistence, there is no better place to visit than its capital, Jerusalem, which is at the heart of the three faiths. I was further inspired by my Jewish friend Peter, who said that the land offers opportunities to understand the perpetual connections between mankind and God.

Sacred to Jews, Christians and Muslims from all over the world, Jerusalem is a 3,000-year-old metropolis, sprayed on the hills and sprawling with limestone buildings which wrapped a sense of holiness around me the moment I stepped in, though I belong to none of these religions. There is a sense of sanctity about the place, and it made me feel that I was entering an imaginary abode of the gods. Similar emotions were experienced by some Buddhist visitors from Japan, whom I came across during my stay.

The place is the common reference point for Jewish Joshua in New York, Christian Anna in Lisbon and Muslim Hassan in Syria, because they are all descendents of the patriarch,

Abraham, and his children, Ishmael and Isaac. Physically
the land is dotted with synagogues, churches and mosques,
almost holding each other's arms like brothers, though we can
guess there are invisible walls of distrust between them.

While taking in the sights of the metropolis, I witnessed
a flow of devoted Jews, dressed in long black coats and
hats, white-bearded Greek Orthodox priests wearing black
cassocks, and Muslim clerics in long robes, crossing each
other. I didn't see them talking to each other, or exchanging
any greetings — their manner seemed like that of brothers in
a feud over family property to which they've all laid claims
of ownership. For them, the esteemed property is the land
that the Lord showed to Abraham, that God promised to
Moses.

Like many, I kept wondering about what actually attracted
the mighty empires to fight for this tiny piece of land — was
it just the religious credence which derives from the belief
of the religious, like my friend Peter, that the land is blessed
with God's physical presence?

The Jewish kings, Solomon and Herod built wondrous
temples in Jerusalem to house their God on the site where
legend says Abraham was about to sacrifice his son Isaac; but
unfortunately, they were later destroyed by foreign invaders.
Nothing remains today, except part of a retaining wall which
is famously known as the Western Wall or the Wailing Wall,
revered by Jews, who congregate there and weep for the
destruction of their sacred temples

'A divine presence still remains here for us,' said Ben,
my Jewish guide who escorted me. So strong is their faith
that, as a tradition, they write messages on pieces of paper
and squeeze them in the cracks of the wall, and believe
that God will respond to them. When I observed their
extreme devotion, it was hard for me not to accept their firm
conviction about empathy with God; rather, it inspired me

to do what they were doing. While wedging my paper in one of the cracks, I could make some sense of what Peter meant by 'the perpetual connection' between mankind and God. I guessed that he was referring to the spark from the great quantum of energy that leads humans to seek self-realisation.

What impressed me most was that anyone could be a part of the tradition of the tucking-of-a-note-to-God. It was open to all, even if you were not connected with the land or religion, implying that Almighty God and divinity are above all of that.

'Even the Pope did it during his visit in March 2000,' said Ben. That historic visit, being the first ever by a pontiff to a Jewish state, made newspaper headlines around the world. Interestingly, the Pope's prayer to God was later taken out, made public and the piece of paper now resides in the Holocaust Museum in Jerusalem.

It reads: 'God of our fathers, you chose Abraham and his descendants to bring your name to the nations. We are deeply saddened by the behaviour of those who in the course of history have caused these children of yours to suffer. And asking your forgiveness, we wish to commit ourselves to genuine brotherhood with the people of the covenant.'

Next to the Western Wall, within the same precinct, the Muslims built the grand Dome of the Rock and Al Aqsa mosque, the third holiest shrine for Muslims after Mecca and Medina, as they believe that their prophet Mohammed visited the site in his fabled night journey from Mecca to heaven, as described in the Koran. Every day, at prayer time, devoted pilgrims throng there.

For Christians, every inch of the land is holy, as it is marked by the footsteps of Jesus who was born in Bethlehem, ten miles out of Jerusalem, but crucified and resurrected in Jerusalem.

St Helena, mother of the Byzantine Emperor Constantine built a church at the site. When inside, my guide, Ahmed, pointed me to a silver star on the floor of the cave and whispered in my ears, 'That's exactly where God became flesh.' Which God? I thought it must be the Almighty God who unites faiths and people. I pushed my way through the devoted pilgrims, placed my forehead on the star and came out spiritually hyped with an electrifying sensation.

I had similar feelings when I touched the Stone of Unction inside the Church of Holy Sepulchre in Jerusalem where, after his crucifixion, legend says Christ's body was anointed by several mourners, including Mother Mary. Interestingly, the key of this church has, for centuries, been held by a Muslim, who opens the doors every day, in the morning.

Via Dolorosa (in Latin it means 'Way of Sorrow') is a narrow pathway in Jerusalem, of special significance for Christians, it being the stretch along which Jesus took his last fateful walk, carrying the cross from the point of his trial to that of his crucifixion. 'Walking along this path is an invigorating experience for Christians,' said Ben, as we marched along. 'It connects them with the pain and humiliation that Jesus had to bear.' I am a non-Christian, but my experience was no different. I collected a handful of dust from the pathway, thinking that one or two of those particles might have the footmarks of God.

What was most striking to me was that, on a Friday afternoon, when rabbis were preparing for their holy Sabbath at the Western Wall, priests were getting ready to lead a poignant procession carrying crosses down Via Dolorosa, and clerics were inviting thousands of devotees for the afternoon prayer service at the Al Aqsa mosque. They were all getting ready to pray to God, but differently, as their faiths taught them. I wondered, if they realised, in the core of their heart, that their faiths are flowers of the same tree. At that very moment I heard the ringing of the church bells, resonating with the prayer call from the mosque. I rushed up to the Western Wall and heard a group chanting from the Torah. I started seeing rays of hope, of reconciliation in the horizon and felt that, perhaps, the wisdom of brotherhood will one day unite the descendants of Abraham — a hope expressed by the Pope in his prayer note.

Sandip Hor

Unity, Diversity, and Other Contradictions

*If God be within the mosque, then to whom does this
world belong?
If Ram be within the image which you find upon your
pilgrimage,
then who is there to know what happens without?
Hari is in the East: Allah is in the West. Look within
your
Heart, for there you will find both Karim and Ram;
All the men and women of the world are His living
forms.
Kabir is the child of Allah and of Ram: He is my Guru,
He is my Pir.*

Kabir

I grew up in a Hindu household. Our home (and my father
moved a dozen times in his working life) always had a prayer
room, where paintings and portraits of assorted divinities
jostled for shelf and wall space with fading photographs

of departed ancestors, all stained by ash scattered from the incense burned daily by my devout parents. Every morning, after his bath, my father would stand in front of the prayer room wrapped in his towel, his wet hair still uncombed, and chant his Sanskrit mantras. But he never obliged me to join him; he exemplified the Hindu idea that religion is an intensely personal matter, that prayer is between you and whatever image of your maker you choose to worship. In the Indian way, I was to find my own truth.

Like most Hindus, I think I have. I am a believer, despite a brief period of schoolboy atheism (of the kind that comes with the discovery of rationality and goes with the acknowledgment of its limitations — and with the realisation that the world offers too many wondrous mysteries for which science has no answers). And I am happy to describe myself as a believing Hindu, not just because it is the faith into which I was born, but for a string of other reasons, though faith requires no reason. One is cultural: as a Hindu I belong to a faith that expresses the ancient genius of my own people. Another is, for lack of a better phrase, its intellectual 'fit': I am more comfortable with the belief structures of Hinduism than I would be with those of the other faiths of which I know. As a Hindu, I claim adherence to a religion whose rituals and customs I am free to reject, a religion that does not oblige me to demonstrate my faith by any visible sign, by subsuming my identity in any collectivity, not even by a specific day or time or frequency of worship. As a Hindu, I subscribe to a creed that is free of the restrictive dogmas of holy writ, that refuses to be shackled to the limitations of a single holy book.

Above all, as a Hindu I belong to the only major religion in the world that does not claim to be the only true religion. I find it immensely congenial to be able to face my fellow human beings of other faiths without being burdened by the conviction that I am embarked upon a 'true path' that they have missed ... Hinduism asserts that all ways of belief are equally valid, and Hindus readily venerate the saints, and the sacred objects, of other faiths.

How can such a religion lend itself to fundamentalism? That devotees of this essentially tolerant faith have desecrated a shrine and assaulted Muslims in its name is a source of shame and sorrow. India has survived the Aryans, the Mughals, the British; it has taken from each — language, art, food, learning — and grown with all of them. To be Indian is to be part of an elusive dream we all share, a dream that fills our minds with sounds, words, flavours from many sources that we cannot easily identify. Muslim invaders may indeed have destroyed Hindu temples, putting mosques in their place, but this did not — could not — destroy the Indian dream. Nor did Hinduism suffer a fatal blow. Large, eclectic, agglomerative, the Hinduism that I know understands that faith is a matter of hearts and minds, not of bricks and stone. 'Build Ram in your heart,' the Hindu is enjoined; and if Ram is in your heart, it will little matter where else he is, or is not.

Shashi Tharoor

The Talking Tree

Everybody says that I am the perfect daughter. The perfect Indian daughter, that is. I suspect it is because I was a good student who chose to study engineering, and got the perfect job in a multi-national organisation. Soon, I was living and breathing work twenty-four hours a day. As time passed, my circle of friends grew smaller, and responsibilities at work grew bigger. I never stopped to take a break; nor did I realise that life was just passing me by.

Once, my cousin Raghav came to stay with us for a few weeks. He is one of the craziest people I have ever met in my life. He is always talking to anybody who will listen, even animals and trees. We have fish, turtles and dogs as pets and Raghav will spend hours talking to all of them. My brother, Abhishek, and I used to call him 'Paagal Raghav' (Crazy Raghav). My mother, however, always thought that he was special, and encouraged us to involve him in our activities. On that visit of his, finally fed up of his silly antics, Abhishek and I cornered him and started pulling his leg.

'Hey Raghav, we noticed you like talking to the fish and dogs in our house. So, do they talk back to you?' Abhishek asked.

'Sure,' replied Raghav seriously. 'Just like us, animals and trees possess consciousness too. The only difference is that our bodies are all different. If you don't believe me, try talking to trees. They are really good listeners.'

'Of course they are. They can't talk back, can they?' I snickered.

Raghav said, 'Come on, Shruti, just talk to a tree for five minutes.'

'You must think I'm as crazy as you,' I muttered.

'I think you should do it. Talk about your thoughts and feelings to the trees. They all listen, you know. Sometimes, they even respond. I'll take you out to your favourite mithai shop if the tree doesn't talk back. That's a promise. And if it does, you owe me lunch.'

'All right, I'll do it. I'm always ready for a treat.'

And a few minutes later, I found myself standing in front of an absolutely beautiful green mango tree on the street near my house. I stood there for some time without speaking. Then, I looked to the left and right, embarrassed. Finally, I mustered enough courage and said, 'Hello, Tree. How's your day going?' I listened and listened, but there was no response from the tree.

I heaved a sigh, resigned myself to the inevitable and went on, 'Well, my name is Shruti and I am twenty-four years old. I love reading, playing table tennis, listening to the radio and singing along with it. I have a cousin called Raghav, and he says that you will listen to me.' Slowly, I started opening up and talked about things that were important to me. I talked about how I loved squirrels, how I missed my grandparents, how much fun I have with my best friends, and the boys that I liked.

As I was getting ready to leave, I suddenly remembered Raghav's remark that trees respond to conversations. I turned to the tree and said, 'Tree, you never said a word. How do I know you were even listening to me?' Then, I heard the crackle of dry leaves underneath the tree. As I looked towards the noise, I saw a small squirrel peeping out from the bottom of the trunk. There we were, a little squirrel and a short, bespectacled girl from two completely different worlds, just staring at each other. Usually squirrels scurry away when they know that someone is watching, yet this one kept looking at me, relaxed and unafraid, and it was as if we each understood the other. Everything seemed to be at a standstill and I was filled with complete awareness.

It came to me in an epiphany that the tree was acknowledging our conversation through the squirrel. Many creatures lived in and around the tree — crows, pigeons, squirrels, rats, bandicoots, dogs, even the occasional cat. Perhaps, some would call it a coincidence, but I believe that the tree 'chose' a squirrel because it had really listened and heard me talk about my love for them. I remained rooted to the spot, knowing that I had finally understood that there is such a thing as universal consciousness. All we need to do is learn to break away from our busy schedules and spend a little time to view things with 'the seeing eye'. And every now and then, we just might feel His presence, and learn to connect more harmoniously with our real self and the world around us.

I took Raghav out for lunch that day!

Shrutkeerti Khurana

A Dip of Reaffirmation

You have to grow from the inside out. None can teach you, none can make you spiritual. There is no other teacher but your own soul.

—*Swami Vivekananda*

I am a journalist by profession and at heart, and religion and spirituality had never played much of a role in my life. It was with resignation that I gave in to my mother's wish that we should go down to a remote temple in Thirunelly in Kerala to participate in the rites for my grandfather's death anniversary. Appoopan, as we called him, used to be a hardcore communist and a senior journalist who always spoke up and wrote against ritualistic customs and practices. It was in his footsteps that I too had followed. So for me, this trip to Thirunelly was more of a chance to meet the rest of the family than to bow my head to multiple deities.

The routine, on such occasions, is simple. We are supposed to wake up at five in the morning and leave for the temple, which is right on top of a steep hill. Once we climb to the peak we are to take a dip at the Paapanashini stream and then perform the rites before heading to the temple. The sceptic in me had made me turn to the Internet to look up information on the place before heading out, and I had seen pictures of a clean-looking stream with a heavenly glow. While I was not sure whether the stream would live up to its name's literal translation of being a cleanser of sins, it looked good enough to take a dip in. I was willing to give it a try.

The next day I was ready at five in the morning, grumbling about it even as I started the steep climb up. With every step, however, I felt my resentment melting away. With every step, I could see people who had turned up for a reason. There were people who had small urns of ashes in their hands — there to immerse the mortal remains of their loved ones in the Paapanashini so that they would have a happy afterlife. There were young couples with small babies who were being fed their first morsels of rice, ever. Families like us who were there to perform the rites on death anniversaries. And people who were simply there to pray. And it seemed to me as if they were there to shed their past and wash away their perceived sins, and to ask for a better future.

While reflecting on the pull of faith, I headed with my family to the stream to start the rites. It had taken us a hundred stone steps and a forty-minute barefoot hike over boulders and rocks to get there. And the first glimpse of the stream was nothing like the images I had seen on my computer. The Paapanashini or the 'cleanser of sins' turned out to be a small pond diverted from the original river with a spring flowing into it but with no outlet. And not just that. The constant flow of devotees for their ritualistic dip had made the waters a muddy brown. This was not what I had expected, yet egged on by the others I cautiously felt my way into the waters of the pond. The water was freezing and as I looked around I could see water bugs making their way towards me.

I gathered my courage and made my stipulated three dips in rapid succession. It was when I took my third deep breath after I completed my dips that I realised something: all the three times when the muddy waters had closed around me, the sole thought in my mind had been, 'Oh God, please give me the faith to trust you to take care of me.' And as I pulled myself out of the rocky pond, I could not get over the fact that a self-proclaimed agnostic like me, who had long echoed the quote that religion is the opium of the masses, seemed to have the same thoughts that most pilgrims at Thirunelly must have. It is a strange feeling when you regain the faith you think you no longer possess.

After taking our dips, my family (from my seventy-year-old great-aunt to my nine-year-old cousin) huddled in a shivering line along the narrow and rocky banks of the Paapanashini, the stream that was the source of the waters that accumulated in the pond. Dripping wet and freezing, we sat facing the plantain leaf, which had a mixture of rice, boiled rice, gingelly seeds, basil leaves and karuka grass.

I had a vague memory of participating in such a ritual. But it was probably the sheer lack of anything urban at the spot that forced me to actually focus on the ritual. When you are shivering in the middle of a dense forest on the banks of a stream, being prompted to remember all those who have died in your family, it seems next to impossible to tune out and distract yourself.

My Appoopan died suddenly at the office, when I was in the fourth standard, on the second day after my school re-opened. I remember being brought home in the middle of school to my mother who was distraught yet holding fort — taking calls, informing relatives and taking care of the million things that had cropped up. My grandmother, who was always seen as one of the most capable individuals in the family, suddenly crumpled. And as I waited for my cousins to come from various parts of Kerala, I was also waiting for my grandfather to wake up and say he was joking and that everything was fine. But he never did and that was the first time I realised how unfair life could be.

All this had been pushed into cold storage for almost sixteen years and all of it came rushing back as I started on the motions of a ritual I never understood the significance of. And then it was almost like my mental floodgates opened and everything I had pushed aside came flowing out. I was trying to remember every little thing that had broken my heart. I needed the pain to ooze out and leave my system. I had had enough of keeping it in shady recesses only to have it come out when I least expected it. It was time to spring-clean and throw out the ever-lurking pain that would emerge at the slightest opportunity. I finally understood that the monotony of rituals have a deeper significance than the literal meaning I had ascribed to them. As I chanted the hymns with my family, I found it easier to purge my memories. I had pushed my belief system away, but it felt like it had somehow found me and enveloped me in a bear-hug, cushioning me from the raw pain I felt at saying goodbye to my repressed recollections.

I finished the mantras and gently placed the leaf with the rice and seeds on the waters of the Paapanashini. And as it bobbed up and down to its final destination, I knew I could now truly start again from scratch. No holds barred.

Shweta Ganesh Kumar

Running into God at Pondicherry

*You meet God in a moment of time. And often, he is
the man sitting beside you.*

— *Kabir*

Late on a weekday night, our six-year-old daughter Ananya
announced that she was going to read a story 'all by herself,
without help'. We were thrilled, of course, at her sense of
adventure and this first sign of independence where reading
was concerned. With our son Aniruddha, we had barely
noticed his transition into literacy. He was a fluent reader,
and reading had come to him easily. With Ananya, on the
other hand, it had been a bit of an uphill climb. She loved
books and insisted that my husband or I read to her every
night. She saw life through literature, and her conversations
were often peppered with 'literary' references. She was quick
to remember Hansel and Gretel when she was scolded for
scattering bread crumbs on the floor. But it had taken some
prodding to get her to read. Words were hard, sentences
impossible. They must have seemed to her like hills she

couldn't possibly climb! Which was why I was delighted and absurdly proud that night. As it turned out, Ananya read not one but three stories printed in a big, child-friendly font 'all by herself, without help'. But apple carts are set up to be upset, and this one I was rejoicing over was no exception.

When she was done reading, Ananya turned to us and complained that her eyes were smarting. Unmindful of how late it was, I propped her up twenty feet away from an eye chart pasted in our kitchen, and asked her to read from it. My husband stood over her as she read, prodding and cajoling her every now and then. Ananya didn't make it past the fourth line.

Panic. Guilt. Little things falling into place. More guilt. Perhaps Ananya's reluctance to read, her annoying tendency to skip an entire word or line, was connected to poor vision. We should have caught on earlier. How could we have missed this? What an insensitive mother I had been! Would she go through life wearing thick glasses? And so on....

Granted I was over-reacting to what is really a very common and minor problem: Aniruddha told us that most of the children in his class wore glasses. But then, attachment is a strange thing. So is this business of being a parent. Other children wearing glasses are always *other* children wearing glasses. I told myself, of course, that Ananya's case was a bit different. We had adopted her when she was one — a scrawny little thing with eczema on her scalp and wounds on her face. She had blossomed now into a spunky little girl, full of energy and life. But during her early months in the orphanage, she must have been low on nutrition. Had that affected her eyesight?

We took Ananya to not one but two ophthalmologists. Both confirmed that she had weak eyesight. We also learnt that one of her eyes was considerably weaker than the other. Ananya was probably using only one eye! The other eye, the ophthalmologists warned us, could soon turn 'lazy'. They wrote out prescriptions for glasses and recommended a multivitamin syrup.

I had great faith though, in the kind of vision therapy advocated by Dr Bates, and offered by the School of Perfect Eyesight, one of the departments of the Aurobindo Ashram at Pondicherry. According to the Bates school of thought, spectacles were not a solution for weak eyesight. Over time, your eyes would get increasingly dependent on them. It was a bit like walking with a crutch. The thing to do was to change your habits of seeing, and train your eyes to see properly.

I had had first-hand experience of the Bates method, having undergone a course to correct my own astigmatism at the School of Perfect Eyesight. I phoned the school and got an appointment for Ananya. She was to undergo a six-day course.

Ananya and I checked into one of the ashram guesthouses, visiting the School of Perfect Eyesight for an hour every morning and another hour every afternoon. Ananya's favourite breakfast spot was the crowded Adayar Ananda Bhavan restaurant on Nehru Salai. She was an unswerving idli-dosa loyalist. On our third morning at Pondicherry, we walked up as usual to the restaurant. We were a bit late and there was a long queue at the counter. I elbowed my way to a corner table and positioned Ananya there with strict instructions not to wander off. After a wait of ten minutes, I managed to get our two plates of dosa.

As I approached the table, I found an old man talking to Ananya. She was usually shy with strangers. But in this case, she was actually chatting with him. They fell silent as I approached. I smiled tentatively at the man. Being city-bred, I have been brought up to be suspicious of strangers. But instinctively, I trusted this man. He was frail and bent with age. Judging by his clothes, he appeared to be from a lower-middle-class family.

'She is a good, sweet child,' he smiled, gesturing in Ananya's direction. I nodded proudly. 'Where are you from, Ma?' he asked.

'Madras,' I said.

'So you are not from Pondicherry. Why have you come here?'

I explained to him briefly why I was there. We were running late, but somehow, I let myself be drawn into conversation with him. Then, it was my turn to pose some typically Indian questions. 'Are you from here?'

He looked at me for a moment. 'I am from Madras too, like you. I am here to take care of my son. He is in hospital.'

'What happened?'

'They amputated his leg,' he said. 'He fell off a moving train, somewhere near Chidambaram. He was brought here. This was closer than Madras.' His voice dipped as he spoke. I stopped chewing on my dosa. Ananya was playing with her food. I let it pass. Around us there was a crush of people hoping to grab a seat. The clatter of vessels. Billing counter noise. Someone yelled, 'Oru plate pongal — one plate pongal.'

'How old is he?' I asked the man.

'Forty,' he said. 'He is a railway employee like me. I retired from service years ago. I have to be around him now, all the time. Round the clock.' I didn't ask him any more questions. What was there to ask or say? There I was worrying myself sick and obsessing over my daughter's small problem, and here was an old man whose son had just lost a leg.

'Where are you from, originally? I mean, what is your hometown?' the man asked then.

'Tiruthirapoondi village, Thanjavur,' I said, adding for good measure, 'but I have never been there. I am really from Madras.'

He disregarded my answer. 'Don't mind my saying this,' he said, 'but take the child to the Mariamman temple there. It will cure her eye problem. The Goddess is a great healer. Take this as advice from a grandfather.'

'Thank you,' I said, 'I will. And please wish your son from me.' He broke into a toothless smile, a smile of great radiance. We parted ways after that.

It is unlikely that I will run into him again, but now and then, I wonder how he is ... this man who rose above his own pain to think of my daughter.

K. Srilatha

My God or Yours?

There was a time when he was in a coma for three days. When he woke up there was a lot of pain. He was allowed only sips of water for a while and around midnight the doctor said that he could have a cold drink. He asked for a Pepsi. The ICU was on the second floor and the nearest shops were far away. For three days I had been standing beside him and my feet were swollen and I was worn out. I wasn't sure I had the strength to walk to the shops and back. Seeing Kumar so restless and desperate, I picked up my bag and sent up a little prayer saying, 'Please help.' This prayer was a kind of reflex action and I didn't really expect an answer.

As I walked through the corridor, I heard a voice calling me. I turned and saw a man standing there. He was clad in a spotless white kurta and dhoti and looked like an angel. 'I heard that your husband was very ill and I came to see if you needed any help,' he said. The man was my tailor. I asked him to get a can of Pepsi for my husband. Despite my battered frame of mind, and all my pain and fears, I knew that God had heard my prayer and had sent an angel to minister to me in my hour of need.

It was cold and damp where I stood and, for the first time since my husband was admitted in the hospital, I began to cry. Everything seemed so hopeless and sad. After a while, a feeling of warmth enveloped me. My tiredness, fears and tears gradually vanished.

My husband died, and many years later, a chance meeting with the tailor who helped me, brought into focus something that had been haunting my mind. He said, 'While I was shutting up shop for the day, God told me to come to you.' *Which God*? I wondered for a long while. I had been brought up in a tradition which told me that there is only one God, and here was my Hindu tailor, telling me that God spoke to him and sent him to me. God certainly spoke to me too that day, so which God were we both referring to?

This sent me on another search of learning and spiritual experiences and, as I interacted with friends of other religious traditions, I began to see that their needs and faith struggles were similar to mine. Their search for God was similar to mine too. Sometimes, our paths converged and we walked the same way. Sometimes, we followed a different route. I learnt that our destination however was the same.... A closer relationship and communion with God, the Creator of heaven and earth and all the universe.

Usha Jesudasan

The Seeds of Hope

When one loses the deep intimate relationship with nature, then temples, mosques and churches become important.

— *Jiddu Krishnamurti*

I grew up on a farm with my mother. She was highly educated, but she chose to be a farmer, because she believed that the highest state of human evolution is to be a peasant.

My mother always wore khadi. When we wanted nylon she said: 'I'll buy you nylon. But you know, if you buy nylon, some industrialist will get another Mercedes, and if you buy khadi, some woman's chullah will get lit. You decide.' That was a profound lesson in simple living. My parents also taught us fearlessness. Acting by your conscience, doing the right thing without being afraid of the people around you. That's been an important lesson for me, because you can't take on the Monsantos and Cargills of the world without rising above fear.

Also, the concept of the divine, the workings of a larger universe and so on, were very present at home. My parents were thoroughly non-religious, but deeply spiritual. They exposed us to the best and most authentic spiritual teachers as part of our upbringing, be it Anandamayi Ma or Swami Sivananda, for instance.

Growing up in the hugely ecological environment of the Himalayas and in a home of a spiritual nature, I knew from very early on that I would dedicate my life to the exploration of nature. So my life has been about the search for the understanding of the workings of nature and, of course, of its preservation. I started alone, but even at the toughest moments something would occur, showing me there is grace at work. I have been working on tough issues, fighting powerful adversaries, hell-bent on destroying the planet. I have had to deal for instance for more than twenty years with companies patenting and genetically engineering seeds, which to me are amongst the most criminal corporations in the world. And there is no way my limited brain would have come up with solutions. But I managed, again, because of that grace at work.

Spirituality to me is the awareness of the connectedness and creativity of the universe; and built into that creativity, is a sense of the divinity that pervades the entire cosmos. I would not be here without it. I can feel it especially at some very crucial moments, when I am very aware of my smallness, my helplessness, my sense of inadequacy — and am then made adequate to the challenge, way beyond my objective capabilities.

At one level, all the work I do in ecology is a material expression of my spiritual quest. The fact that I save seeds as a resistance to patenting and genetic engineering is a recognition of the sacredness in every seed. But I do not have daily rituals, meditations or prayers of any sort. I simply stop at times of the day, to hand over my life and reconnect.

I don't think you can be a deeply ecological person without being a deeply spiritual one. Spirituality for me is all about connecting, and about a widening circle of sympathy and compassion, which includes the entire earth. The notion comes from a very ancient category in Indian thought. Just like Chief Seattle talked about being in the web of life, in India we talk about vasudhaiva kutumbakam, which means the earth family. Indian cosmology has never separated the human from the non-human — we are a continuum.

◆

Over the past three decades, I have tried to be the change I want to see. When I found global corporations wanted to patent seeds, crops or life forms, I started Navdanya to protect biodiversity, defend farmers' rights and promote organic farming.

Obviously when you are up against powerful interests, there are greater chances of failure than success. But I've learned from the Bhagavad Gita and other teachings of our culture to detach myself from the results of what I do, because those are not in my hands. The context is not in your control, but your commitment is yours to make, and you can make the deepest commitment with a total detachment about where it will take you. You want it to lead to a better world, and you shape your actions and take full responsibility for them, but then you have detachment. And that combination of deep passion and deep detachment allows me always to take on the next challenge because I don't cripple myself, I don't tie myself in knots. The awards don't matter, the brickbats don't matter, the lousy rumours don't matter. Nothing affects you. I function like a free being. Getting that freedom is a social duty because we ought not to burden each other with prescription and demands. I think what we owe each other is a celebration of life, and to replace fear and hopelessness with fearlessness and joy!

Vandana Shiva

Once, in a Little Village .

Many years ago, my friend Suguna called from the US to announce that she had decided to come to India to 'find' her 'native place'. (Presumably, her family had 'misplaced' it several generations ago when they had set off to spread themselves the world over.) She had very few clues as to where it was, and all of them pointed towards the boondocks of Tamil Nadu. 'I need to go and pray to our family deity there,' she explained. I merely listened on autopilot until she said, 'And you're coming with me, of course.'

'No way!'

'Think of all the punya....'

'I don't want to, unless it comes with a proper loo.'

But Suguna begged and pleaded and slapped on enough emotional blackmail to make me fall in with her plans. And we set off soon after she arrived — I guess madness is the best cure for jet lag. As the relatives she'd been hounding for help with her quest had given her wildly conflicting directions, we travelled in circles and squares ... in loops and hoops ... with dust in our hair and face and clothes. Stripped fields. Skeletal animals. Roads that led nowhere.

I began to wonder whether her family deity wanted to be found at all.

That morning, as we approached one of the many villages on our way, we found that preparations had been made for a festival at the crumbling temple there. And, on an impulse, Suguna asked the taxi driver to stop. 'Come on, let's go and see what's happening,' she said.

People were standing around, looked somewhat preoccupied. Nevertheless, we two strangers were immediately welcomed and invited to participate in the temple festival. From the conversation fizzing around us, we learnt that the musicians who were expected to take part in the festivities had not arrived as yet, the puja couldn't begin without the music — that was the practice — and it was getting late. The auspicious time would soon pass, unless they managed to find a way out of the impasse.

Suddenly, we noticed a middle-aged man walking towards the temple. Unlike the others, who were probably in their best clothes, he looked unwashed and unkempt, and not all there. Everyone murmured and tch-tched. 'Didn't you pay him off yesterday?' asked someone.

'I did. So why hasn't he left?'

We gathered that the man had camped in the village for a few days with his bellows and other paraphernalia to give the gigantic brass vessels in which the prasad had to be cooked the mandatory coating of 'lead'. He'd spoken to no one except to fix his price, and although his work passed muster, he'd get drunk every evening, and scream curses through the night. Or so we were told. No wonder, the last thing they wanted was for him to turn up and wreck their festivities.

The man walked to the temple steps before the others could collect their wits to say something. But he did not go in. Standing there in the open, he bowed to the deity inside, then looked up at the sky for a moment, and spreading his hands in supplication, he began to sing. The shadows of the leaves from the nearby bilva tree flickered and lingered on his face, and from deep within that sunken stomach, those hunched shoulders, that head poking forward, from inside all of him, the music swelled and soared. The angry murmurs, the yelping of the dogs … everything was stilled except for the pure notes of Thyagaraja's song:

> Helpless have I wandered, day by day. I now seek
> Refuge in you,
> Come to my rescue.

No one spoke or moved even when the song came to an end. It was still there in the temple stones, in our skin, our minds, in the sudden silence.… He took out the money that he had tucked away in a cloth pouch at his waist — it was probably all that he had earned on the job there — left it in the brass plate inside the temple, and started walking away. Several voices called out to him to stay, but he neither looked back nor paused. In minutes, he was gone.

Everything there had changed somehow. The priest carefully put the man's offering in the hundi, and said, 'We can start the puja now.'

◆

Perhaps, it wasn't all that astonishing that a person with the face of a ruffian could sing like an angel. We've all heard such stories, of course. What was unusual was the way things turned out after that, for his offering proved to be the 'seed money' that paved the way for something much bigger.

When Suguna went back to the US, she wrote about this incident in a local newspaper. Unexpectedly, it jogged the conscience of someone from that village, who happened to read it. All along, he'd only had vague thoughts of his 'native place' and his family deity, but now, he decided to do something more and spoke about it to others. By some strange coincidence, a couple of them knew people whose ancestors had migrated from there, and tipped them off. They were so inspired by the story that they got together and raised money to renovate the temple and put in a borewell for the use of those who lived in the village.

Suguna never did find the whereabouts of her family deity, although she had shown others (who had not even been looking!) the way to theirs. 'Oh, well,' she sighed. 'God works in mysterious ways!'

Veena Seshadri

Sisters and Goddesses

On the edge of the jungle lay a small wooden temple. It was late evening, and the sun had already disappeared behind the palms. The light was fading fast, and the hundreds of small clay lamps lined up on the wooden slats of the temple all seemed to be burning brighter and brighter, minute by minute.

The oiled torsos of the temple Brahmins were gleaming too. They had nearly finished the evening ceremony — surrounding the idol of the Goddess Bhagavati with burning splints as they rang bells, chanted and blew on conch shells. The ritual prepared the Goddess for sleep.

Only when it was over, and the doors of the inner shrine were sealed for the night, were they able to tell me about the Goddess they served. Bhagavati is the pre-eminent Goddess in Kerala, the most powerful and beloved. In some incarnations, it was true, she could be ferocious: a figure of terror, a stalker of cremation grounds who slaughtered demons without hesitation or compassion.... But, in other moods, Bhagavati could be supremely benign and generous — the caring, loving, fecund mother — and this was how her followers usually liked to think of her. For many, she was the deity of the land itself: the spirit of the mountains, and the life force in the soil. In this form, Bhagavati is regarded as a chaste virgin and a caring mother, qualities she shares with her sister, whose enclosure lies a short distance down the road.

'Yes, yes, the Virgin Mary is Bhagavati's younger sister,' explained Vasudeva, the head priest, matter-of-factly, as if stating the obvious.

'But, for sisters, don't they look rather different from each other?' I asked.

'Sisters are often a little different from each other,' he replied. 'Mary is another form of the Devi. They have equal power.' He paused. 'At our annual festival the priests take the goddess around the village on top of an elephant to receive sacrifices from the people. She visits all the places, and one stop is the church. There she sees her sister.'

'Mary gets on an elephant too?'

'No,' he replied. 'But when the goddesses visit each other, the sacrifice in the church is just like the one we have here: we light lamps and make an offering. The priests stay in their church, but the congregation of the church receives us, and makes a donation to the temple.'

'So relations are good?'

'The people here always cooperate,' he said. 'Our Hindus go to the church and the Christians come here and ask the Goddess for what they want — for everyone believes the two are sisters.'

This was something I had seen for myself ever since I had arrived in Mannarkad, a small village eighty kilometres to the south of Kerala's capital, Trivandrum. In the large courtyard of the church — newly rebuilt and enlarged around a medieval core — many of the worshippers were Hindu rather than Christian.

'I have come here from seventy kilometres away,' said K.N. Prakashan, a middle-aged school teacher. 'Yes, I am a Hindu, but Mary is our holy mother. She is your mother and my mother, too. I believe she is a powerful goddess. Every time I come, I ask her to let the sufferings go from my life.'

'And does she answer your prayers?'

'Of course,' replied Prakashan. 'It works. Otherwise I wouldn't be coming back here.'

No less surprising were the Hindu customs practised by the church's congregation. The devotees coming in and out proudly told me that during the annual festival of Our Lady, the pilgrims would all take a ritual bath, shave their heads and eat only vegetarian food to purify themselves. They would join processions under torches, banners and coloured silk umbrellas of exactly the sort used by Hindus in their temple processions. The church also had a reputation for its powers of exorcism — the Christians sharing the Hindu belief that certain rituals can rid a possessed person of an unwanted spirit.

All this was mixed up with forms of devotion usually specific to the Orthodox churches. Booths along the side of the courtyard sold bronze plaques of arms, legs, eyes, hearts and other body parts to place in front of a holy icon to remind the saint to cure a particular ailment — something practised in Greek and Syrian Orthodox churches across the Levant.

The Christians seemed wholly at ease with the idea of praying alongside Hindus. 'I believe Mary is more generous to the Hindus than she is to us,' said Thomas Daniel as he prayed at the stone cross at the back of the enclosure. 'Yes, we also believe Bhagavati and Mary are twin sisters.'

'So you believe in the Hindu gods, too?'

'Yes, of course. Those gods are there. I go to the temple with my Hindu friends, though I don't tell the priests. And I participate in their festivals, though I don't give offerings.'

Thomas smiled. 'This has been passed from generation to generation.... All the people of Kerala believe in all of the gods.'

Kerala is the greenest state in India: hot and humid, still and brooding. The soil is so fertile that as you drift up the lotus-choked backwaters around Mannarkad, the trees close in around you, a vault of palm and bamboo. Mango trees hang heavy over the fishermen's skiffs. All around this central part of Kerala live the St Thomas Christians — so called because they believe that St Thomas, the apostle of Jesus who famously refused to believe in the resurrection 'until I have placed my hands in the holes left by the nails and the wound left by the spear', came to India from Palestine after the resurrection, and that he baptised their ancestors.

Over the centuries, almost every Western traveller to southern India, from Marco Polo to the first Portuguese conquistadors, told the same story of Thomas' missionary journey. According to the Anglo-Saxon Chronicle, King Alfred sent Bishop Sighelm of Sherborne 'to St Thomas in India'; years later the bishop returned, carrying with him 'precious stones and the odiferous essences of that country'. In Kerala, St Thomas is said to have converted the upper caste Brahmins with the aid of miracles and to have built seven churches.

Whatever the historical truth, there can be no doubt that Christianity has deep roots in the soil, in all probability stretching back to the first century AD. Over the centuries of unusually close coexistence, the Hindus and the Christians of the region have found their myths and their rituals fusing slowly together. There may be violence between Christians and Hindus in some parts of northern India, but there has never been any serious tension between the two faiths here in Kerala. Until recently, the St Thomas Christians were awarded places of honour in the great temple processions and the churches were allowed to borrow the temple elephants for their own festivals.

When the Portuguese arrived in India in the sixteenth century they criticised the St Thomas Christians' clergy for the many 'pagan' practices they had adopted: ritual ablutions, the casting of horoscopes in the Hindu manner, the belief in the transmigration of souls — traditions which survived into the twentieth century, some of them still common today.

The same fusion of Hinduism and Christianity is seen in the Christian art of Kerala. Every church in the region has a large stone cross in its churchyard; but these unambiguously Christian symbols rise out of lotus-shaped Hindu bases, decorated with lion-headed, fish-bodied makaras, cows, elephants, tigers and dancing girls. Paired peacocks are especially popular, doubling as they do as eucharistic symbols and vehicles of the God Murugan, son of Shiva.

◆

As we walked along the village boundary, through pepper and rubber plantations, groups of devotees were waiting for the annual visit of their deity. Trestle tables had been loaded with burning lamps and offerings — coconuts and bananas, baskets of puffed rice and jaggery. Each time the elephant stopped, offerings would be given and blessings received. Then more firecrackers would be let off — scaring the children and grazing goats — and on the procession would trundle.

'She is the mother of the village,' said Saraswati Amma, an old lady waiting on her veranda for the Goddess, with her grandchildren around her.

'I have always heard that the two Devis of the village are sisters,' said Raji. 'If you go to the temple you must also go to the church, otherwise one of the sisters will be jealous.'

'It's true,' said Susheela. 'They say that if you want your prayers answered you must pray at both the temple and the church. They say that if you light a lamp at the temple, that light also can be seen flickering in the church, and vice versa. The two are really one....'

William Dalrymple

More Chicken Soup?

Share your heart with the rest of the world. If you have a story, poem or article (your own or someone else's) that you feel belongs in a future volume of Chicken Soup for the Indian Soul, please email us at cs.indiansoul@westland-tata.com or send it to:

Westland Ltd
S-35A, 3rd Floor
Green Park Main Market
New Delhi 110 016

We will make sure that you and the author are credited for the contribution. Thank you!

Contributors

George Abraham is an advertising professional and motivational speaker, who also writes on sports and disability. He conducts training programmes for the visually impaired, is the founding chairman of the World Blind Cricket Council, and has set up Project Eyeway, a single stop information source on the eye and blindness. He can be contacted at george@eyeway.org.

Anu Aga, after retiring as chairperson of Thermax Limited, continues to be on the company's board of directors. She is now chairperson of the Thermax Social Initiative Foundation, which runs the CSR activities of Thermax. She is also closely associated with the Teach for India initiative, and is involved in causes promoting communal harmony and human rights.

Shinie Antony has worked with the *Economic Times*, the *Financial Express*, the Indo-Asian News Service and Amar Chitra Katha in an editorial capacity, and is the author of *Barefoot and Pregnant*, *Planet Polygamous*, *Kardamom Kisses* and *Séance On A Sunday Afternoon*. She won the Commonwealth Broadcasting Corporation's Asia Award for Short Story Writing in 2002. You can reach her at shinieantony@gmail.com.

Akber Ayub is a mechanical engineer by profession, an ex-marine engineer, ex-industrialist, college faculty member, and now a writer. He has written and edited coffee-table books on travel and is the author of a textbook on marine engineering. He can be reached at akbersait@yahoo.co.uk.

Megha Bajaj is, above all else, a seeker. She is the author of the book, *Thank You, Cancer*, which aims at showing people that the human spirit is strong enough to overcome any challenge known to man. She is also the founder of an organisation called Spread Your Wings, which is a unique body-mind-spirit class for children. You can contact her at megh83@hotmail.com.

Indu Balachandran quit her job in advertising (she was VP and creative head, JWT, Chennai) to follow a passion — travel writing. She now reviews eco-friendly hotels all over India (www.travelto-care.com) and can't think of a better job in the world! She contributes regularly to *The Sunday Hindu*, and you can read her travel-blog at www.idiva.com. She can be reached at indubee8@yahoo.co.in.

Srilatha Batliwala is a Bangalore-based social scientist and gender expert who has worked as a grassroots activist, gender-equality advocate, and women's studies teacher and researcher. She is currently Scholar Associate with Women's Rights in Development; and Research Fellow at the Hauser Center for Nonprofit Organizations, Harvard University. She has published on a range of civil society and women's issues. Her work can be viewed at www.genderatwork.org, or at www.awid.org. You can contact her at sribatli@gmail.com.

Dr Kiran Bedi is India's first woman police officer. The reforms that she instituted in Tihar jail, Asia's largest prison, and her innovative methods of policing have been recognised with several awards, including the Ramon Magsaysay Award. Kiran Bedi has written a number of books, anchors radio and television shows, and is a popular speaker. She is the founder of two NGOs — Navjyoti and India Vision Foundation. Her website: www.kiranbedi.com.

Preeti A. Bhatt is a teacher who is passionate about creative writing and loves to experiment with meaningful theatre to help her students think with conviction. She also brings theatre to the streets for rousing public awareness on various issues in society. Preeti currently works as the cultural coordinator of St Kabir, a reputed school in Ahmedabad, and may be reached at preetibhatt11@ yahoo.co.in.

Kalyani Candade is a copywriter, travel writer and process trainer. With the army for a past life and adventure in the present, the outdoors and writing are in her blood and bones. Together with her husband, she has co-founded Wildertrails, their outbound organisation, and believes that her work offers her the rare privilege of intimate insights into the human psyche and nature. You can check out more of her writing at http://thewandererwithin. blogspot.com.

Mathew Chakola is a champion chess player, gourmet cook, raconteur, bibliophile — and an engineer. His passion, however, is paper, and Chakola is one of the biggest producers of roofing felt from recycled paper in the US, where he lives in Maryland. He is also the author of *The Indian Boy Without Feathers*, an inspirational book on how to fight fair and win. He may be reached at mchakola@aol.com.

Annie Chandy Mathew was a teacher for twenty-three years and has been a student all her life. She now runs Unisun Publications, which is based in Bangalore.

William Dalrymple is a historian and writer who was born in Scotland, and wrote his first book, the highly acclaimed bestseller, *In Xanadu*, when he was twenty-two. This was followed by other books, such as *City of Djinns*, *From the Holy Mountain*, *The Last Moghal*, *White Mughals* and *Nine Lives*. Dalrymple has won several prestigious awards for his writing, including the Duff Cooper Prize, the Thomas Cook Travel Award and the Wolfson Prize for History. His website: www.williamdalrymple.uk.com.

Mahesh Dattani is one of India's best-known playwrights writing in English. He is also a film maker, script writer and director. His plays include *Final Solutions*, (for which he won the Sahitya Akademi Award), *Dance Like a Man*, and *A Muggy Night in Mumbai*. His film, *Mango Souffle*, was adjudged best motion picture at the Barcelona Film Festival. You can reach him at mahesh.dattani@gmail.com.

Esther David is a sculptor, art critic, columnist and the author of several books including *The Walled City*, *The Book of Esther*, *By the Sabarmati* and *My Father's Zoo*, and co-author of *India's Jewish Heritage, Ritual, Art and Life Cycle*. She belongs to a Bene Israel Jewish family of Ahmedabad, where she grew up amidst a zoo created by her father.

Khursheed Dinshaw is a Pune-based editor and freelance writer with more than 526 published articles in major Indian newspapers and magazines. An avid traveller, she writes on lifestyle, travel, health, food, trends, people and culture. She can be reached at khursheeddinshaw@hotmail.com.

Geeta Doctor is a journalist and writer. She describes herself as a lifestyle journalist whose commentaries on life, literature, the arts and society have always sought to be provocative and controversial. She lives in Chennai.

Shweta Ganesh Kumar is a freelance travel journalist and writer who lives in the Philippines. She has worked with CNN-IBN as a desk editor and as a city correspondent. After two years with the mainstream media, she joined Greenpeace India as a communications officer. An active volunteer, she blogs about life and her experiences at http://simplyspeaking.blogspot.com.

Tenzin Gyatso, the Fourteenth Dalai Lama, is considered, by the people of Tibet, their temporal and spiritual leader. Yet, he describes himself as 'a simple Buddhist monk'. He has received several awards, including the Nobel Peace Prize, in recognition of his message of peace and compassion, non-violence and religious harmony. The Dalai Lama has also written more than seventy-two books. His website: www.dalailama.com.

Anand Halve is a management graduate by education and a brand consultant by profession. He is a co-founder of chlorophyll brand consultancy, and has served on all the major advertising industry bodies. Halve has authored *Planning for Power Advertising*, which is used as a textbook in several management schools. He is visiting faculty at IIM, Ahmedabad, and writes Urdu poetry in his free time. He may be reached at anandhalve@gmail.com.

Anjum Hasan has written short fiction, travel essays and book reviews, and her poems have appeared in national and international anthologies and journals. Her first novel, *Lunatic in my Head*, was short-listed for the Crossword Fiction Award, and her second novel, *Neti, Neti*, was long-listed for the Man Asian Literary Prize. She has also published a book of poems, *Street on the Hill*.

Sandip Hor is passionate about writing. He is an intrepid traveller who has left his footprints in twenty-six countries in five continents, and has described his remarkable experiences in over ninety articles published in India, Australia, Singapore, UK and Fiji. He is an engineer, and has been living in Australia for the last twenty-five years with his wife and two kids. He may be reached at sandiphor@hotmail.com.

Maya Jayapal is the author of three books — *Old Singapore* and *Old Jakarta* and *Bangalore: The Story of a City*. She is also a prolific contributor of travel and other articles of human interest to newspapers and magazines. Maya is a counsellor, living and practising in Bangalore.

Usha Jesudasan is a writer and inspirational speaker who lives in Vellore, Tamil Nadu. She writes a column for the *Hindu* called 'The Ahimsa Way', mainly on issues of peace and harmony. She is the author of Value and Peace Education textbooks for schools in India, and holds workshops to help people accept and be comfortable with relationships. You may contact her at ushajesudasan@gmail.com.

Shaizia Jifri has run a store, driven an auto rickshaw across India and Nepal in a rally, managed a vegetarian restaurant and guesthouse in the temple town of Tiruvannamalai, worked for an ad-film production company in Mumbai and as a freelance writer. In between, she has worked for event management companies, hired out her services as a graphic designer, acted, and also done a stint as an art director for a short film. Currently, she teaches drama to children and works for a theatre company based in Mumbai. She may be reached at shezjifri@gmail.com.

Kabir, fifteenth-century mystic, poet and saint called himself 'the child of Allah and Ram' and was a bridge between Hindus and Muslims, as he was revered by both.

Dr A.P.J. Abdul Kalam was the eleventh president of India. He has worked in ISRO and DRDO, and played a crucial role in the development of the country's indigenous satellite launch vehicle, missile and nuclear weapons programmes. Scientist, philosopher and educationist, Dr Kalam is a recipient of the Bharat Ratna award. He has written several best-selling books, including *Wings of Fire* and *Ignited Minds*. His website: www.abdulkalam.com.

Dr Malavika Kapur retired as professor and head of clinical psychology, National Institute of Mental Health and Neurosciences, Bangalore. She is the author of several books, including *Mental Health of Indian Children* and *Learning from Children What to Teach Them*. Her other interests are fiction writing (she also writes stories for children), and trekking in the foothills of the Himalayas.

Maulana Wahiduddin Khan is an Islamic scholar who has made peace and inter-faith harmony the mission of his life. A recipient

of several national and international awards, the Maulana set up
the Centre for Peace and Spirituality in order to promote and rein-
force the culture of peace. The Maulana has translated the Koran
into English, Hindi, Urdu and Arabic and authored more than 200
books. You can find out more about him at www.cpsglobal.org.

Shrutkeerti Khurana worked as a radio jockey and software professional before pursuing her MBA. She currently lives in Austin, Tex-
as. You can find out more about her at http://ScribblerInTheWoods.
com/. She can be reached at shrutkeerti@gmail.com.

Leela Krishnamohan has a Master's in English literature and lin-
guistics and a senior diploma in French. After attending a teachers
training course in Paris, she taught French at the Alliance Française
for ten years and continues to keep in touch with the language. She
is married, has two children, and lives in Bangalore.

Mini Krishnan sources and edits literary translations, and is the
series editor of a multi-author, multi-faith series of Peace Education texts for Indian schools — *Living in Harmony*. She writes on
translation and peace advocacy, both of which she sees as nation-
ally integrating forces. She is on the National Translation Mission
and on the Curriculum Advisory Board, NCERT. She worked for
Macmillan India for twenty years and is currently with Oxford
University Press. Her email is minik@satyam.net.in.

Major A.J. Kuryan (Retd) served in the Indian Army for over
two decades as a frontline infantry commander, and took part in
operations in India and overseas. He has a post-graduate degree
in management and, during the last fifteen years, has been part of
one of the leading financial service providers.

Vanishree Mahesh is the proprietor of EasyLib.com, an online
library in Bangalore. She can be reached at help@easylib.com.

Gayatri Makhijani has lived in Mumbai all her life. In the city's
splendour, she discovered her love for God, swimming, reading,

writing and people. She works with a digital advertising agency, enjoys music and loves watching the rain. She can be reached at makhijani.gayatri@gmail.com.

Indu Mallah is a writer, literary critic, poet, and social activist. Several of her short stories have been broadcast over BBC World Service Radio, and her novel, *Shadows in Dream-time*, has won wide critical acclaim.

Dr Sonal Mansingh is a renowned bharatanatyam and Odissi dancer. Dance has taken her all over the world, and brought her many honours, including the Sangeet Natak Akademi Award, the Padma Vibhushan, and the Kalidas Samman. In 1977, she founded the prestigious Centre for Indian Classical Dances, in New Delhi.

Dr Ketna L. Mehta is the founder trustee of the Nina Foundation, which is dedicated to the rehabilitation of people with spinal cord injury. To find out more about its activities, visit www.ninafoundation.org.

Asha Menon writes for the weekend supplement of *The New Indian Express*. She may be reached at ashasmenon@gmail.com.

Saeed Mirza is a pioneer of New Wave cinema in India. He has made several award-winning films such as *Albert Pinto ko Gussa Kyon Aata Hai?* and *Mohan Joshi Haazir Ho*, documentaries, and popular TV serials such as *Nukkad* and *Intezar*. He is the author of *Ammi: Letter to a Democratic Mother*.

Sudha Murty, award-winning author, social worker and philanthropist, has an M.Tech degree in Computer Science. She is the chairperson of Infosys Foundation, which is involved in a number of social development initiatives. Sudha Murty writes both in English and Kannada, and her books include *Mahashweta* and *Wise and Otherwise*.

Anita Nair is the best-selling author of *The Better Man, Ladies Coupe* and *Mistress*. Her most recent book, *Goodnight and God Bless*, is a collection of literary essays. Her books have been translated into more than twenty-nine languages around the world. Her website: http://anitanair.net.

Manjula Padmanabhan is a writer and artist. Her books include *Getting There*, *Kleptomania* and *Escape*. *Harvest*, her fifth play, won the first prize in the 1997 Onassis Award for Theatre in Greece. She has illustrated twenty-five books for children, and her most recent picture book is *Where's That Cat?* You can visit her blog at www.marginalien.blogspot.com.

Bachendri Pal is the first Indian woman to climb Mount Everest. She has led the Indo-Nepalese Women's Everest Expedition; an all-women rafting expedition down the Ganga; and the seven-month-long Indian Women's First Trans-Himalayan Journey. She is director of the Tata Steel Adventure Foundation and also chief of adventure programmes, Tata Steel Ltd. You can find out more about her initiatives at www.tsafindia.org.

Makarand Paranjape is a professor of English at Jawaharlal Nehru University, New Delhi. A critic, poet, fiction writer, and literary columnist, he has over 30 books, 100 published academic papers, reviews, notes, and popular articles to his credit. His latest book is *Another Canon: Indian Texts and Traditions in English*. His websites: www.makarand.com and www.samvadindia.com.

Tanushree Podder is a nomad at heart and loves nothing more than travelling and writing. She also revels in delving deep into the history, culture and cuisine of the places she visits. After an MBA and eight years in the corporate sector, she quit her job to take up writing, and is the author of seventeen books including two novels, *Nurjahan's Daughter* and *Boots, Belts, Berets*. She can be reached at tanushreep@aol.in. Her website: www.tanushreepodder.webs.com.

Preeti Prabhu has a Master's in engineering, and now works for Oberthur Technologies. She is a Sri Sri Yoga teacher on weekends, and currently, an MBA student as well. She lives with her husband and eight-year-old daughter in Singapore.

Shubha Priya loves to travel and start a fresh life in different lands, while exploring the cultural diversity of our planet. She has worked as an advertising creative director in Jakarta, studied graphic and web design in the San Francisco Bay Area, and is currently a freelance writer residing in the UAE. She is also a contributing writer with www.traveltocare.com. She can be reached at shupri@gmail.com.

Prof Sudharani Raghupathy is a legend in the field of bharatanatyam. She has also been a senior teaching associate of Indian Studies (Professor) at the Colgate University, New York. In 1970, Prof Sudharani Raghupathy founded Shree Bharatalaya, a teaching-cum-research institution for nurturing the fine arts. She has received several awards including the Padma Shri and the Sangeet Natak Akademi Award.

Ratna Rajaiah is a graduate of IIM, Kolkata. She spent several years in advertising before quitting to make television shows and write for various publications, such as *Mid-Day*, *The Hindu* and *India Today*. She now writes a weekly column in the *Bangalore Mirror* and her earlier column in *The New Indian Express* will soon be published as a book. She may be reached at ratna.rajaiah@gmail.com, and you can check out her writing at http://choti-moo-confessions-of-a-bigmouth.blogspot.com.

Sandhya Rajayer is living her top five passions: health, wealth, well-being, personal development and travel. She is the author of the 2002 Gourmand Award-winning cook book, *Healthy Cooking: More Than 100 Smart Ways to Good Health*. She freelances for international magazines, and creates web content and script multimedia presentations from her home in Bangalore. She can be contacted at rajayers@gmail.com or you could call 0 99800 74081.

A.N. Ramachandran is a retired engineer interested in spirituality and the philosophy of Hinduism. He may be contacted at: anramachandran@yahoo.com.

Padma Ramachandran was a member of the IAS. She was the first woman in Kerala to become district collector and, later, chief secretary to the government. She has been vice chancellor of the Maharaja Sayaji Rao University of Baroda; and director of the Asian and Pacific Centre for Women and Development in the United Nations ESCAP, at Bangkok; and is now a member of the UGC's national consultative committee on Capacity Building for Women Managers in Higher Education. She is the author of *Public Administration in India* and co-authored *Education in India*.

Jamuna Rangachari has authored two books for children, *One* and *The Magic Liquid*. She is the assistant editor of *Life Positive* and has also written for the *Times of India*, *Hindustan Times* and other publications. She can be reached at jamuna.rangachari@gmail.com. Her website: www.jamunarangachari.com.

Dr Swarnalatha Rangarajan is an assistant professor at the Department of Humanities and Social Sciences, IIT, Madras. She was a Fulbright visiting scholar at Harvard University where she took a course in advanced fiction writing. Her short fiction has appeared in publications such as *The South Asian Review*. She is the editor of *The Indian Journal of Ecocriticism* and is currently working on her first novel.

Janardhan Roye is a freelance writer-photographer whose work has appeared in publications in India and abroad. He writes on an extensive range of topics. This Bangalore-born management professional now spends more time on writing, photography and 'giving back to the community'. He can be contacted at janardhanroye@gmail.com.

Monideepa Sahu is a former banker and internationally published writer of fiction and non-fiction. Her short fiction has been accepted by several literary publications, such as *Temenos, Apocalypse, Urban Voice* and *Hobart*. *The Riddle of the Seventh Stone*, her fantasy/ adventure novel for younger readers, is due soon. You can reach her at monideepa.sahu@gmail.com and check out her blog at www. monideepa.blogspot.com.

Saniya started writing poetry in Marathi during her schooldays, and later turned to other genres. Her work includes eleven short-story collections and three novels. Her fiction has also been adapted for making television serials. Saniya has received twelve literary awards including the Maharashtra State Awards; and some of her stories have been translated into Hindi, Kannada, English and German. She can be reached at saniya1011@gmail.com.

Shevlin Sebastian is a senior journalist with *The New Indian Express* in Kochi. He has published more than 1,500 feature articles on social problems, personalities, spirituality, travel, humour, and sports. He is also the author of four novels for children. You can visit his blog at www.shevlinsebastian.blogspot.com.

Priyanka Seshadri lives with her parents in the US and is currently in her first year of college in Northwestern University, Chicago, where she will be studying biology and business. She runs, plays tennis and has been writing since her schooldays.

Sri Sri Ravi Shankar is a spiritual teacher and the founder of the Art of Living Foundation, the International Association for Human Values, and numerous charitable organisations. His universal message of peace, service, and holistic living has attracted followers across the globe, and the attention of world leaders and international humanitarian organisations. For more information, check out his website: www.srisri.org.

Ayesha Sharma is a television anchor and producer who lives and works out of New Delhi. Born in an Army household, she spent her childhood moving between various little towns in India and went to six different schools. Whether it's backpacking alone in Europe, drifting on the Nile in Egypt, or riding her motorcycle to the far reaches of Ladakh, there is little she has turned down in life. You can reach her at ayeshasharma.mail@gmail.com.

Dr Vandana Shiva is an award-winning environmentalist, scientist and author. She has been mobilising small farmers to reclaim their rights to life and livelihood, and has been working to counter the perils of globalisation. Her books include: *Water Wars: Privatization, Pollution, and Profit*; *Stolen Harvest, The Hijacking of the Global Food Supply*; and *Soil Not Oil*. Navadanya, a network of seed banks and organic producers across the country, is her brainchild, as also the learning centre, Bija Vidyapeeth.

Arun Shourie is an author, editor and Member of the Rajya Sabha. He was a Minister of State in the previous government and, earlier, an editor of *The Indian Express*. He has received several national and international awards including the Padma Bhushan, the Magsaysay Award, the Dadabhai Naoroji Award, and International Editor of the Year Award. He is the author of several books such as *Hinduism: Essence and Consequence* and *Religion in Politics*.

Moid Siddiqui, managing director of Intellects Biz, has served corporate India in senior- and board-level positions for over three decades. He has authored fifteen books; nine on management (including his two award-winning books, *The Brave New Manager* and *Corporate Soul*) and six on spirituality. He may be reached at moidsiddiqui@yahoo.com and reachus@intellects.biz.

Jaswant Singh, after a stint as an Army officer, has served seven terms in Parliament, and headed six core ministries of the Government of India, including External Affairs, Defence and Finance. He is a columnist, bibliophile, skilled horseman and polo player, and the author of several books such as *A Call to Honour* and *Jinnah: India Partition Independence*. He may be reached at jaswant@sansad.nic.in.

Rocky Singh is an internationally certified consultant in the fields of HR and business process. He is also a wildlife enthusiast, ornithologist, scuba dive master, and single handicap golfer. His passions are food and travelling, and he combines both in the popular TV show, *Highway on My Plate*, which he anchors with his friend, as they hitchhike and eat their way across the country.

Karuna Sivasailam is a freelance editor. Apart from the spoken and written word, her other great passions are music, nature and gardening. She lives in Bangalore and can be contacted at karuna-siva@gmail.com

Anuradha Sivasundar, a postgraduate in nutrition and dietetics, is a yoga practitioner and teacher, healer and counsellor. She writes regularly for *Self Knowledge*, a spiritual magazine. She is also a webmaster doing freelance work.

Dr K. Srilata, poet, fiction writer and translator, is an associate professor of English at IIT, Madras. Her debut novel, *Table for Four*, was long-listed for the Man Asian Literary Prize, 2009. Her books include, *The Other Half of the Coconut: Women Writing Self-Respect History*, and an anthology of poetry titled *Seablue Child*. She has also co-edited *Rapids of a Great River: The Penguin Book of Tamil Poetry*.

Avinash Subramaniam is a writer. He has just finished rewriting his first novel, *11, Alexandra Road*. That apart, he is a regular contributor to OPEN magazine and numerous unknown causes. He lives online and his address is ubermaniam@gmail.com.

Swami Sukhabodhananda, an international management and spiritual guru, is the Founder Chairman of the Prasanna Trust. He has studied the scientific aspects of meditation and psychology, and conducts self-development and management programmes. He is the author of several best-sellers such as *Oh, Mind Relax Please!* and *Oh, Life Relax Please!* You can find out more about him at www.prasannatrust.org.

Pingali Surya Sundaram worked as an officer in the Indian Audit and Accounts Service. He took up the task of translating spiritual books after his retirement, and won the Sahitya Akademi Award for his translation of Sri Krishna Bhikshu's biography of Sri Ramana Maharishi, *Sri Ramana Leela*, into English.

Eshwar Sundaresan is an award-winning writer. He has written several short stories and is the author of *Bangalored*, a book on the expats living in Bangalore. He may be reached at eshwar.sunda-resan@gmail.com.

Brinda Suri is a media professional who has worked in diverse editorial capacities in the country's leading newspapers, for over a decade. A university gold medallist in history, she switched to travel writing to pursue her interest in exploring places and cultures. She can almost always be found sniffing around for a fascinating story. You can read more of her writing at brindasuri. blogspot.com.

Rabindranath Tagore, poet, philosopher, artist, musician and writer, was awarded the Nobel Prize for Literature for his collection of poems, *Gitanjali*. He established Shantiniketan, an institution that blends the best of Indian and western education (near Bolpur, Bengal), and later set up the Visva Bharati University there.

Madhavi Tata, a journalist by profession and a writer by accident, feels that words begin touching the soul when she looks at them through the lives of other people, every day. And therein lies the constant inspiration to write. She lives in Hyderabad, her birthplace by accident and her place of work, also by accident. She can be reached at mad.tata@gmail.com.

Sumaa Tekur is a Bangalore-based writer and journalist who is on an exciting inner journey of self-discovery. She tries hard to listen to her instinct on most days and believes that reiki has changed her life. She occasionally reads Tarot cards for friends. It is her goal to be conscious, alive, and aware in the present moment, every day. She can be reached at sumaatekur@gmail.com.

Mother Teresa was an Albanian nun who came to India to serve the poorest of the poor. A symbol of compassion, she established the order of the Missionaries of Charity in Kolkata, and set up 610 foundations in 123 countries to serve those in need. After her death, Mother Teresa was beatified by the pope. Find out more about her at www.motherteresa.org.

Hormis Tharakan served in the Indian Police Service and retired in 2007.

Shashi Tharoor is the Minister of State for External Affairs. Earlier, he was the UN under-secretary for communications and public information. He has written several books including *Bookless in Baghdad* and *Kerala: God's Own Country*, and novels such as *The Great Indian Novel*, *Riot* and *Show Business*.

K.R. Usha is a writer and editor. Her fiction includes the novels, *Sojourn* and *The Chosen*. Her third book, *A Girl and a River*, won the Vodafone-Crossword Award, 2007, and was shortlisted for the Commonwealth Writers Prize, 2008.

Shreekumar Varma is a novelist and playwright. His plays include *Platform*, *Midnight Hotel*, *The Dark Lord* and *Bow of Rama*. *Lament of Mohini* was his first novel and his recent book, *Maria's Room*, was long-listed for the Man Asian Literary Prize. He has also written a book for children, *The Magic Store of Nu-Cham-Vu*. He is married and has two sons. His website: www.shreevarma.com.

Suma Varughese is the editor-in-chief of *Life Positive*, a body-mind-spirit magazine. An ardent seeker of the spirit, she considers it her mission to help raise human consciousness and pave the way for a New Age. Her other great mission is to support the underprivileged and generate greater social equity. You can check out her blog at http://travellinglight-suma.blogspot.com/.

B.G. Verghese is a columnist, author and visiting professor at the Centre for Policy Research in Delhi. He started his career with the *Times of India* and served as information adviser to Prime Minister Indira Gandhi before going on to edit the *Hindustan Times* and *The Indian Express*. He won the Magsaysay Award in 1975, and is associated with a number of NGOs.

Prof Susan Visvanathan teaches sociology at JNU, and is the author of *The Christians of Kerala* and *Friendship, Interiority and Mysticism*. She has also written several novels.

Zai Whitaker works at the Kodaikanal International School, where she teaches English as a second language. She is also a writer and her books include *Andamans Boy*, *Kali and the Rat Snake*, and *Cobra in my Kitchen*. Her particular interests are natural history and Adivasi communities.

Purnima Yogi is a mass communications professional with over twenty-five years of experience in the print and electronic media as producer, writer, editor, translator and teacher. However, her only identity at present is that she is a follower of her Guru Shri Shri Nimishananda of Bangalore. You can check out her blogs at http://purnima-says.blogspot.com and http://gurunamana.blogspot.com.

PERMISSIONS

Fate or Faith? Reprinted by permission of Preeti A. Bhatt. Published in *Consecration* magazine in 2004. © 2004 Preeti A. Bhatt.

The Weekend Surprise. Reprinted by permission of Karuna Sivasailam. © 2009 Karuna Sivasailam.

Full Circle. Reprinted by permission of Shubha Priya. © 2009 Shubha Priya.

Son, Mothers Only Give. Excerpted from *Guiding Souls (Dialogues on the Purpose of Life)* by A.P.J. Abdul Kalam. © 2005 A.P.J. Abdul Kalam. Published by Ocean Books Pvt. Ltd. Reprinted by permission.

Stop! Reprinted by permission of Jamuna Rangachari. Published in *Life Positive* under the title 'Teaching Stories', in 2008. © 2008 Jamuna Rangachari.

The Blessing. Reprinted by permission of K.R. Usha. © 2009 K.R. Usha.

Hug Your Enemies. A version of this story appeared in *Soul Inc.* by Moid Siddiqui. © 2007 Moid Siddiqui. Published by Wisdom Tree. Reprinted by permission.

Not in the Words We Speak but in Our Deeds. Reprinted by permission of Saniya. © 2009 Saniya.

Doing the Right Thing at the Right Time. Reprinted by permission of Shinie Antony. © 2009 Shinie Antony.

Beyond the Call of Duty. Reprinted by permission of Usha Jesudasan. © 2009 Usha Jesudasan.

Give Till It Hurts. Excerpted from the Nobel lecture by Mother Teresa. From *Nobel Lectures, Peace 1971-1980.* © 1979 The Nobel Foundation. Published in http://nobelprize.org. Reprinted by permission.

It Will Come to Us. Excerpted from *Life Beautiful* by Sri Sri Ravi Shankar. © 2009 The Office of His Holiness Sri Sri Ravi Shankar. Published in www.srisri.org. Reprinted with permission.

Me, My Bike and the Road Ahead. Reprinted by permission of Ayesha Sharma. © 2009 Ayesha Sharma.

Daffodils in December. Reprinted by permission of Indu Mallah. © 2009 Indu Mallah.

Tara. Reprinted by permission of Leela Krishnamohan. © 2009 Leela Krishnamohan.

Light on a Hill. Reprinted by permission of Susan Visvanathan. © 2009 Susan Visvanathan.

Home Thoughts. Reprinted by permission of Maya Jayapal. Published previously in *Tehelka* magazine in 2008. © 2008 Maya Jayapal.

I Am a Lotus. Reprinted by permission of Mahesh Dattani. Published previously in *The Week* in 2009. © 2009 Mahesh Dattani.

Looking for God on Brigade Road. Reprinted by permission of Mini Krishnan. Published previously in the *Deccan Herald* in 2008. © 2008 Mini Krishnan.

Shades of White. Reprinted by permission of Monideepa Sahu. A briefer version of the story was published in *BTW* magazine in 2008. © 2008 Monideepa Sahu.

The Meaning of Life. Discourse by Swami Sukhabodhananda published in the *Times of India* and www.prasannatrust.org in 2009 under the title, 'Try New Combinations, Be Creative in Life'. Reprinted by permission of the Prasanna Trust. © 2009 Prasanna Trust.

Thy Will Be Done. Reprinted by permission of Suma Varughese. Excerpted from a longer article published in *Life Positive* in 2008. © 2008 Suma Varughese.

Yoga and Rollerblading. Reprinted by permission of Preeti Prabhu. © 2009 Preeti Prabhu.

Their Lives or Ours?. Reprinted by permission of Major A. J. Kuryan. © 2009 Major A. J. Kuryan.

Nature Cure. Reprinted by permission of Zai Whitaker. © 2009 Zai Whitaker.

Hijacked!. Reprinted by permission of Sudharani Raghupathy. © 2009 Sudharani Raghupathy.

The Red Rice Granary. Excerpted from 'The Red Rice Granary' in *How I Taught My Grandmother to Read and Other Stories*. Published in Puffin by Penguin Books India in 2004. Reprinted by permission of Sudha Murty. © 2004 Sudha Murty.

Once Upon a Time. Reprinted by permission of Sandhya Rajayer. © 2004 Sandhya Rajayer.

Don't Worry, Jesus. Reprinted by permission of Annie Chandy Mathew. © 2009 Annie Chandy Mathew.

Yatra. Reprinted by permission of Karuna Sivasailam. © 2009 Karuna Sivasailam.

The Sufi. Reprinted by permission of Makarand Paranjape. © 2007 Makarand Paranjape.

Do Unto Others. Excerpted from 'Quest for Eternal Youth' in *Ghosts and Other Friends* published by Dronequill in 2009. Reprinted by permission of Malavika Kapur. © 2009 Malavika Kapur.

Remembering Alicia. Reprinted by permission of Priyanka Seshadri. © 2009 Priyanka Seshadri.

Vivekananda Every Day. Published by Sri Ramakrishna Vijayam in 2009. Author not mentioned. Transcreated from the Tamil version by A.N. Ramachandran. Reprinted by permission of Sri Ramakrishna Vijayam. © 2009 Sri Ramakrishna Vijayam.

Speaking in Many Tongues. Reprinted by permission of Swarnalatha Rangarajan. © 2009 Swarnalatha Rangarajan.